D1356962

OXFORD STUDIES IN THEOLOGICAL ETHICS

General Editor
Oliver O'Donovan

OXFORD STUDIES IN THEOLOGICAL ETHICS

The series presents discussions on topics of general concern to Christian Ethics, as it is currently taught in universities and colleges, at the level demanded by a serious student. The volumes will not be specialized monographs nor general introductions or surveys. They aim to make a contribution worthy of notice in its own right but also focused in such a way as to provide a suitable starting-point for orientation.

The titles include studies in important contributors to the Christian tradition of moral thought; explorations of current moral and social questions; and discussions of central concepts in Christian moral and political thought. Authors treat their topics in a way that will show the relevance of the Christian tradition, but with openness to neighbouring traditions of thought which have entered into dialogue with it.

PERSONS

The Difference between 'Someone' and 'Something'

ROBERT SPAEMANN

Translated by Oliver O'Donovan
from *Personen: Versuche über den Unterschied zwischen*
'etwas' und 'jemand'

OXFORD
UNIVERSITY PRESS

OXFORD
UNIVERSITY PRESS

Great Clarendon Street, Oxford OX2 6DP

Oxford University Press is a department of the University of Oxford.
It furthers the University's objective of excellence in research, scholarship,
and education by publishing worldwide in

Oxford New York

Auckland Cape Town Dar es Salaam Hong Kong Karachi
Kuala Lumpur Madrid Melbourne Mexico City Nairobi
New Delhi Shanghai Taipei Toronto

With offices in

Argentina Austria Brazil Chile Czech Republic France Greece
Guatemala Hungary Italy Japan Poland Portugal Singapore
South Korea Switzerland Thailand Turkey Ukraine Vietnam

Oxford is a registered trade mark of Oxford University Press
in the UK and in certain other countries

Published in the United States
by Oxford University Press Inc., New York

© Klett-Cotta. 1996 J. G. Cotta'sche Buchhandlung Nachfolger GmbH, Stuttgart

The moral rights of the author have been asserted
Database right Oxford University Press (maker)

First published in English 2006

All rights reserved. No part of this publication may be reproduced,
stored in a retrieval system, or transmitted, in any form or by any means,
without the prior permission in writing of Oxford University Press,
or as expressly permitted by law, or under terms agreed with the appropriate
reprographics rights organization. Enquiries concerning reproduction
outside the scope of the above should be sent to the Rights Department,
Oxford University Press, at the address above

You must not circulate this book in any other binding or cover
and you must impose the same condition on any acquirer

British Library Cataloguing in Publication Data

Data available

Library of Congress Cataloguing in Publication Data

Data available

Typeset by SPI Publisher Services, Pondicherry, India
Printed in Great Britain
on acid-free paper by
Biddles Ltd., King's Lynn, Norfolk

ISBN 978-0-19-928181-7

Translator's Preface

I began translating selected chapters from Professor Spaemann's *Personen* for the purposes of teaching, finding nothing in the English language that would bring certain important questions and arguments so effectively to the notice of my students. But although many of the chapters are effectively free-standing and can be profitably used this way, I found that in order for them to make their full effect, I needed constantly to be explaining the rich and eclectic approach to philosophical anthropology that gave them their context. It began to seem a pity that these explanations should not be given in the author's own way, rather than in mine. As news got round that a translation was afoot, the number of enquiries I received confirmed my expectation that Professor Spaemann's thought, already known from the translation of his *Happiness and Benevolence*, would find a ready interest in the English-speaking world. In carrying through this demanding, though always stimulating and educative task, I incurred various debts: to the author himself, who has been generous with his advice and graciously relaxed in allowing the English language to do its own thing when it cannot easily match his German step by step; to Dr Bernd Wannenwetsch and Dr Holger Zaborowski, whom I have consulted on points of detail; and to Dr David Leal, who read the whole manuscript through with great care, his philosopher's weather-eye cocked for solecisms. To James Mumford, who prepared the Index, special thanks are due. To Lucy Qureshi and the Delegates of Oxford University Press, who have been prepared to venture on what is now a rather unfashionable enterprise, permitting theologians and philosophers who read no German to encounter the work of a major contemporary thinker, salutation is in order from author, translator, and readers alike. In the hope of assisting English-speaking readers to find their way back to the original, page numbers from the German edition, published by Klett-Cotta of Stuttgart in 1996, are included in the margin.

O.M.T.O'D.

The publication of this work was supported by a grant from the Goethe-Institut.

Contents

Introduction

Within the universe of things that exist, 'persons' have a special position. They do not compose a natural kind. We need to know what kind of being anything is *before* we can know whether it is 'something' or 'someone', i.e. a thing or a person. What does it mean, then, to speak of 'someone', and so admit a claim on his or her part to a distinctive status?

Ever since Boethius's famous definition of the person as 'the individual substance of a rational nature', philosophy has attempted to identify the attributes that license us to apply this term to certain beings.[1] Such attempts have taken two routes. On the one side there have been those that sought precision about what it means to be 'rational', *rationabilis* in Boethius's definition. Thinkers of the English-speaking world, from Locke to contemporary analytical philosophy, have led the way in elaborating a range of predicates supposed to define personality. Strawson, for example, sees it as essential that persons are bearers of mental and physical predicates simultaneously, not mere 'thinking substances' in Descartes's sense.[2]

Certainly, it is important to distinguish a philosophy of the person from an account of subjectivity or consciousness; but if the expression 'mental predicate' is taken to include every kind of subjective experience, Strawson's definition is too broad. Even robins, we may presume, have some kind of subjective inwardness. Other authors

---

[1] Boethius, *Contra Eutychen et Nestorium* 3.

[2] P. F. Strawson, *Individuals* (London: Methuen, 1959), 104: 'the concept of a person is to be understood as the concept of a type of entity such that *both* predicates ascribing states of consciousness *and* predicates ascribing corporeal characteristics, a physical situation etc. are equally applicable to an individual entity of that type'.

have attempted to establish what gives inwardness the marks of personality: self-consciousness, memory, a relation to one's life as a whole, an interest in one's life. Max Scheler long since defined persons as the subjects of a *variety* of intentional acts.[3]

The other route to understanding the idea has focused on the social character of personal existence. There are only *persons*, in the plural. Persons are not persons merely on the basis of some specific difference that marks them out. Mutual recognition is determinative. The status of personal existence depends on a communicative event. It is easy to see how this line of thought derives from Fichte and Hegel. But since Hegel absorbed personal status finally into an all-encompassing rational Universal, the 'personalism', so called, of the early twentieth century achieved its distinctive profile only with the decline of Hegel's influence.

Intellectual preoccupations with the concept of the person have, until the present day, assumed a somewhat theoretical and academic character. But in recent years, unexpectedly, that has changed. The term 'person' has always (since Boethius) served as a *nomen dignitatis*, a concept with evaluative connotations; in the wake of Kant it became the central plank in the foundation of human rights. Now its function has been reversed. Suddenly the term 'person' has come to play a key role in *demolishing* the idea that human beings, *qua* human beings, have some kind of rights before other human beings. Only human beings can have human rights, and human beings can have them only as persons. The argument then runs: but not all human beings *are* persons; and those that are, are not persons in every stage of life or in every state of consciousness. They are not persons if from the first moment of their lives they are refused admission to the community of recognition, for that is what makes human beings persons. And they are not persons if, as individuals, they lack the features that ground our talk of human beings as persons in general, i.e. if they never acquire or lose, temporarily or permanently, the relevant capacities. Small children are not persons, for example; neither are the severely handicapped and the senile. In the view of Derek Parfit, by far the most unflinching adherent of this line of

---

[3] Max Scheler, *Formalism in Ethics and Non-formal Ethics of Value*, tr. M. S. Frings and R. L. Funk (Evanston, Ill.: Northwestern University Press, 1973[5]), 382–3.

thought, one ceases to be a person when asleep or temporarily unconscious.[4] There is no reason to ascribe such a thing as a 'right to life' to human beings in such conditions; that would even be immoral, a kind of unjust partisanship for one's own species which has become known, in the disparaging term coined by the Australian animal-rights philosopher Peter Singer, as 'speciesism'.[5]

The public horror provoked by these suggestions should not be allowed to conceal the fact that a genuine theoretical dilemma has presented itself. That is not unusual when cultural axioms that hardly seemed to require theoretical elucidation are suddenly put in doubt. What Lübbe calls the 'incredulity-defence' (*Verblüffungsresistenz*) is, no doubt, the first requirement of the situation; but it cannot 11 substitute for serious thinking. Even 'axiomatic' beliefs need justifying in the long run, if they face a challenge. It is true that Aristotle, the great interpreter of the Hellenic way of life, thought that anyone who said one might kill one's mother needed correction, not argument; but Socrates, by contrast, was grateful to those whose provocative questions gave rise to deeper exploration of the foundations of intuitive certainties. Some axioms prove unfounded in such circumstances, and so forfeit their axiomatic status.

Are all human beings persons? It is clear that if we say Yes, we are making some prior assumptions. One is that, although persons relate to one another a priori through mutual recognition, recognition is not an antecedent condition for being a person but a response to a prior claim. Another assumption is that though we concede this claim on the basis of specific attributes, the demonstration of these attributes is not a condition for recognition in each case; membership of the species that typically displays them is sufficient. And this in spite of the fact, and because of it, that persons do not relate to their species in the same way that members of other species do. Persons are 'individuals' in an unparalleled sense. And it is precisely for this reason that we recognize persons not by their individual demonstration of the specific features, but simply by their membership of the species. This paradox is among the conclusions to which the reflections to be developed in this book will lead us.

---

[4] Derek Parfit, *Reasons and Persons* (Oxford: Oxford University Press, 1985²).
[5] Peter Singer, *Practical Ethics* (Cambridge: Cambridge University Press, 1993²).

These reflections are prompted by a challenge to our cultural tradition and its developed understanding of humanity and human rights. But it does not follow that they should be understood as a defence of that tradition. For the tradition itself has developed the potential for its own destruction, not least by separating and isolating consciousness and subjectivity from the concept of life. Life is not an attribute or property which may or may not pertain to a given existent. Life is, as Aristotle wrote, 'the being of living things'.[6] Persons are living things. Their being and the conditions of their identity are the same as those of living creatures of any species. Yet they are grouped not in a species or a genus, but in *community*, open in principle to those of other species, a community where each member occupies a unique and distinctive position entirely his or her own. To occupy such a position is what it is to be 'someone' rather than 'something'.

What do we mean when we speak of 'someone'? How did this talk of 'persons' arise? What are its assumptions? What does it imply, and what does it preclude? These are the questions around which the following reflections circle. Persons are not something *else* the world contains, over and above inanimate objects, plants, animals, and human beings. But human beings are connected to everything else the world contains at a deeper level than other things to each other. That is what it means to say that they are persons.

---

[6] Aristotle, *De anima* 415ᵇ13: τὸ δὲ ζῆν τοῖς ζῴοι τὸ εἶναί ἐστιν.

1

Why We Speak of Persons

I

The meaning of the word 'person' is exceptionally dependent upon its context. For the most part we speak of persons to denote human beings, referring, for example, to 'eight persons at table'. In such a phrase the word 'person' is not emphatic, but rather the opposite. 'Eight human beings at table' would be more forceful and strike a somewhat more solemn note. 'Eight persons' is abstract and impersonal, simply a way of counting. It would seem rather pretentious to speak of a human-to-human, instead of a person-to-person, telephone call.[1] And the phrase 'this person' is especially impersonal—either bureaucratic or deliberately dismissive.

In other contexts, however, the contrary is true, and especially when the word 'person' functions as a predicate, *i.e.* when it is said that some specified subject 'is a person'. The recent proposal to replace the expression 'human rights' with 'personal rights' illustrates a use of language in which 'persons' are those human beings, and only those, who are distinguished by certain qualities. And the reply

---

[1] [It is impossible to reproduce with the English 'person' the range of uses of the noun *Person*, partly because English commonly substitutes the collective noun 'people' for the plural in a casual sense. Here the author suggests that we would speak casually of inviting eight people (*Personen*) to dinner rather than eight human beings (*Menschen*), and that we would not think of calling a 'passenger train' (*Personenzug*) a 'human train' (*Menschenzug*). Below he contrasts the weighty attribution of personal existence to the merely formal entry of a name in the *Personenstandsregister*, i.e. the register of births, marriages, and deaths. And finally he refers to the term with which the cast list is commonly headed in German theatre programmes, *Personen.*]

that *all* human beings are persons, treats the term 'person' as a *nomen dignitatis* in just the same way. To ascribe 'personal existence' is to recognize that someone can claim a certain kind of treatment from anyone who encounters him.

Traces of an older and different use of the term may be found in the heading of a list of characters in a play: *dramatis personae*. 'Persons' in this context are precisely *not* persons, i.e. human beings. They are roles, distinct from the actors who present them. We see something like the same use in St Paul's remark that 'God does not look upon the person.'[2] If we ask what God *does* look upon, 14 the answer must be that he looks precisely on 'the person' in the modern sense. Finally, and not only for the sake of completeness, we must remember the grammatical expressions, 'first person', 'second person', 'third person', which have come to assume a decisive importance in our contemporary use of 'person'.

The discussion that follows will principally have to do with the sense of the word 'person' used as a predicate, when we say that this or that subject 'is a person'. This sense sheds some light, however, on the secondary use, when we employ it impersonally for the purposes of numerical identification.

'Person' is not a classificatory term, on the one hand, identifying a particular *this* as *such* a thing. 'X is a person' does not answer the question 'What is X?', as do 'X is a human being' or 'X is a lampstand'. In order to know whether X is a person, we must first know whether X is a human being or a lampstand. The term 'person' does not identify an X as a such-and-such; it says something further about an X already specified as a such-and-such. On the other hand, it does not ascribe some further property to X, for there is no 'property' of personal existence. On the contrary, it is on the basis of certain definite identifiable properties that we are licensed say of some Xs that they are persons.

What are these properties? And when we have established them, what does the predication of personal existence add? We begin with a preliminary and unsystematic collection of pointers.

We need some preconception to help us embark upon our exploration, an idea of what we are searching for. And this lies to hand in

---

[2] Galatians 2: 6 [where Paul's Greek has πρόσωπον the Latin Vulgate *personam*. 'God does not recognise these personal distinctions' NEB.]

the phenomenon that we have already noticed, that the word 'person' is applied in a peculiar way. On the one hand, it ascribes a special value, on the other serves for numerical indexing, ignoring distinguishing features. On the one hand, it is not a classificatory term, identifying any X as belonging to some class of thing; on the other, it 15 is not a property, but denotes the bearer of certain properties. If we refrain from dismissing these two patterns of use as simple equivocations and pay attention to what connects them, we have our first pointer in the right direction. A person must be someone who is what he is in a *different way* from that in which other things, or other animals, are what they are.

What do we mean by 'a different way'? Perhaps a line from *The Magic Flute* can help us. Sarastro's well-known aria commending philanthropy, 'Within this hallowed dwelling is heard no rage or strife', ends with a sentence that sounds odd, but which everyone will understand: 'Whoe'er these truths will not maintain, doth not deserve to be a man.'[3] 'Being a man' is here represented as a privilege, something one can forfeit. We understand readily enough what it might mean that a man did not deserve to be a prince; but who is there that could deserve, or not deserve, to be a man? 'Man' is a classificatory term that specifies *a limine* who is in a position to deserve or not deserve things. It is a substance-term, in Aristotle's language, distinguished by not being a predicate of any other thing but identifying things that may then be the subject of predicates.[4]

We can clarify the point by thinking of a dog, who is sometimes a barking animal and sometimes a not-barking animal. When not barking he continues to exist; but the moment he stops being a dog, we say that 'he' is no more. To this paradigm one might object: he has simply stopped being a *dog*, just as when he is not barking he has stopped being a *barker*. In ceasing to be a dog he has not vanished into thin air, but has changed into something else, a corpse initially and compost later. There is an underlying material substrate of which one can predicate dogginess at first and decomposition afterwards. But this line of thought is successfully rebutted by Aristotle's distinction between two kinds of change, coming-to-be and ceasing-to-be

---

[3] E. Schickaneder and W. A. Mozart, *The Magic Flute* no. 15.
[4] Aristotle, *Metaphysics* 1017^{b}10.

on the one hand, alteration on the other.[5] When a human being dies, we do not say that some thing, a piece of spatio-temporally localized matter, has altered its condition; we say that someone, a human being, has ceased to exist. The classificatory term is what gives primary *a limine* specification to any X of which we propose to say anything. The stuff of which X is composed is referred to simply as 'the stuff of X'. It is not the true subject of our predication. 16

So when Sarastro says, 'Whoe'er these truths will not maintain, doth not deserve to be a man,' he does not mean that some piece of matter defined by space–time coordinates has forfeited manhood as a man may forfeit princedom. A piece of matter has nothing to do with deserving or forfeiting. Only a *man* can deserve or forfeit manhood, which is what makes Sarastro's saying paradoxical. To be able to deserve or forfeit, one must be a man already. Yet we have an intuitive grasp of Sarastro's meaning, and that is because we do not think about a man's relation to manhood in the same way that we think of a dog's relation to dogginess. We think in terms of a mental self-differentiation, something we never conceive of in the relation of other individual members to their kinds. A man is obviously not a man in the same way that a dog is a dog, i.e. simply and solely by being an instance of the species.

This becomes clearer when we consider the application of the term 'human'. In one sense anything that human beings do is human, even those peculiar atrocities of which animals are incapable. But we do not use the word like that. We use it as a normative term to differentiate kinds of conduct of which we approve from others of which we disapprove. Sometimes this rule of speech is interestingly reversed, as when we call some kinds of conduct 'human' which we disapprove of to a degree, but wish to excuse: 'to err is human'. But such excusable conduct is always a breach of the norm through weakness. We do not use the word 'human' of malicious breach, though malice, too, is characteristic of human beings. On the contrary, we call the most perversely malicious kinds of behaviour 'inhuman'. Inhumanity, it is clear, is a trait specifically restricted to the human race.

---

[5] Aristotle, *De genesi et corruptione* 314ª1–315ª25.

II

These paradoxes, then, provide us with a first pointer to something that makes us designate instances of *homo sapiens* not only with the species-name, 'man', but as 'persons'.

As a rule we make a distinction between men and animals. But 'man' is first and foremost a zoological species-term, and ancient and medieval philosophy treated 'man' as one among the animal species, *animal rationale*. The fact that for us the word 'animal' (*Tier*), like *bestia* in Latin, carries the connotation of 'non-human', makes us prefer the formal expression 'living creature' (*Lebewesen*) when we want a category embracing both men and animals. This again reveals how a man instantiates the human species in a different way from that in which individual members of other species instantiate theirs.

This peculiarity can be clarified by the way we refer to ourselves with the personal-pronoun 'I'. 'I' is an ostensive term. When we say 'I', we are not referring to '*an* Ego'—a pure invention of the philosophers!— but to a particular living creature, a particular human being identified by other speakers with the use of a personal name. But when this particular human being identifies the selfsame person that he or she actually *is*, the term 'I' is used. And the account to be given of this 'I' is anomalous in two respects.

In the first place, nobody can doubt that 'I' refers to something real. The same cannot be said about 'he', 'she', 'it', 'this', 'that', or even 'you', which may all on occasion refer to imaginary objects. But anyone who says 'I', exists. That is the truth behind Descartes's celebrated *Cogito ergo sum*.

But what do we mean, 'exists'? Who is it that says 'I' and exists, and what is he? One can imagine someone saying 'I' and not knowing the answer to this, or getting it wrong. And that is the second anomaly with this personal pronoun. To identify a thing, as we have observed, means to identify it qualitatively as a such-and-such, to situate it as 18 a member of a kind by the use of a classificatory term. But that is not true of identification with the personal pronoun 'I'. Someone may be mistaken about who and what he is, ignorant of his position in time and space; robbed by an accident of memory and sight, he may ask, 'Who am I?' 'Where am I?', even forgetting that he is a human being.

Yet there is no unclarity about who 'I' refers to. 'I' simply picks out an item regardless of its qualitative features; it refers to the speaker, irrespective of what the speaker may be besides.

We should not make the mistake of thinking that 'I' refers to a purely mental *res cogitans,* or to a bare existent without a nature, which must, as it were, first realize itself *ex nihilo* as some thing with some nature. That is to misunderstand the phenomenon. It is not insignificant that when the victim of amnesia asks, 'Who am I? Where am I?', he presumes he is *someone,* with characteristics of *some* kind, situated *somewhere* in the wide world. He does not think of himself as 'an Ego'. If he is conscious at all, he is aware that he is more than consciousness. Yet the knowledge of who and where he is has not kept up with the knowledge *that* he is. He cannot identify himself by qualitative distinguishing features. I know that I have a nature of a certain kind and with certain characteristics; but this nature is not simply what I am. When I say 'I am', I have not said enough to plot my coordinates in time and space; but I aspire to plot them.

The human being, then, is not what he is in the same way as everything else we encounter is what it is. Our talk of 'persons' has to do with this phenomenon. Pointing in the same direction is the universally attested idea of metamorphosis. In Kafka's *novella* 'Metamorphosis' a man is transformed into a giant insect. Such transformations crowd the pages of folk-tale and myth—we may think of 'The Frog King' or 'Brother and Sister'. Ovid collected a series of transformation-myths in his *Metamorphoses,* and from more recent literature we should mention Guimaraes Rosa's short story 'My Uncle the Jaguar', a monologue in which the reader 19 accompanies the narrator through his transformation into a jaguar. What is going on in these stories?

It is not what Aristotle calls 'substantial change'. Substantial change consists in the ceasing-to-be of one thing, and the coming-to-be of another out of the material substrate of the first. The one thing is finished with; the other has taken its place. The material continuum between the two is what Aristotle calls *hylē,* 'matter', and the matter of which the two successive substances are composed is the only continuous element. In nature we experience such changes constantly. An organism disintegrates and turns to loam, and this in turn provides material for a new organism. But that is not the stuff of nightmares, myths, or literary fantasies.

The distinctive feature of metamorphosis is that the subject himself, not only a material substrate, survives the transformation. The subject exists at first as a human being who says 'I', and subsequently exists as an insect, frog, hind, jaguar or even, in Ovid, a tree. The interesting thing is that only human beings undergo metamorphosis of species with their identities intact, and they may on occasion be changed back, or 'set free'. We do not find animals transformed into men unless they were men before. Abstract individual identity is a feature of dreams, too, where we encounter someone whom we know to be so-and-so, though he has no resemblance to the person in question at all. We simply know that it *is* this person. But what is it that we know? What does it mean to say, it *is* this person, whose name we know but with whom the image in our dream very clearly has nothing in common? This is another case of abstracting individual identity from qualitative similarities. It does not matter that all these examples are fictive. The point is simply that though the abstraction is possible only because human beings have qualitative attributes, qualitative attributes do not define personal identity. *Who* we are is not simply interchangeable with *what* we are.

Generally speaking the same conception of metamorphosis is at work in ideas of reincarnation—most strongly, naturally, in those 20 where men are reborn as animals. In Western doctrines a human being comes back only as another human being, but with such new characteristics as prompt us to distinguish his individual identity from an identity of quality. In Indian doctrines, on the other hand, Sarastro's line is taken literally: someone 'does not deserve to be a man' *next time*, and so comes back as something else, yet without ceasing to be the selfsame someone.

III

There is a third angle, finally, from which I would like to approach the phenomenon of inner difference between the human subject and himself.

Any entity in nature displays what it is by what it does, by its manner of expressing itself. As the scholastic adage had it: *agere sequitur esse*.[6] But this applies in the strictest sense only to the objects of physics. Even plants and animals display what we call 'deviation from type'. Even animals are not simply 'what they are'. To a certain extent they may fail to realize what they are, for what they are is not accounted for wholly in terms of how they display themselves. No, essentially the animal is an 'inside', something that 'goes out for' (*Aussein-auf*), or pursues things. Only when we treat it as such do we take it seriously as a *living* creature. Normally we speak of the pursuit of living things as 'drive' for self- and species-preservation. Not as though this purpose was actually present to the animal as an idea; the ideas that are present to animals are food, mate, prey, peril; it is only we, the observers, for whom these drives function as a system explained by the theory of evolution. But be this explanation as it may, wherever there is teleological destination, the pursuit of something, there is the possibility of failure.

In physics there is no such thing as failure. In the physicist's realm only the physicist fails, nature never. To fail in anything, a thing must pursue it. A three-legged hare is a 'malformed' hare or an 'unlucky' hare, because three-leggedness is more than simple deviance from a statistical norm; it means the hare is less well adapted to its ecological niche than a four-legged hare, less well in itself, with slimmer chances of survival. To 'go for', to 'fare well', to 'fare ill': all these expressions point to the same inner difference between what a living creature *properly* is, and what it *actually* is. Human beings are living creatures, too, and so participate in this difference that Aristotle says is characteristic of all higher life-forms, the difference between *zēn* and *eu zēn*, living and living well.[7]

Human beings are apparently unique in being conscious of this difference. In speaking about animals we are forced back upon one of two possible analogies: an analogy with our own human experience, or an analogy with machines, which are systems that appear such only to our view. That is to say, the phenomenon of pursuit, the specific difference introduced by 'drive', is discernible only to

---

[6] Thomas Aquinas, *Summa contra gentiles* 3. 69.
[7] Aristotle, *De anima* 434ᵇ21.

the kind of being that rises above this difference and relates to the form of its own animal life at a higher level. In pain, for example, human beings can see something beyond the sheer impairment of their vitality. Defence or evasion are not their only reactions. They can expose themselves to pain deliberately; they can take a negative view of life as the condition of pain; or else, in a kind of selective self-negation, they can distance themselves from this or that property, wish or drive, regretting that they are as they are, and wishing they were different. When we say that someone must learn to 'accept himself', we are not recommending the closing-up of this inner difference, a return to blind self-assertion, the response of defiance when criticized for some inconsiderateness: 'That's just the kind of person I am!' 'The kind of person I am' is only the other side of 'the kind of bastard he is!', which is how we nail someone pitilessly to the character revealed in his behaviour and deny him the possibility, which forgiveness could facilitate, of appearing in a different light. No one is simply and solely what he is. Self-acceptance is a process that presumes non-identity with self, and must be seen as the conscious appropriation of the non-identical—in Jung's term, 'integration'.

Harry Frankfurt has developed a similar line of thought in speaking of 'secondary volitions'.[8] This is the phenomenon of taking a position on our own desires and acts of will. We can desire to have, or not to have, certain desires. We evaluate not only the objects of our desires, but our desires themselves. When we succeed in bringing our desires into line with our evaluation, we feel free; when we do not, we experience impotence, like addicts and compulsive offenders who have wills that run counter to their own wills. One can even desire to desire something without the will to gratify the desire, merely willing to experience it. When Odysseus wanted to hear the Sirens and experience the longing that their song aroused, he took careful precautions not to fall victim to that longing: he had his companions chain him to the mast of the ship, their ears stopped up, his unstopped.[9] Plato in the *Laws* suggests that where possible young people should be administered anxiety-producing drugs, to train

[8] *Journal of Philosophy* 68 (1971), 5–20.
[9] Homer, *Odyssey* 12.

them in the cool-headedness to do what they see to be good and right in the teeth of anxieties.[10] Secondary volitions are not simply stronger resolutions that prevail within the parallelogram of motives. In fact, they do not always prevail, in which case we may try to manipulate the parallelogram itself, by organizing a system of rewards and penalties for ourselves to reinforce desirable but weak first-order resolutions, when the crunch comes, with another first-order resolution. The damage smoking does to one's health may often not be a sufficient motive to overcome the desire to smoke; but one may compensate by a device that rewards abstinence, so that the anticipated reward is enough to enable one to give up smoking. In secondary volitions we treat ourselves as we would another person whose behaviour we seek to control. In this, however, we come up against an unbreachable boundary. It lies beyond our control to alter the fundamental direction in which we influence ourselves. If it were not so, we would face the problem of an infinite series 23 of willings-to-will.

At this stage of our initial exploration we cannot go into the nature of this primary, spontaneous movement that is distinct from all its objective indications. The point to grasp is simply how it demon-strates the self-differentiation of a human subject from everything that may be true *about* him. This, it seems, is fundamental to our talk about persons. We are familiar with this self-difference from discus-sions of 'reflection'. But reflection is only one of its manifestations. Our existence is marked by interior difference even when we are not reflecting; it makes reflection possible, but does not depend on it. Reflection is turning in on oneself, but we can also describe difference as coming out of oneself, as the 'de-centred position', in Helmut Plessner's term.[11] Here the decisive factor is not the use of 'I' in speaking of oneself, but the use of the third person. Small children regularly speak of themselves in this way, which is more remarkable in some respects even than the use of 'I'. To speak of oneself in the third person is to step out of the central position that all living things in nature occupy in relation to their environments, and to see oneself

[10] Plato, *Laws* 1. 648A–C.
[11] Helmut Plessner, 'Die Stufen des Organischen und der Mensch', *Gesammelte Schriften* iv (Frankfurt: Suhrkamp, 1981), 360 ff.

with other people's eyes as something 'out there'.[12] For this one must adopt a point of view from outside one's own organic centre. Morality is possible only with this capacity for self-objectification and self-relativization; only on these terms, too, is speech possible. Speech differs from the cries of living things in nature, in that it anticipates the standpoint of the one who is to hear what is spoken. When someone says 'I am in pain', that statement is not merely a cry by other means. The immediate expression of pain must be suppressed, in order to form a communication about the pain as an event in the world and to make that communication intelligible to another. To this end, far from merely 'expressing ourselves', we must submit to a prescribed system of rules that makes understanding possible. Correspondingly, the system of speech itself prompts the emergence of self-difference, the distance from ourselves that gives rise to our talk of 'persons'.

As human beings we are aware of another's gaze fixed on us. We 24 are aware of the gaze of *all* others, the gaze of all *possible* others, the 'view from nowhere'. That we experience this gaze and know about it, or believe we do, makes it impossible to understand ourselves as mere organic systems that constitute their own environment, where every encounter has meaning only in relation to the system's requirements. Stepping out of our organic centre, we stand in a dimension where there is no 'natural' decision about what has significance, and what the significance is. The medium of understanding itself is not given in nature, for there is no natural human speech. But neither is speech an invention. It is a presupposition of our entering the communicative event in which we realize ourselves as what we are, as persons.

But why '*persons*'?

---

[12] Cf. Robert Spaemann, *Happiness and Benevolence*, tr. J. Alberg (Edinburgh: T & T Clark, 2000).

2

Why We Call Persons 'Persons'

I

In our first approach to our subject we assembled some peculiar features that help us understand why human beings, ourselves among them, are classified not only biologically as a particular mammalian species, but in a different kind of class altogether, the class of 'persons'. But is it correct to say that persons constitute a class? It is an intriguing question. On the one hand, 'person' functions like any other term we use to classify particular entities. We can ask which particulars belong to the class, and what features qualify them to do so; we can ask whether human beings are the only constituent members of the class, and indeed whether all human beings are members of it. On the other hand, there are two factors that make it awkward to speak of persons as a class.

First, when we describe particular individuals as 'persons', we do not *mean* that they belong to a certain class, or are instances of a generic category. What this word means is that their relation to what they are—to the class or species to which they belong—is not the normal relation that members have to their class, that of 'falling within' it. Persons do in fact invariably belong to some natural species, but they do not belong to it in the same way that other individual organisms belong to their species.

The second reason which makes it ontologically awkward, though logically unobjectionable, to speak of persons as a class, is that when we apply the term 'person' to individuals we accord a special status to them, that of inviolability. To accord this status is to accept an obligation to acknowledge its relevance. We can declare that someone is a king, a city-freeman, or an officer, and yet be opposed to kings and officers and think the title 'freeman' an anachronistic survival. 26 But if we do not intend to *respect* human beings as persons, we either deny that they *are* persons, or we consider the designation vacuous and unserviceable. To employ the term 'person' is to acknowledge definite obligations to those we so designate. The decision as to who these are depends, of course, upon certain describable features; but while personhood corresponds to these features, it is not itself a specifying feature, but a status—the only status, indeed, that we do not confer, but acquire naturally. (Which does not mean that it is an endowment of nature. The distinction is the same as in the case of language: it is natural for the human race to communicate linguistically, but there is no language given us in nature.)

Since 'person' is not a descriptive term, it cannot be defined ostensively, by reference to simple qualities such as colour, nor narratively, by telling a story to fix its reference. The phrase, 'the Battle of the Teutonburger Wald', carries a story with it; and whether that phrase refers to something real depends on whether the story is true. The same applies in principle to natural kinds. They, too, have their story, and the theory of evolution is one possible attempt to tell it. But with terms that have a normative content it is a different matter. True, to make their meaning understood we must again tell a story; but this time it is not the story of the referent, but of the term itself.

From our considerations up to this point it would seem obvious to conclude that the term 'person' belonged among these normative terms. In fact, as we shall shortly discover, it belongs to a third class altogether. For the present, however, it is enough to establish that the use of this term does have a normative implication. To ascribe 'personhood' (in the thematically substantive sense we are discussing) is more than to declare something to be the case. It is to make a demand. And to understand the demand, we must see how it arose.

The history of the term 'person' is a circuitous one, and in retracing 27 it we are drawn briefly into the heart of Christian theology. Without Christian theology we would have had no name for what we now call 'persons', and, since persons do not simply occur in nature, that means we would have been without them altogether. That is not to say that we can only speak intelligibly of persons on explicitly theological suppositions, though it is conceivable that the disappearance of the theological dimension of the idea could in the long run bring about the disappearance of the idea itself.

Plato never once conceived the thought that we have when we use the term. He had, to be sure, put behind him the Homeric view of man as a theatre for the play of uncontrolled forces. This view it is that earns Homer his banishment from Plato's republic as a bad educational influence. Human autonomy is the concern of Plato's Socrates, too, in his struggle against sophistic rhetoric. The speech of Gorgias in praise of Helen denied autonomy and the responsibility that accompanied it: Helen was possessed, not by supernatural powers but by words; the irresistible speeches of Paris left her no freedom of choice in yielding to him.[1] Plato, for his part, knows of speeches to which one can only yield; but these are the speeches that make one wise, and to yield to them is not to yield to the speaker, but to the very same truth the speaker has yielded to. It is the truth that makes us free: to yield to it is to do what one wills. Rhetoric is the art of producing an appearance of truth, and so impelling people to do what they would not will if they knew the truth. And that is to do what they do not *really* will; for to do what one wills, one must know what one does. Which is why Plato also banishes the poets, with their divine inspiration, from his city. For even if they speak the truth, they do so not because they know the truth, but because they are possessed by some power, and lack the means of telling where this power is taking them. Because their speech is not really *theirs,* it cannot stand up to the acid test of Socratic dialectic, which tests speech for its truth.

For Plato, then, the wise man is free. He, and he alone, does what he wills. That is no accident; it is because he himself is the ground of his actions. But what does it mean to say, 'he himself'? Here, without doubt, we embark upon a train of thought that will lead to the person; yet it is clear that this precise thought was never entertained by Plato. Talk of a man's ruling himself means, for Plato, that he is ruled by that part of the soul which can give instruction and wisdom about what is worth every man's seeking. He is ruled by reason. Autonomy is simply reason's dominion. But reason is a common

---

[1] Gorgias, *Reden, Fragmente und Testimonien,* ed. T. Buchheim (Hamburg, 1989), 3 ff.

possession, the organ of truth that all share. The particular individual is of no significance in comparison with the universal idea, a nothing that exists only to realize and implement the real thing, which is the idea. In Plato's republic only the lower classes have individual fulfilment of some kind—marriage, possessions, enjoyment, etc.—as the goal of their existence. Their share in truth is to let themselves be ruled by those who have put individuality behind them and have only the universal in view, those with no personal ties, family, or possessions, who are concerned only to implement the idea of justice in the republic. Plato's demand for a regime of philosophers is tantamount to rejecting the rule of men by men, for the regime of philosophers is a regime not of men but of the idea. We do not imagine, after all, that Pythagoras exercises personal rule just because everyone admits the force of Pythagoras's Theorem.

II

The polarity of universal and individual, of class and member, leaves open for Plato the possibility that an individual human may rise above individuality, above being simply a unit in a class. By comprehending universal nature itself in thought, one may break out of particularity. But one thing never enters Plato's mind: that someone who in this way 'achieves the Universal' attains a *higher level of being than the Universal itself.* That the justice realized and made concrete in a just man is more than the idea of justice; that the man who dies for his fatherland is more than his fatherland. As an atomic particle, he merely contributes to the whole, the people; but in realising his contributory role, he himself becomes a totality, compared with which the people is only an abstraction. Hegel coined the term *der* 29 *Einzelner* ('the Individual') for one who, having taken the Universal into himself and realized it, attains a standing beyond the opposition of particular and universal. Persons are 'individuals' (*Individuen*), not in the sense that they are *instances* of a universal concept, but as the particular individuals they are, who in an individual and irreplaceable way *are* the Universal. They are not parts of a larger whole, but totalities. In relation to them everything else is only a part.

For persons, then, self-determination does not mean that there is a truth beyond the individual, which is the really important thing, and that individuality is comparatively unimportant, arising only at the level of the senses. That is how things appear in Plato: reason is the medium of the universal, and where reason rules, man is free. But why are so many people not ruled by reason, if the point of reason is to rule? If we reply, 'Because they refuse reason', Plato will not understand us. For everyone wills what is good for him, and what is good for him is simply what is good in itself. If people refuse *that*, it can only be that they do not know it. Why do they not know it? At this point ancient philosophy begins to go round in circles.

The answer of the New Testament to this question is as follows: They do not know it because they refuse to know it. They 'loved darkness rather than light'.[2] The first thing that the Holy Spirit reveals, according to the Gospel of John, is the meaning of sin: that 'they do not believe in me'.[3] This way of speaking is as un-Socratic as could be conceived, and is the source of the discovery of the person. Underlying it is this thought: it is not the lottery of nature, a function of the genes and education, that determines whether or not the absolute claim of the rational good prevails in any human life; the basis lies in the human being him- or herself. Following the New Testament, Christianity calls this basis 'the heart'. Unlike reason, which is by definition always rational, but is sometimes unenlightened and ineffective in exerting control, the heart is always in control, but makes its own decision as to who or what it will accept direction from. On what basis does it make that decision? On the basis that it is a heart of such and such a kind, with such and such a 'nature', about which it can do nothing? No. According to this account the heart is not a nature. There is no condition of the heart, no specific quality, that could be a basis for defection from good or for love of darkness. The heart is its own basis, and needs no further basis. There is no equivalent in the conceptual or terminological repertoire of antiquity. The heart's identity goes deeper than every specific quality. This gives voice to a real discovery about human existence, a discovery corresponding to the experience of gratitude that someone is the way she is, and of blame, to oneself or another, simply for being

---

[2] John 3: 19.   [3] John 16: 9.

the way we are. Certainly, in the New Testament, too, evil is closely associated with ignorance. But in the New Testament evil is the basis of ignorance, not, as for Plato's Socrates, ignorance the basis of evil. That explains the difference between the hard words of Jesus against his opponents and the friendly, ironic way that Socrates speaks of his.

The term 'heart' underlies the later development, and so amounts, more or less, to the discovery of the person. To strengthen this observation, the decision between good and evil, light and darkness, is not a decision about an idea, but about a person, who is the ultimate revelation of the truth. The Johannine Christ sees sin as actually consisting in the fact that 'they do not believe in me'. In another place he can say: 'If I had not come...they would not have sin.'[4] Knowledge of the truth is thought of as a personal act of belief. Truth itself appears not as the universal that is greater than any individual, but as the unique countenance of another individual person.

III

It took several centuries for thought to digest the experience that found expression here, and to integrate the new concept within the ancient terminology. How did the Latin word *persona* acquire a key position in this process? Its roots, like those of the Greek *prosopon*, lay in the world of the theatre. It meant the 'part' as distinct from the 'player'. It is, in fact, precisely the term that may still appear today at the head of a list of characters in a play: Dramatis Personae.[5] Originally the *persona* was simply the mask through which the actor spoke; later it was extended to mean a role in society, the social position one held. One of the decisive elements in our modern concept of the person, that of non-identity, was already present: the actor is the performer, not what is performed. But in contrast to our modern usage, the person was not what lay *behind* the role and made

---

[4] John 15: 22.
[5] [The author alludes here to the German words 'die Personen und ihre Darsteller' which appear on a theatre programme where we would find the words 'the Cast'.]

the performance possible. It was the role itself, and what lay behind the role was 'nature'. Antiquity knew no way of getting behind the nature of a man or woman, no way of regarding the nature itself as object. Nature is the bottom line, factually and normatively. The *persona*, therefore, was a secondary, assumed identity, weaker than the natural identity. So Seneca can write: 'No one can support a part for long. Pretence quickly gives way to nature.'[6]

All the same, this secondary identity, the role one performs, is something one is responsible for. The actor must play his part according to the book, and the Stoics compared the right conduct of life with a good performance in the theatre. This was to promote an indirect relation of the agent to his primary ends. The primary ends of the human agent as an animal organism are to sustain life. But as an intelligent being the human agent has a special end, beautifully foreshadowed by his nature, which is to act *intelligently*. Cicero, too, suggests that we owe something to our *persona*, the part that we play; for our duties, *officia,* are determined by our roles.[7] In the modern conception of an 'official' we still detect the ancient idea of the person.

The philologists of Alexandria based themselves on the concept of the person as role when they distinguished the three possible positions in the speech-act as the 'first', 'second', and 'third person', an idea taken over by Latin grammarians, who referred to a 'threefold nature of persons': the person who speaks, the person who is spoken to, and the person spoken of. In the case of the second, and especially the third, a person may be substituted for by another living creature or a thing.[8]

The third step to note is the use of *persona* in Roman jurisprudence of the imperial age. Here for the first time we find *persona* as equivalent to a human agent, designating either the distinctive status of the freeman as opposed to the slave or that of the human agent as

---

[6] Seneca, *De clementia* 1. 1. 6: *Nemo potest personam diu ferre. Ficta cito in naturam suam recidunt.*

[7] Cf. Cicero, *De officiis* 1. 2. 4: *nulla enim vitae pars neque publicis neque privatis neque forensibus neque domesticis in rebus, neque si tecum agas quid, neque si cum altero contrahas, vacare officio potest in eoque et colendo sita vitae est honestas omnis et neglegendo turpitudo.*

[8] See 'Person', in the *Historisches Wörterbuch der Philosophie,* vii, ed. Ritter and Gründer (Basle: Schwabe, 1989), 269–83 (M. Fuhrmann) and 283–300 (B. Kible).

opposed to all other entities. In the jurists the word *homo* applies principally to slaves, or else to biological members of the human race to whom no definite status is assigned. On the other hand there is also a distinction made between 'persons' and 'things', in which all human beings, slaves included, are 'persons'. Slaves are 'persons subject to another's right' (*personae alieno iuri subiectae*), as opposed to 'persons of their own right' (*personae sui iuris*).[9]

What all these ancient applications of the word have in common is that, though they refer to human beings and sometimes to all human beings, they view them not as instances of a kind or examples of a general concept, but as bearers of a social role (in the widest sense) or as occupants of a legal status. Behind this role and presupposed by it, there stands the bearer of the role, the human nature itself. In Stoicism, however, there is a conception of human nature itself as acted out like a part; and what the subject of *this* performance may be is left entirely in the dark. Actually, there seems to be no subject at all, for the Stoic determinism and fatalism made it all come down in the end to a matter of destiny whether the performance would succeed or fail, and wisdom was nothing in the last resort but the unprotesting acceptance of this universal destiny.

IV

To understand the shift of perspective by which the term 'person' came to mean a subject relating to its nature like an actor to a role, we must examine the way the term was used in speculative Christian doctrine in the first centuries after Christ. There were two occasions on which it was serviceable in resolving paradoxes that arose in the attempt to think consistently about statements of the New Testament and their interpretation in the church.

The first paradox arose in the course of an endeavour to reconcile an uncompromising Jewish monotheism with statements in the New Testament where Jesus describes himself as 'one' with the Father, or tells the disciples that 'he who has seen me has seen the Father'.[10] The

---

[9] Gaius, *Institutiones*, I. 10 f., I. 48, I. 142.   [10] John 10: 30, 14: 9.

prologue of John's Gospel speaks of the Logos become flesh in Jesus simply as 'God'. On the other hand Jesus speaks of God as his Father, and addresses the Father in prayer; which ruled out the idea that Jesus was simply a theophany like those in ancient mythology, an earthly appearance of God the Father.

Furthermore, the New Testament speaks of the 'Pneuma', or 'Spirit' of God poured out upon mankind through Christ, and even accords the Spirit hypostatic existence as a reality distinct from the Father and the Son. In John's Gospel Christ speaks of the 'Paraclete', and of the 'Spirit of truth' that the Father will send in his (Christ's) name, who 'will teach you [*sc.* his disciples] all things'.[11] The earliest Christian theologians were unswerving monotheists. They understood it as their task to conceive the unity of God consistently with the distinction of Father, Son and Pneuma, and this they did by understanding the latter as a distinction *within* God. Here they were assisted by such sayings of Jesus in John's Gospel as, 'Before Abraham was, I am.'[12] The 'I' of Jesus in this text is identified with the Logos in the prologue of the Gospel: 'In the beginning was the Logos, and the Logos was with God, and the Logos was God.' This Logos, it goes on, 'became flesh'.[13]

We must, of course, observe the connection between this text and later Neoplatonism—at least so far as its reception in the Hellenistic world is concerned, though the New Testament, too, belongs to the Hellenistic world! Plotinus's theory of the primordial One and its emanations affords a special point of comparison. From the One is derived Intelligence, or *Nous*; from *Nous* is derived the World-Soul. Christian thinkers, especially those from the Greek-speaking East such as Origen and the Cappadocians, are clearly influenced by the idea of eternal emanation from the One. But in their hands it undergoes a series of modifications. A radical break is introduced between the first two emanations and all that follows them, right down to the level of matter. These lower entities were no longer seen as 'emanations' deriving from the higher by logical and ontological necessity, but, following the conception of Genesis, they were described as 'creation'. They arose not from necessity but from a free decision of God. The Absolute, the One, has decided—from

---

[11] John 14: 26.   [12] John 8: 58.   [13] John 1: 1, 14.

eternity, to be sure, but in complete freedom. The metaphor of emanation, 'flowing out from' godhead, is replaced by the metaphor of calling-forth from nothing. The Godhead itself, meanwhile, understood as the subject of something like free decision, can no longer be conceived as a Monad without self-mediation. For the implication of that conception was that the Other proceeded from the One immediately and necessarily. The first emanation, the Logos, makes it possible for the One to be *known* as One, since without the Logos the One cannot know itself. But according to Plotinus the One does not know itself; even the dawning of its consciousness lies beyond its own horizon. Christian thinkers, on the other hand, conceive of the One as God. They thus conceive it as having this mediation *within* itself, so that it knows and affirms itself. The implication of which is that the first two emanations—not freely posited creations but necessary self-articulations of the divine being—are conceived not as a declension from the One to lower levels of potency, but as consistent with the continuing self-possession of the One, which contains its own Other in itself. Logos and Spirit are, so to speak, the same One another time. They are not three instances of the concept 'god', i.e. three gods. That would be inconsistent with biblical monotheism, and would destroy the idea of the One.

To approach the same point from the opposite end: in Platonic, Aristotelian, and also Neoplatonic thought, the replication of one and the same thing many times over requires a medium distinct from the multiplied form, providing, as it were, a dimension within which the form can multiply itself. Leibniz, in abandoning this concept of an indeterminate material, also denied the possibility that there could be a plurality of individuals numerically but not qualitatively distinct. What the Greeks called the three 'hypostases' of the godhead, however, were distinguishable only numerically. The infinite potency of the One allowed of no replication, only of inner differentiation, so that unity came to be thought of as a process of self-mediation, an eternal occurrence. In other words, unity was thought of as *life*. The One is no longer the inexpressible, ceasing to be One as soon as it is expressed. It is self-expressing. This inner distinction is not to be thought of in qualitative terms, as though the hypostases were different from each other. In that case the Source would not recognize and express itself fully and completely in the Logos, and the Logos would be somehow different from the one whose Logos it was. In Christian understanding the Logos is not different from the Father, but 'other than' the Father. The distinction is simply the asymmetry of the relation: the Father begets the Son, and the Son does not beget the Father. When all is said and done, it is a purely numerical distinction. (We have to remind ourselves that these highly speculative distinctions were so much part of the air they breathed in Constantinople of the fourth and fifth centuries, that, as Gregory of Nyssa tells us, one would be drawn into discussion of the essential likeness or unlikeness of the Father and the Son in the godhead before one had an opportunity to ask for a loaf of bread![14])

Yet how are we to think of a purely numerical distinction of emanations and origin without imagining a spatial separation? The Greek theologians called at this point on the abstract concept of 'hypostasis', which meant something like a self-standing existent. Western theologians, following the North African Tertullian, took up the grammarians' analysis of the speech-act and its associated concept of a 'person', applying it even to Old Testament exegesis, in asking especially of the Psalms, where it is often unclear at first glance who the 'I' is, 'Who is speaking? What about? And to whom?'[15] It is Tertullian, too, who replaces the Greek conception of hypostasis with the less abstract and speculative 'person'. The grammarians' 'person' is not affected by the distinction of one from another. The same individual can be spoken of now in the first, now in the second or third person, and persons are distinguished only by their relative position in a given speech-situation. The Johannine discourse of the divine Logos made the speech-situation a natural model for the mystery of divine self-constitution.

'One being, three persons' is the formula on which Christian orthodoxy settled. 'Being' was not meant in the sense of Aristotle's 'second *ousia*', a general, multiply instantiated kind of being, indifferent to its instances, even to how many of them there might be. It was meant in the sense of a 'first *ousia*', a particular, individual

---

[14] Gregory of Nyssa, 'On the Divinity of the Son and the Holy Ghost', *PG* 46.557 f.
[15] Tertullian, *Adversus Praxean* 11. 4.

kind of being, which exists in the manner that the persons who realize it transmit it to one another in a definite order, having their reality in self-giving and self-receiving. The difference between the person and its condition, or the kind of being it is, is found immediately in the fact that a person so understood can only be thought of in relation to other persons, i.e. in plurality. When a later neoscholasticism taught that 'natural reason' could attain the conception of God as one person, its doctrine was incompatible with the idea of a free creation. A God who was *one* person would *necessarily* have finite persons as his correlate.

V

For a second time in the history of Christian theology the concept of person served to resolve a paradox thrown up for thought by the consciousness of faith. This had to do with how Jesus Christ could be thought of as at once the incarnation of the eternal divine Logos and as man in the true and proper sense, not as a hybrid of some third kind. Here, too, there were dramatic and prolonged controversies, brought to an end at the Council of Chalcedon by the use of a formula developed by the Greek Church Fathers: Jesus Christ had two 'natures', divine and human. The uniting of these two natures in an individual could not involve conflation, but was a matter of their both being 'had' by one 'person'. This person was the divine person: his existing relation to the divine mode of being was by 'having' it; now, in the incarnation it was thought, he related to a finite and created nature by 'having' that, too.[16] The personal name Jesus does not refer to a form of being, but to 'someone', one who bears it. So one can say 'Jesus is God', and (against the protest of the Nestorians) 'Mary is God-bearer, *theotokos*.'[17] What is born is not something, but someone, someone named by a personal name or personal pronoun. That is how Jesus can say of himself in St John's Gospel, 'Before Abraham was, I am'. It was the concept 'person', the equivalent of the

---

16 Symbolum Chalcedonense, in Denziger, *Enchiridion Symbolorum* 300–3.
17 Denziger 250.

Greek *hupostasis*, that made it possible to understand the application of the personal pronoun in this statement without making Jesus appear as a theophany clothed in human form. For the first Christians this point was decisively important, since it decisively excluded all associations with ancient mythology or borrowings from that source to clarify the Christian faith. Zeus appears as man, as cloud, as swan; but Zeus *is* none of these things. When he comes to Leda in the form of a swan, he begets a demigod. Jesus was never revered as a demigod. He is wholly human, with human soul, human spirit, and human will. This was now expressed in terms of his possession of a human 'nature'.

Phusis, or nature, is the term that is opposed to 'person' in Christology, where in the doctrine of the Trinity the opposition had been with *ousia*, or being. *Phusis* is the *ousia*, or being, of finite things, of things subject to becoming and passing away. Yet *phusis* is also used more or less unspecifically as a general term for whatever answers the question, 'What is that?' Cicero wrote a book *De natura deorum*, and we find similar references in Christian texts, especially in Christology, to 'divine nature'. The original sense of *phusis* as a principle of growth, becoming and passing away, has been ironed out into a concept of nature as everything that is what it is of itself—unlike artefacts.

In the sixth century Boethius, precisely in the context of Christological debate, made a list of various meanings of 'nature', and distinguishes four. First, nature means *every intelligible reality*, everything that answers the question 'What is that?'—irrespective of whether it is a substance or a property we are asking about, so that one may speak as well of the nature of a colour as of the nature of the gods. A second sense is more restricted: nature refers to *things*, i.e. substances, whether material or immaterial. More specifically still, in the third place, the term is applied to all *non-artificial* bodies. In the fourth place, finally, *natura* indicates not the concrete thing but the general form or kind of being to which it belongs, that by which the specific difference of one kind is determined in relation to all other kinds. This last meaning of nature it put to service by Boethius in his definition of 'person', which laid down a benchmark that was to last for a thousand years. In this definition, personhood is the specific way that 'rational natures' are concrete and individual:

'the individual substance of a rational nature'.[18] The word *substantia* is one Latin translation of the Greek *ousia*. The other translation is *essentia*, being. It is not possible to draw a sharp and unambiguous line between these two, for usage is variable, and can often only be understood by retranslation back into Greek. In the context of the doctrine of the Trinity *substantia* and *essentia* are equivalent, referring to the one divine substance in three hyypostases or persons; but here Boethius plainly uses *substantia* in the sense of a *hypostasis* as distinct from a kind of being, which he calls *natura*. What he means by substance is explained in the same text two pages later where *substantia* is replaced in the definition by *subsistentia*—the direct equivalent of *hypostasis*.

What does it mean to say that rational natures exist as persons? Of course, 'person' here is a *nomen dignitatis*; rational natures command a definite kind of respect. But the primary sense of Boethius's definition is ontological: the *natura rationalis* exists as a being-in-itself. But that is to say that an individual existing in this way cannot be displayed in full by any possible description. No description can replace *naming*. A person is *someone*, not *something*, not a mere instance of a kind of being that is indifferent to it.

VI

Boethius's definition, though by no means always unchallenged, lies behind all medieval discussion of the person, which is dominated as a result by the relation of qualitative and numerical identity, i.e. of description and naming. Richard of St Victor may be singled out as a critic whose objections amount in fact to a deepening of Boethius's intention. He raises difficulties about the application of the term 'substance', not noticing that Boethius himself makes it interchangeable with 'subsistence'. A person, Richard writes, cannot be a substance, only the bearer of a substance, for which he appeals for support to the canonical phrasing of the doctrine of the Trinity,

---

[18] Boethius, *Contra Eutychen et Nestorium* 3: *personae est definitio naturae rationabilis individua substantia*.

where the three divine persons are distinguished from the one divine substance. 'Substance', Richard goes on, denotes a something, a *quid*, a given *case of X* where there could in principle always be *other* concrete cases of X. 'Person', on the other hand, stands for 'a property of a unique subject'.[19] What 'person' means, then, is something that essentially cannot be encapsulated in description, however carefully specified, but must by definition belong to a unique individual in each case. Richard now offers his own definition: a person is 'a sole and self-standing existent in a singular mode of rational existence'.[20] Personhood is a mode of existence, not a qualitative state. It is the sustaining of existence as a particular individual—*existence*, not *essence*.

It is well known that the distinction of essence and existence in medieval philosophy arose in the context of defining contingency. This distinction has an obvious phenomenal basis in the way persons experience themselves. There is a well known essay of Thomas Nagel, 'What is it like to be a bat?'[21] Nobody would ask what it is like to be a car. Being a car is not like anything, because a car does not *exist* in other than a purely logical sense. The kind of thing indicated by the word 'car' is instantiated at a given space–time situation just for us who look on a certain arrangement of pieces of metal as a car.

Natural beings, on the other hand, exist in other than a purely logical sense. For them there is something 'it is like' to be themselves. We can, of course, never know what it is like to be a bat. We can only understand the question by analogy, from knowing what it is like to be a human being, or, more precisely, what it is like to be *this* human being. And here we make a distinction between the self that sustains existence, on the one hand, and *what* it is that exists, on the other. We say that someone finds life difficult, or that someone takes his or her own life, and in some stages of life we feel that simply existing is an effort. These expressions are all paradoxical. They speak of existing as an activity which subjects perform, though in order to perform any activity, a subject must exist first, while the 'activity' of existing is apparently a condition for there to be a subject to exist. We would do

[19] Richard of St Victor, *De Trinitate* 4. 6: *proprietas qui non convenit nisi uni soli.*
[20] 4. 24: *existens per se solum iuxta singularem quandam rationalis existentiae modum.*
[21] *Philosophical Review* 83 (1974), 435–50.

better to say that the 'what' of the subject's existence is a 'way of being'. In the case of the bat it would seem that its being is wholly swallowed up in its way of being, wholly accounted for as 'living'. Human beings, on the other hand, exist by distinguishing their being from their specific way of being, their specific 'nature'. Their nature is not what they *are*, pure and simple; their nature is something that they *have*. And this 'having' is their being. To be a person is the form in which 'rational natures' exist.

'Being' in the sense of 'existence' is predicated of different beings in different ways. Aristotle writes: 'Life is the being of living things'.[22] A lion does not *exist* on the one hand, *live* on the other; it exists only by living, and while it lives. But we have no analogous word for the being of persons, and if we wanted to invent one, we would immediately find ourselves in the midst of a controversy. There is a school of thought—it is the school of John Locke—for which the existence of persons is no less distinct and separate from that of other living creatures than we generally conceive the existence, i.e. the life, of living creatures as being from the inert objectivity of a corpse.

There will be more to say of this later. At this point we simply keep to the thesis of Richard of St Victor, that personhood is the mode of existence of a rational nature, and that it is peculiar to this mode of existence to be defined singularly, not as a kind of thing that could in principle appear in multiple copies. We are pointed in the same direction, though with greater perspicuity and clarity, by St Thomas Aquinas's observations on the same topic. He follows Boethius's definition in designating a person as a 'substance', but stipulates that it is *substantia prima*, Aristotle's 'first *ousia*', i.e. a concrete individual. While the word 'man' denotes a species, a natural kind defined by the specific predicates of its members, 'person' does not denote the kind, but the member of the kind, and not *as* a member of the kind, but as an individual. Person, writes Thomas, is not a *nomen intentionis*, but a *nomen rei*. That means, not a concept, but a name, a name for an indeterminate individual (*individuum vagum*). While the expression 'a particular man' can be applied to many men, it does not *mean* all of them, but only one, without saying which. Every man is 'a particular man'. But we can refer to men

---

[22] Aristotle, *De anima* 415^{b}13.

in the aspect of their being men, and we can refer to them in the aspect of their being so many unique individuals, each one of which *could* be referred to by a proper name. The word 'person' refers to a man *in the aspect* of one who bears a personal name. ' "A certain man",' Thomas writes, 'refers to human nature, or an individual in the aspect of its nature, together with the mode of existence that belongs to individual beings. The noun 'person', on the other hand, is not used to refer to an individual in the aspect of its nature, but to a thing which subsists *in* that nature.'[23] 'Person', then, is not a generic term, but a 'generalizable proper noun'.

Why can we call on such a generalizable proper noun only for individuals with a 'rational nature'? Because individuals with such a nature have a different kind of relation to their nature from other individuals. They are more than mere 'instances of...'. This difference is explained by Thomas when he writes that persons are individuals who 'exist *per se*' and have mastery of their own actions. Their actions do not simply proceed from their nature. 'Not only are they acted upon, like other things, but they themselves act.'[24] Events involving them do not simply happen, as with other beings; they act for themselves. That means, they are free.

To be 'a beginning of rest and movement' is, according to Aristotle, the nature of each thing; but these fit that description in a different way. Natural substances have a kind of 'beginning', a 'principle', in themselves, which is what Aristotle means by *phusis*.[25] So we could even say that only persons fully realize the concept of natural substance. In fact, of course, the paradigm on which Aristotle has based his concept of substance is the human being. If Thomas, by contrast, says that natural objects 'are acted upon' and that 'something happens' involving them, that is for two reasons: in the first place, the nature of any animal is imposed on it from

---

[23] Thomas Aquinas, *Summa Theologiae* (ST) 1. 30. 4: *Hoc tamen interest, quod aliquis homo significat naturam, vel individuum ex parte naturae, cum modo existendi qui competit singularibus; hoc autem nomen persona non est impositum ad significandum individuum ex parte naturae, sed ad significandum rem subsistentem in tali natura.*

[24] 1. 29. 1: *quae habent dominium sui actus, et non solum aguntur, sicut alia, sed per se agunt.*

[25] Aristotle, *Physics* 192^{b}14: τά μεν γὰρ φύσει ὄντα πάντα φαίνεται ἔχοντα ἐν ἑαυτοῖς ἀρχὴν κινήσεως καὶ στάσεως.

without, reproduced as a rule through sexual generation; in the second place, this nature that originates apart from us programmes in advance the specific reactions of the animal to external stimuli. An animal of one species reacts aggressively, where the animal of another species turns tail. A nature is a principle of specific reaction. With the concept of the person, however, we come to think of the particular individual as being more basic than its nature. This is not to suggest that these individuals *have* no nature, and start out by deciding for themselves what they are to be. What they do is assume a new relation to their nature; they freely endorse the laws of their being, or alternatively they rebel against them and 'deviate'. Because they are thinking beings, they cannot be categorized exhaustively as members of their species, only as individuals, who 'exist *in* their nature'. That is to say, they exist as persons.

3

How We Identify Persons

I

Words referring to classes of things, or 'classificatory' terms, are used in two ways: to indicate the particular entity that belongs to the kind in question, e.g. a particular apple; and to indicate the kind, the 'what it is', that makes this entity a such-and-such. In the one case we say 'this apple' or 'there is an apple lying there'. In the other case, we say 'this is an apple', or 'that is an apple lying there'.

Recent trends in logic have dispensed with this alternative by explaining the first case in terms of the second. For 'this apple is red', we are to understand, 'this is an apple, and this is red', which has the advantage of bringing out the implicit assumption that when we utter the sentence 'this apple is red', the thing we are talking about is actually an apple. So, should the supposed apple turn out to be a pear, the statement 'this apple is red' is not simply meaningless, but false.

But here there arises a difficulty. In the version, 'this is an apple, and this is red', how do we decide what 'this' stands for, if it is not 'this apple'? Imagine someone pointing to an apple and saying, '*this* is an apple'. We could suppose he was referring to a red patch on the skin, or to the round shape, or to the fact that it was given as a present (so that the word 'apple' on his lips meant 'gift'). What he intends by 'this' becomes clear only when we already know that it is an apple he is talking about, or at least a fruit. In the latter case we can represent his meaning in some such form as, 'this fruit is an apple'. But then the logician wants to translate this into 'This is a fruit, and this is an apple', so that the problem confronts us over again. What Quine has called 'indefiniteness of reference' is closely connected with the fact that in original acts of naming we cannot identify without ambiguity *this thing here* that has to be named. Every statement of the type F*x* appears to be circular, since to say anything about *x* we must know already what *x* is. 44

Furthermore, we must know *who is talking* about 'this thing here', if we are to know what thing he is talking about. 'This thing here' bespeaks a relation to the position of the one who is pointing at it. We must follow his gesture if we are to understand what he is referring to. A singular object can be identified only in relation to someone who identifies it, and only by being classified as a such-and-such. But this rule does not apply to the one who points. He is in the peculiar position of being able to refer to himself *without* classifying himself in relation to a kind and *without* clarifying his position in relation to the position of anything else. 'I' refers to a singular being without any elucidation of its meaning or any indication of its material content.

Persons are singular in an unparalleled fashion. Duns Scotus wrote of their 'ultimate solitude', St Thomas of their 'incommunicability'.[1] Yet self-identification cannot occur solipsistically. It necessarily implies the existence of others and the possibility of being available to their knowledge, as we shall shortly have occasion to demonstrate.

Somone coming round after a swoon may ask other people where he is, what time it is, even who he is. One of the mistakes for which Locke is responsible is to conceive of personal identity as constituted wholly by self-consciousness and memory. It is not up to me alone to decide whether I am the person who did, or did not do, this thing or that. But what criterion do others have for my identity? Only an *external* criterion—namely, the identity of my body as a continuing existent in space and time.

The question of personal identity assumes a decisive importance in cases of so-called 'split identity', where two subjects actually appear to communicate with one another in one body. Are we dealing in these cases with two persons? There is no one who thinks so. We prefer to speak of an illness, which we try to cure; if the cure succeeds, we do not suppose we have finally eliminated one of the two persons.

[1] Scotus, *Reportatio Parisiensis* 1 d. 25 q. 2 n. 14; Thomas, 2 *Sent.* 3. 1. 2.

And the patient him- or herself can often take this same observer's view, for example in seeking medical help. If the observer's view were irrelevant to identity, we would have no right to say that the patient was psychotic and suffered from delusions.

It makes no difference to an animal how an observer may describe 45 it. Correspondingly, there is no observer's view that can tell what it is like to be that animal or an animal of that species. But we humans can talk with one another about ourselves. You and I can discuss you, or we can discuss me. For the view from inside the outside view is relevant, and makes a difference, while the view from outside, not least the view of the physician, needs what information it can get about the inside view. This interaction of perspectives is what creates the very possibility of psychiatry. For what psychiatry brings into its objective observer's view is precisely the view from inside.

II

When personal identity is treated as no more than a *consciousness* of personal identity, one fact is generally overlooked: we identify with ourselves over time without being conscious of all our previous states. The psychotic may look back on a psychotic episode as his own, as we may all look back on a dream as our own, without a subjective continuum to link our dreaming to our waking. We remember our dream, but remember it *as* a dream. This is the only way we can integrate it as a part of our experience into our biography, even though we did not experience it as a dream while we were dreaming it.

From Descartes's philosophy of subjectivity to the contemporary philosophy of mind, which constructs the identity of 'I' upon the criterion of immediate self-presentation, our moment-by-moment states of conscious self-presentation are treated as an irreducible last frontier, to which the dimensions of past and future relate only as 'extasies' of the present. Thoroughgoing solipsism always involves isolating the present instant, something Descartes was aware of when he had to support the continuous unity of consciousness by appealing to the truthfulness of a God who would never allow our memories systematically to play us false. With the concept of the person, however, this thoroughgoing solipsism/instantialism is already left behind. The 'solitude' of the person, of which Duns Scotus speaks, is tied up with its incommunicability. It is not defined in qualitative terms, which would mean that its uniqueness was in the end contingent; it is defined by a 'place' in the universe which it alone 46 occupies. This place, again, is defined by a situation relative to all other places; the person is defined by relation to everything else that can never be that person. And this is not a delivery of external observation alone; the person knows the uniqueness of his or her place and of the unsubstitutability of its relation to everything else, and so of his or her essential uniqueness. Since it is a relational uniqueness, it cannot be conceived apart from the external aspect of the person, mediated primarily through the body. The body of a human being with a split personality is not a split body, unless there are instances of 'brain-split', a problematic conception that cannot be taken up here. The fissure of the so-called multiple personality is an illness—and not the illness of two 'I's, but the illness of a single person.

III

The doppelgänger, or split personality, leads us to another discovery. The two distinct 'I's are, inevitably and as such, *different*. Were they not different, they would be identical. To this case we may correctly apply Leibniz's principle of *identitas indiscernibilium*, the identity of whatever is not qualitatively different. The numerical distinction of the two 'I's is no more than a function of their qualitative difference. Within the person a drama is played out. What appears within the drama as two subjects, substantially distinct, is in reality only two aspects of one subject, though qualitatively so disparate that it seems for the moment impossible they should ever be integrated. But even in this case, to integrate them is the task we face. All qualitative differences may be thought of as complementary. In our discussion of Christology we saw how two integrated natures came to be thought of as united in a single person. These natures must be thought of as different; for if they were alike, there would be no sense in thinking of them as two.

The qualitative difference of the two split parts of the 'I' allows us to interpret the development of split personality as a problem in the constitution of an existing substantial unity. Two (qualitatively) different objects may exist side by side without being related in any way; but if a relation arises between them, they lose their independent status and are integrated into a higher unity, in which they are no more than constitutive 'moments'. But the relation of persons is not like this. In the first place, it is not entered into but is there from the start. Each person stands in a relation to each other a priori. Even when we take no notice of another person, it is not that there is no relation, but that the relation is of a certain kind. Furthermore, the relation does not result from qualitative differences that repel or attract. There are, of course, repulsions and attractions between persons, which have their source in qualitative differences. But these are based on a fundamental relation, 'recognition' or its refusal, a relation more basic than sympathy or antipathy, than 'elective affinity' or repulsion. Qualitative peculiarities allow persons to engage together in unifying structures, societies, and institutions; but as persons they can never be 'integrated' in a real sense, so that their status is reduced to that of a part in a greater whole. Human beings are parts of a greater whole in many respects. But they know that they are parts, and can will to be parts. It is not that their natural instincts are programmed to function as a part in a whole, nor that their individual orientation is, as seen from outside, merely a function of the whole. They relate themselves to their part-function freely. They may refuse it. Alternatively, they may make their service of the larger whole an integrating constitutive aspect of their own identities, and even give up their lives for it. But even in doing that, they are no longer *mere* parts, but a whole, which cannot be accounted for as a means to an end.

Antagonism and complementarity between persons is always built on qualitative differences. The most intimate of personal communities, that of marriage, presupposes the difference of the sexes. There are many kinds of community that human beings of the same sex can develop, but they cannot become 'one flesh', which is how Paul understands the meeting of the two sexes. We can appreciate why the myth of the androgyne interpreted this form of community as springing from an original identity. Yet different persons cannot be 48 thought of as originally identical. For their status as persons, beings that 'have' their various distinctive qualities, numerical difference is no less decisive than similarity. They are alike in this 'having' of their nature; but it is not an empirical likeness. Empirical observation can only establish unlikenesses. It is, in fact, a great mistake to think we must suppress observations of human differences if we are to do justice to human dignity. The dignity of the person is not touched by such observations, for the dignity of human beings as persons is not an object of observation but of recognition. Kant's remark about existence applies also to the use of the word 'person' as a *modus existendi*: it is not a real (i.e. factual) predicate.[2] If we say that someone is a person, we are saying that he or she is someone, a unique Individual; and this cannot be understood as the chance implication of one predicate, or even of an ensemble of predicates. *What* he or she may be besides does not settle *who* he or she is. The *what* we can observe and comprehend; the *who* is accessible to us only as we recognize something ultimately inaccessible.

Inaccessible not only to outward perception, as are all mental events, but to inward perception, too. Even inward perception has access only to 'real predicates', i.e. what can be determined as fact. Inwardly we see ourselves (as Kant realized) simply as phenomena, and as phenomena we disclose no more than that our properties and states are sustained by *some* subject; they do not take us to *what* sustains them, i.e. to what constitutes our identity. At this point inner perception is as much at a loss as outer. There is no categorical reason why we must know ourselves better than others know us, even though we know ourselves 'from within'. The person is neither within nor without, but transcends the inner–outer difference that is the boundary of the mental sphere. Yet for the purpose of *re*-identifying persons, i.e. of recognizing them as the persons we already know, perception from outside is decisive, which means that physicality is decisive. Physicality enables us to 'place' the person in relation to

---

[2] Kant, *The Only Possible Argument in support of a Demonstration of the Existence of God, Akademic Ausgabe* (*AA*) ii. 73. (*Theoretical Philosophy 1755–1770*, tr. D. Walford and R. Meerbote (Cambridge: Cambridge University Press, 1992), 117–19).

everything else, and simple numerical identity can only be grasped through place.

Solipsism, then, is incompatible with the concept of the person. The 49 idea of a single person existing in the world cannot be thought, for although the identity of any one person is unique, personhood as such arises only in a plurality. That is why philosophical monotheism is invariably ambiguous: either it is advances to become trinitarianism, or it slips back into pantheism. The thought of a single unipersonal divinity depends upon a concept of the person that has lost touch with its historical roots. We began to speak of God as a person only when we began to speak of three persons in one God.

4

The Negative

I

Persons are what they are; but persons are *not only* what they are. They are defined by a difference from what they are, a 'negative moment'. A negative moment, too, distinguishes animate from inanimate beings; but negativity is extended to its furthest point in the person. Persons feel, but they do not only feel; they think, but they do not only think. They think behind their thinking. They think the thought of 'being', a thought with no specific content which directs the attention to nothing in particular, but achieves the distinctness of a thought only by the double step of negation: being *is not* the thought, and the thought *is not* the thing thought about.

Thought itself is defined by a difference from what simply *is*. That difference cannot be composed of what simply is; for the negative cannot be elicited from the positive, though the positive is presupposed in the negative. That is why machines cannot think. Simulation cannot achieve the difference from what simply is; it has to presuppose that difference. Any and every product of a machine is a positive fact in the world, but only a living being can read such positive facts as *signs*, and so transform them into *something thought*. The sign '−' is no more and no less a material product in the world than the sign '+'. Only when a living creature gives it a specific meaning can the negative moment arise. But does it arise at all? Is not 'not' a symbol, too? And what does it mean to 'understand' but to replace an unknown symbol with a known one? Is there anything 'behind' symbols? If there is nothing that symbols symbolize, there are no symbols either, only yet more things-in-the-world. That is how the computer processes them, of course, and if that is what is meant by 'understand', the computer clearly 'understands'. It is pointless to prognosticate what computers will and will not be able to do, what 'intellectual feats' they will never be able to perform. Even today these are in many respects ahead of the intellectual feats that humans perform. Yet it is not pointless to say, 'the computer does not think'. It means it does not *know* it is thinking. And that means it does not *experience* thinking. There is no ghost in the machine.   51

Knowledge is a kind of subjective experience. But all subjective experience is experience *of something*. The basic structure of subjective experience is pursuit, or 'going out for' something, i.e. 'drive'. Drive imports a twofold difference: between the inside and the outside, the difference that lies at the source of space-perception, and between anticipation and anticipated, between the 'already' and the 'not yet', the difference that lies at the source of time-perception.

It is generally supposed that the difference between the inside and the outside is a fundamental characteristic of all systems, not of organic systems only, which are simply a special case of systems in general. Actually the relation is the other way round. Systems are simulations of life. And only for living beings that can see them as such are they systems at all. The thermostat is an arrangement of material elements operating on one another by physical laws in a reciprocally interactive relation with other material elements that do not count as part of the thermostat. That through this interaction the temperature in a given space is kept stable, is a reality only for a being that can compare its conditions at one moment with those at another, with an interest in keeping them uniform. Only living organisms are such beings. Thermostats are thermostats, then— indeed, they are systems at all—only while there are organisms with pursuits, which interest themselves in temperature conditions. The difference between the inside and the outside in such systems is only the projection of the inner–outer difference in ourselves, which is the source of our individuality. The inside and outside of non-living systems, taken on their own, form an undifferentiated continuum.

Were we to think of such systems as having a 'being', or 'self', we would credit them with something which, by definition, no one could have invented. 'Selfhood' means emancipation from the conditions of one's coming-to-be, and this emancipation can only be conceived as a momentary happening, like Aristotle's *genesis*, 'coming-to-be', as distinct from *alloiōsis*, 'alteration'. We commonly speak in this connection of 'emergent properties', meaning properties whose coming-to-be regularly arises out of certain material combinations but cannot be understood as combinations of the properties of the uncombined materials. But properties have to be properties of 52 something. The coming-to-be of a new something, individuation, cannot be described as an emergent property. If drive, or pursuit, individuates experience, life cannot be comprehended as the *property* of an existent but only as its *being*. 'Life is the being of living things.'[1] Persons are living things, and their being is life, their individuation that of a living organism.

Life is the existence of every existent for which there is something 'it is like' to be. 'What is it like to be a bat?' asked Thomas Nagel, and answered that we really cannot know. Daniel Dennett replied that we can learn a great deal from the non-verbal behaviour of bats about what they want, what they are aware of and unaware of, and so on. Compared with ours, the consciousness of such creatures is certainly 'severely disjointed'.[2] In the same way we could in the end learn something about the consciousness of computers, once they achieved the level of consciousness. What, then, distinguishes the pursuits of a bat, or the pursuits of a man, from their simulation in a computer? What does it mean that there is something 'it is like' to be a person or an animal? What does 'experience' mean?

II

Here Heidegger has pointed the way forward, in singling out 'attunement' (*Gestimmtsein*) as a fundamental phenomenon of *Dasein*. It is only through being attuned that we are ever *in* the world, that there is ever a 'world' for us at all.[3] Attunement is not something

---

[1] Aristotle, *De anima* 415^{b}13.

[2] Daniel C. Dennett, *Consciousness Explained* (London: Penguin, 1993).

[3] Cf. *Being and Time*, tr. John Macquarrie and Edward Robinson (Oxford: Blackwell, 1962), 172 ff. [To avoid long explanations I have preferred 'attunement' to Heidegger's English translators' 'mood', which to the casual glance suggests a superficial rather than a fundamental disposition. Tr.]

we bring about; it is not even a distinct occurrence, but lies behind everything of that order. Consciousness, effort, will, knowledge are only what they are as they are embedded in an attunement of which they bear the traces. A computer has no consciousness, does no thinking, makes no efforts for anything and knows nothing, because there is nothing 'it is like' to be a computer. And for this reason the difference between the inside and the outside has no reality for a computer.

For non-personal animals, naturally enough, this difference has reality to the extent that it is transmuted into an inward, experienced difference. Outward complexity must become inward complexity. 53 There is something not identical with the animal that is *to be* experienced, something that has a positive or negative significance for it. This thing is 'to be experienced', indeed, only to the extent that it has a significance. The significance is anticipated through the drive-structure of the individual animal and through the difference, essential for the drive-structure, between striving and satisfaction. This double difference means that negation becomes an inner moment for experience itself. Striving is a necessary but not sufficient condition for satisfaction. Striving for satisfaction is directed to something non-identical, which means that satisfaction is contingent. A living creature is on the lookout for 'input'. Since satisfaction is not the climax of an inner paroxysm but demands the input, the living creature is essentially incomplete. It can never be certain of the input, and so pursues it, which costs effort and sometimes pain, which is the price of going beyond steady-state maintenance. Pain is the form in which the negative intrudes upon straightforward being-in-the-world, and becomes the immediate 'attitude' of subjective experience. Of course, one can point to the functional usefulness of pain in the service of survival, and try to introduce an analogous 'pain-function' in artificial systems. But pain cannot be defined by its function. Pain can outlast its usefulness as a warning sign, and be 'unproductive'. The biologists can tell us why: function in nature is not the same as teleology; pain is in every case what it is, but what it is, its specific quality, is curiously irrelevant to its function. Essentially it is negativity. And pain, which nature abhors, can actually be sought out as such—not for its usefulness but in spite of its usefulness, which is to make us avoid it. Curiosity, which is the hunger for new experience and enhancement of vital sensations, desire for solidarity, the need to punish oneself, the desire to excite pity, or, indeed, masochistic inclination, can all lead us to seek out pain. But, of course, it is *as* pain that we seek it. It is not that pain becomes the same as enjoyment for us; rather, we enclose negativity itself within square brackets, as it were, and introduce it with a plus sign. That is something only persons can do—for they do not simply 54 exist as what they are, but step back from whatever it is they are, from the ensemble of qualitative features they display, and enclose it all within square brackets, placing some other sign, negative or positive, before it.

III

In non-personal animals satisfaction is not tied to striving by defini-tion, by analytical equivalence, or by a natural law. The connection is contingent—yet not simply accidental. The prospects of satisfaction and frustration are not symmetrical. Satisfaction is 'normal'. Normality is the biological equivalent of lawfulness. The biological species are themselves modes of normality; they are normal forms of living creatures, the result of attaining an ecological niche that enables the satisfaction of certain expectations and the survival of the species. Every species-specific ambition is tied to some specific expectation that views the arrival of the expected thing as the normal case, its non-arrival as the deviant case, the anomaly. There is no form of life—human life not excepted—without its own form of normality to give structure to its expectations. To exceed the normal expectation with an abundant input, to which humans respond with a special sense of good luck and thankfulness, carries with it—for men as for beasts—a danger. Their readiness and ability to expend the normal amount of effort and exertion can quickly fall away, so that survival under normal conditions is consequently put at risk. Obviously, this problem does not arise if there is no reason to fear reversion to the earlier conditions, since the surplus itself constitutes a new level of normality. This, however, applies only when the shift in standard is effected imperceptibly and over long periods of time; and the reason is that the outlay of energy and effort within the framework of normality for any given species is not simply an expense to be entered on the debit side, but is necessary as such for maintaining its natural endowment and its sense of wellbeing. That is why human 55 beings exert themselves in sport when they no longer require that degree of physical movement and effort to maintain their existence. A certain measure of negative experience, in the sense of effort, is itself part of the normal condition of living creatures. The discomforts of mountain-climbing are part of the enjoyment. Someone who knows that would never change places with a passenger in the cable-car, who, while, finding every moment of the excursion pleasant, can hardly conceive the exceptional joy to be had from climbing a mountain.

Pain, then, is the irreducible negative, the essential anomaly. Even if it were the statistical norm, it would be so. If 90 per cent of a population suffered from chronic headache, no one would attempt to bring the remaining 10 percent in line with the statistical norm. On the contrary. It is the essence of pain to be abnormal, irrespective of statistics. 'Normality', we see, is not a statistical and quantitative notion; but it is a descriptive, at the same time as being a normative one. The consideration of pain falsifies Hume's assertion that Is and Ought belong to two incommensurable realms, unless— that is—we deploy a strictly 'positive' sense of 'Is', meaning 'in front of our noses', out there in the world of objects and waiting to be stumbled over, in which case pain and negativity no longer count among things that 'are'.[4] Usually, however, we take someone's claim to be in pain at face value as offering information about what is happening in the world, just like the claim to be hungry. But when someone calls, 'Help me! I am in pain!', or 'Give me something to eat! I am hungry!', nobody will ask *why* he wants to be rid of his pain or his hunger. 'Because it hurts!' is not a reason, merely another way of saying that he is in pain. There can be no further reason that could lie behind the demand for action in this case.

Pain is essentially and immediately what we do not want. Of course, there may be reasons why persons refuse to eat, despite the pain of

---

[4] Hume, *Treatise of Human Nature*, 3. 1. 1, ed. L. A. Selby-Bigge (Oxford: Clarendon Press, 1888), 455–70.

hunger. Hunger is only a prima facie reason for eating. But the fact that it is so, determines the way the burden of proof is distributed. When someone is hungry, it is not eating but refusing to eat that demands an explanation, not offering food but withholding it. 56 The negative, as distinct from what simply is, arises only where there is life, i.e. where interests are in play, *already* in play, that is, before a choice is made, a goal is set, or some conscious act of will takes place. Choice, goal-setting, and conscious willing, all presuppose an original going-out-after things. What happens when someone in a state of pathological apathy feels unmotivated and without interests, is that that person sees no reason to will anything or to set a goal of any kind. Even so the person him- or herself may perceive this condition as an affliction and may even be moved sufficiently by the experience to shake it off. And at the root of this we see again the same inner self-difference, the negative moment presupposed by the conscious act of will.

There are, in fact, two things presupposed by a conscious act of will. Besides life as going-out-after things, as drive, there is also the disclosure, which we can never get behind, of a dimension of rational universality, with which the acts of rational beings are implicated *ab initio*. This is no more set in place by a free decision of our own than is the general form of striving itself. Giving a hungry person something to eat is, for a rational being, as little in need of explanation as eating itself is. Persons can extricate themselves from this formal requirement to a certain extent, but not totally. They may act without justification in this or that case; they may plead some pseudo-justification for their deeds that does no more than disguise a particular interest; but they cannot in principle renounce the formal condition of generic rules of action. To do so would be to make themselves invisible as persons and their acts unrecognizable as acts; they would thus exclude themselves from the community of mutual recognition among human persons. The linguistic-communicative structure of rationality has already disclosed this dimension of the rational will. Rationality is a form of life.

5

Intentionality

I

Persons are among those beings that have an 'inward' side, which is to say, they have subjective experience. In place of 'subjective experience' we sometimes speak of 'mental states'. The question of the ontological status of mental states and processes has occupied the philosophy of the modern era since Descartes. With Descartes, for reasons to be explored later, there began a line of thought about the incommensurability of inward experience and outward perception, the psychological (*des Psychischen*) and the physical spheres.[1] To take an example: pain is experienced only by the one whose pain it is. Other people can infer from external perception that someone is in a state such as they themselves experience when they say they are in pain. The external perception may simply be hearing that person say he is in pain, in the absence of reasons to doubt him. But immediate perception of someone else's pain is not available to us.

What does this incommensurability amount to? Mind–body dualism always offered a challenge, inviting us to try to overcome it with a monist thesis. Today we know that mental states correspond

---

[1] [The author uses the terms *das Psychische* and *das Seelische* interchangeably, where English might speak sometimes of the Mind and the mental, sometimes of the Psyche and the psychological, and sometimes, in historical or religious contexts, of the Soul. No attempt has been made to find a uniform equivalent in English for each of the author's terms, which would render his lucid argument unnecessarily opaque to English readers. Tr.]

to specific states of the human brain, which is to say that the mental state and the brain-state always occur together. How is this correspondence to be understood? The attempt to overcome dualism was pursued along two different lines. To Idealists the external representations were epiphenomena of mental processes, to Materialists it was the other way round. To the radical monism of Spinoza both levels of phenomena were appearances of the self-disposition of Absolute Substance, the only appearances accessible to perception among an infinite number of inaccessible ones. In contemporary discussion the monist alternative to dualism is predominantly materialist. But the important thing to see is that every variety of monism starts from a description of the phenomena and a formula- 58 tion of the problem that have originally been determined by dualism. The starting-point, in monism as in dualism, is the existence of two different spheres of experience, conceptually distinct. The disagreement touches only how this difference is explained ontologically: for dualism by two independent entities that mutually condition each other, for materialism by treating the mental sphere as no more than an epiphenomenon of material processes. Even so, however, the epiphenomenon is clearly differentiable from the basic phenomenon. And that seems more or less incontestable, for the experience of anxiety, on the one hand, and the corresponding neurological phenomena, on the other, are set apart, it would appear, by an unbridgeable chasm. We cannot describe them in the same breath. To look at a brain is not to look at anxiety. It is not to look at the thought that Charlemagne was crowned Emperor on 25 December 800. Yet there persists the incorrigible persuasion that in actual fact the one is the same as the other. Admittedly, the persuasion rests on a monist dogma unsupported by argument.[2] Yet the dogma survives, fed by the dualism it rejects. Both dualism and monism come to a stand before the task of thinking the unity of incommensurables. Dualism must give up incommensurability to accommodate interaction of mental awareness and physical events, for a causal relation needs homogeneous entities. Monism is dualist *malgré lui*: since it cannot think subjective experience and matter together as a unity, it downgrades the one to an epiphenomenon of the other. In this way

[2] Cf. Dennett, *Consciousness Explained*, 37.

humanity, as it were, cancels itself out. For what matters about it does not matter after all, since there is nothing *to* matter. What is really there is what physics can tell us about.

It is true that we cannot observe events such as anxiety or thought in the brain. But does that mean that we cannot see anxiety at all? We can recognize anxiety written on a face. We can see when someone is running for his life. We observe people's actions. But physical motions only *count as* actions when they express an intention, i.e. a psychological state. Can we not hear thoughts? What else is it we hear when someone speaks? Of course, we may misunderstand either 59 actions or words. We do not have the actual subjective experience of the other person. But the experience is disclosed, and we understand the disclosure. When we understand words, they evoke in us the thought they express. Dualism dissolves the perception of an action into two elements: first, the perception of a physical motion; second, its interpretation as the consequence, or expression, or accompaniment of mental processes. But neither these mental processes nor the physical events are *acts*. The decisive point is that the mental state underlying the act cannot be described or defined apart from the act it initiates. We cannot refer to an intention to catch the 10.45 train and to run for it without mentioning the train, its departure time, and the hurry; nor can we speak of the 'mental state' of thinking of Charlemagne's coronation without alluding to the coronation of Charlemagne. But it would be a necessary feature of a materialist-monist account of these mental states as states-of-the-brain, that we could refer to them and describe them independently of their intentional object. There would be a corresponding state-of-the-brain for each intention or thought, and it would be possible in principle to decode the whole content of mathematics from the brain of a mathematician and the history of the Thirty Years War from the brain of a historian. Materialist monism fails to emphasize the unity of the inner and the outer as a *teleological* unity belonging to the act as a whole. Instead, it presumes that the two spheres are independently definable, and *then* interprets the mental sphere as a function of the physical. But it could only be a function of the physical if it were not already defined by its intentional relation to physical events.

II

Phenomenal dualism, then, is a condition for ontological monism. It is a necessary condition, but not a sufficient one; for dualism does not *have* to be overcome by monism, and there are serious objections to its being so. Whether it is possible or rational to overcome it, is a matter for experience in the broadest sense to decide.

A dualist description is generally in place where we are dealing 60 with mental states of a non-intentional and non-propositional kind, with pain, moods, or states of diffuse emotional excitement. These states are describable and definable without reference to physical data. They are divided from such data semantically by an unbridgeable divide. But precisely for that reason it is not a priori senseless to account for them, as Spinoza does, as the subjective side of objective physical processes. That they are governed by such processes and may be caused by them or repressed by them, is commonly understood. The discussion of the ontological status of these states, and about whether there exists a mental sphere per se, cannot be settled definitively at this level. It would be unwarranted, however, to conclude from this inconclusive stalemate that materialism had carried the day—for that would beg the question of the burden of proof. Materialist monism is counter-intuitive in all its variations, since it must explain the self-understanding of experience as a self-*mis*understanding, and so it must carry the whole burden of proof. Airy assurances that physical explanations, while not currently available, have not been proved impossible, can never substitute for proof that would meet this burden. Popper has referred to contemporary materialism nicely as an 'promissory materialism'.[3]

It is sometimes argued that a reductionist interpretation of subjective experience and mental states is impossible a priori on linguistic grounds. If this means that we cannot translate statements about subjective experience without loss into the language of objective observation, it is undoubtedly correct. Of course, one might adopt it as a linguistic convention to say 'my C-fibres are firing' instead of 'I am in pain'. But if someone in pain were

---

[3] Karl Popper and J. Eccles, *The Self and its Brain* (Berlin: Springer, 1977), 96–8.

told by the physiologist, 'My investigation does not confirm the firing of your C-fibres,' the sufferer would reply, 'But it hurts, all the same!' Used as a way to assert one was in pain, 'my C-fibres are firing' would no longer be part of the language of objective report, open to correction by observation. We would need to find new ways 61 of reporting objectively observed phenomena that correspond to pain.

But the simple impossibility of bringing subjective and objective language under the same roof does not suffice to defeat reductionism. True, by definition subjective experience cannot be reconstructed and simulated objectively. But that is not what reductionism claims to do. The claim of reductionism is that subjective experience is ontologically irrelevant; that is, there is no *sum* to go with the *cogito*. Epiphenomenalism sees subjective experience as standing in a strict one-to-one relation with objectively observable neuronal processes. But the relation is asymmetric: the neuronal processes affect the experience, but the experience does not affect the neuronal processes. So subjective experience is wholly irrelevant to physical processes in the world, but without constituting its own independent sphere of events. It is an inconsequential secondary phenomenon alongside physical processes.

There are questions to be pursued about the interest driving the reductionist endeavour.[4] It is an interest in a tight physical *nexus* of cause and effect, which accommodates and accounts for 'everything there is'. How does such an interest arise? The tightness of the cause–effect *nexus* is not a result of empirical demonstration; it is a postulate. The interest that drives the postulate is an interest in the continuing expansion of our mastery of nature and the possibilities of control. The discovery of the dependence of mental states on physical processes opens up the possibility of manipulating those states. Pain, to be sure, is not merely a neuronal process, yet pain can be subordinated to such a process as effect to cause, and from that realization there emerge enhanced prospects for combating

---

[4] Cf. Richard Rorty and J. Eccles, 'Mind-Body, Identity, Privacy and Categories', in *Review of Metaphysics* 19 (1965), 24–54. Also Immanuel Kant, *Critique of Pure Reason*, 'On the interest of reason in these conflicts', tr. Paul Guyer and Allen W. Wood (Cambridge: Cambridge University Press, 1998), 496–503.

pain. Yet on the reductionist hypothesis the *desire* to combat pain
becomes pointless. The closed system of cause and effect enhances
the possibilities for interventionist action, while at the same time
destroying the very idea of action. For if action is included in
the closed physical system of causality, it is unintelligible why we
postulate this system—why we make any postulates at all, in fact. It is
unintelligible what it could mean to *assert* such a thing as a closed 62
system of cause and effect. For in all this we are engaged in the sphere
of exclusively mental activity, a sphere that we have just explained
away as ontologically insignificant.

III

It has become evident by this point that we must make a distinction
within the sphere of mental activity between psychological states and
intentional acts. With reference to the former, non-intentional states
of mind, we run straight into the theoretical stalemate about their
ontological status: reductionism cannot translate them conceptually
so as to include them in a discourse of physical events, yet the
position can be more or less consistently defended that the residuum
resisting translation does not really exist.

This position comes to grief, however, if we extend it to acts
of *thinking that...*, *knowing that...*, *judging that...*, and *willing
that...* For without acts of *thinking that...*, even the objective
physical world is inaccessible to us. If *these* are dismissed as contentless epiphenomena, the objective world disappears with them, a world
that is only there *for us* in the first place thanks to such acts. And
the same can be said for all acts of conscious preference and going-
out-after things. If such acts are no more than the subjective side of
neuronal processes to which they are neither here nor there, the
proposition that they are no more than the subjective side of neuronal processes is itself neither here nor there. If there is nothing to
it, then there is nothing to the difference between true and false
assertions, better and worse theories. There may be something in
the world that our value words correspond to, but what they correspond to has no connection with values. *For us* the sign '–' signifies

negation, as opposed to the sign '+'; but in the objective world the occurrence of the minus sign is every bit as positive as the occurrence of the plus sign. Wherever theoretical or practical intention enters the scene, materialist reductionism in all its forms becomes self-contradictory.

Intention can never be described satisfactorily as a psychological state. A reference to *what* the subject of an intentional state is thinking or intending is part and parcel of the definition of that state. The meaning of the formula $\sqrt{16} = \pm 4$ is not only not 63 a brain-state; it is not a state of mind either. It is not a *subjective* condition at all. To understand it, one does not need to project oneself into someone else's experiences; one only needs to know how to handle numbers. We understand an intentional act if and only if we direct our intention at the same object. The refutation of psychologism in logic, with which Husserl and Frege are associated, is among the very few philosophical achievements that have brought an existing debate to a decisive close.

Intention is not a psychological reality, but a spiritual or intellectual one. It is a feature neither of the inward nor of the outer world. It is the basis for the 'view from nowhere'.[5] Nevertheless, there is a connection between intention and psychology that sheds light upon the latter. Intentionality belongs in a certain sense to subjective experience, and so to the life of the mind, but only to the extent that, like states of mind, it can be manipulated by physical intervention. It can be manipulated, however, only negatively. It can be removed, but not positively induced. Knowledge of the fact that Caesar was murdered cannot be produced by stimulation of the brain, and no observation of brain-states could license the conclusion that this knowledge was present. The same goes for all those states of affairs which we wish to bring about by acting or wish to be brought about without our acting. Practical intention differs from theoretical intention chiefly in that the non-identity of its object with a state of the subject is not simply implied, but expressed as the defining content of the act. To 'will' something means willing *that that thing should not remain* a mere something-in-the-will. A will or

[5] Alluding to the well-known title of a book by Thomas Nagel (Oxford: Oxford University Press, 1986).

a wish that did not will or wish *that*, would not be a will or wish at all. But it is equally true that to 'think' something, and to think at the same time that one's thinking it was merely a subjective state, would not be to think it at all, but at most to imagine it. The difference is only that in thinking something, as opposed to willing something, the non-iden-tity of thinker and object of thought is not *explicitly* constitutive of the act itself.

Nevertheless, intentional acts and intentional attitudes are still 'in the mind' to the extent that it is an event of subjective experience when we form them. Assent to a proposition, i.e. the habitual knowledge of some fact, has in common with psychological attitudes that they affect the emotional disposition of the subject immediately, 64 and can be 'erased' by external manipulation. Moreover, psycho-logical mechanisms can of themselves bring about such erasures, that is, in forgetting or suppressing things.

The connection between intentionality and psychological states can be illustrated from another angle. We know psychological states only by being aware of them *as* psychological states. That sounds trivial. We know chickens only by being aware of them *as* chickens. What is the difference? If we know of chickens in the farmyard, we know of the existence of chickens as a fact independent of our knowing it. To the fact itself it makes no difference whether anyone is aware of it. It is different with the awareness of psychological states. Our knowledge of these is part of the states themselves. True, we can discover later that we were hungry or had a slight headache before we were aware of it. But our dawning awareness of hunger *is* hunger. Hunger is not found out about, like some object in the world; it is something that I *have*. The having of hunger is actualized in a dawning awareness of it. Was the hunger not mine, then, before I became aware of it? That would be quite wrong. For it is not *any* hunger that I discover and appropriate as I become aware of it, as it is *any* chicken that I import into my field of observation; what I discover is that *I* am the one who has had this hunger, even before I was aware of it. Only of *my* hunger, mine from the outset, can I become aware. But what does 'my' hunger mean? That we cannot say precisely. We can only say that there is a hunger which, when it surfaces in consciousness, surfaces in my consciousness as my hunger. *Awareness* of life is the irreducible paradigm for life

and experience of every kind. Intentionality does not attend to non-intentional experience as an object 'out there', indifferent to our awareness of it. Intentionality is simply the most intense mode of experiencing. Only at a certain level of intensity does subjective experience become self-aware; but when it does, awareness is a quality of the experience. We can say, 'I become aware of my experi- 65
ence', but also, and with no less justification, 'my experience is aware of itself as my experience'.

This casts new light back on the ontological status of psychological states. The reductionist attempt to treat them as ontological phantoms, seen without being believed, comes to grief if there is actually no clear dividing line between states of mind and awareness of states of mind. We have no idea what states of mind of which no one was aware could be like. We only know that our awareness of states of mind, an awareness whose irreducible ontological status is beyond question, is an aspect of those very states. Intentionality is not itself a psychological state; but a psychological state is something with intellectual potential, and we cannot say what it is in itself without alluding to this potential.

We can illustrate this by the phenomenon of ambition, or drive. Living creatures are characterized by direction-towards, by pursuit of things. If we are to be clear what it means to pursue something, we must speak of conscious willing and acting. This has led some people to conclude that the only form that end-directedness can have is the conscious choosing and willing of ends. All other use of teleological language is taken to be improper or, at best, metaphorical. But this will not do, for we can only bring our will to a resolution in the first place as we experience within ourselves an interest that is already there. Without such an interest the world would be a matter of indifference to us; we would have no reason to will one thing rather than another. But in order to describe this interest, we resort to a vocabulary borrowed from the sphere of conscious acts of will which we then apply in a way that excludes the actual moment of intentionality. It may be objected that such a use of the vocabulary would simply destroy its meaning, leaving us with nothing said; but this cannot be sustained. For the conscious act of will finds in itself a tendency the phenomenology of which is to be anterior to consciousness and to 'come to itself' in the moment of dawning consciousness. To express what it is before it becomes conscious means finding some way of expressing what can only achieve definition when expressed. Nicolai 66 Hartmann, like Heidegger, has maintained that we have no categories in which to speak about life with any adequacy.[6] The dualism of *res cogitans* and *res extensa* implies that life is not a *clara et distincta perceptio*, but can be given definition from the point of view of consciousness only by way of negation. We may note, in addition, that early modern philosophy attempted to eliminate not only the concept of finality but that of potentiality, too. But we can speak sensibly about life only if we mean *potentially conscious* life. And that means: life with the experience of potential intentionality.

IV

This seems to me to resolve the disagreement between Husserl and Brentano about the problem of intentionality. For Brentano intentionality is quite simply the distinguishing feature of the psychological sphere, while for Husserl it is only one type of subjective experience among others.[7] In fact, as we have seen, there exist psychological states and experiences without any intentional character. But how are these distinguishable from physical events? Only by our ability to 'get inside' them—right inside, as it were, so that we experience them as our own. And if we do get inside them, they become objects of intentional acts—not in the same way that external objects are, but by acquiring a new quality as they become so. They become events of consciousness, events of conscious identification, in fact, with these experiences. It is true of all psychological events, then, that they are *potentially* intentional. Yet intentional acts are only one kind of psychological experience, and we may even entertain some initial doubt as to whether they properly

---

[6] Nicolai Hartmann, *Philosophie der Natur* (Berlin: de Gruyter, 1956), 29 f.; Martin Heidegger, *Being and Time*, tr. John Macquarrie and Edward Robinson (Oxford: Blackwell, 1962), 75.

[7] F. C. Brentano, *Psychology from an Empirical Standpoint*, ed. L. McAlister (London: Routledge, 1973); E. Husserl, *Logical Investigations*, ii, tr. J. N. Findlay (London, Routledge, 1970).

belong to the sphere of the 'psychological' at all—and to this doubt we can only reply that we lack the categories to specify the soul and the subjective life, yet cannot dispense with talking of soul and subjective life as that sphere of personal centredness which stands between us and the myth of the ghost in the machine, a myth that Leibniz already understood to be inconsistent with our experience of the world.

Talk of persons aquires theoretical force in connection with inten- 67 tionality and intentional acts. Such acts forbid us to treat the actor as no more than a living, feeling object, the receptacle of psychological states, susceptible of sensations such as pain and so, perhaps, to be handled with care, yet not one with whom we could enter into an exchange *about* something, not even about his pain. Persons, *qua* persons, are precisely not encountered in this way. They are encountered only in the context of a world that is common to them and to us. They are encountered in such a way that we understand them only when we 'look in the same direction', i.e. enter into their carrying out of their intentions.

If this account were all that was needed, however, we would extend the concept of person and personal communication rather beyond its customary boundaries. We are in just the same position *vis-à-vis* a bird that builds a nest: we cannot understand it at all unless we understand it *as* building a nest, i.e. teleologically. But 'teleological' and 'intentional' do not mean the same. The bird does not need an *idea* of the nest it is building. And so we cannot enter into communication with it about its end and the means it adopts to achieve it. Neither can other birds. With dogs and horses to an extent, and in a decisive way with primates, we can engage in more intensive forms of communication. But this communication is confined to matters bounded by the context of the animal's 'subjective' sensations. Intentional objects do not stand forth purely and simply as what they are, so that the concept of 'intention' can be used here only in an analogical way. True, higher animals do something akin to recognizing states of affairs. A dog 'thinks' that his master has taken a certain path, and so looks for him at a certain place. But what we notice is simply that he runs off in a certain direction which he would not take if he had not seen his master leave the house. In reading this as 'thinking', or 'striving', we are imposing an interpretation that suits persons very well but cannot uncomplicatedly be transferred onto other animals.

It is a feature of persons that they are subjects of different and clearly distinct kinds of act. In particular, the acts of thinking, preferring, and willing in any human being are independent vari- 68 ables. This, perhaps, is the clearest indicator of personality. Let us imagine a creature with only one kind of act at its disposal—say, that of theoretical thought. There would certainly be a subject of the thinking, a 'centre' to which the thought-acts clung. But this subject would be simply a constitutive element of the thinking itself. The theoretical *cogitare* would have the *form* of a *cogito*, true enough; but in this case the phenomenon would be more closely reflected by the Latin syntax that 'submerges' the *ego*, as it were, in the verb. The 'I' would belong to the act of cogitation for as long as that act persisted, but would have no independence of it, no 'substantive reality'. It would begin and end with it. And in that case there would be no reason to speak of anything like a 'person'.

But have animals not advanced beyond this stage? They seem both to will things and at the same time to have thoughts about how the world is made—at least to the extent that this determines the path they must take to get what they are after. What distinguishes them from human beings, though, is that willing and thinking are not *independent* variables. It is always a package, in which what the animal 'thinks' is related to how it is to reach its goal, or to avoid whatever it wants to avoid. Its ambition, however, is confined within the limits of what its natural conditioning prescribes for it, and cannot transcend the given *conditio animalis*. Its 'thoughts' about the world are strictly functional, and have to do with the conditions for fulfilling its wishes. And so talk of intentional acts is not warranted in connection with animal intentionality, however justified it may be to speak of their recognizing states of affairs.

Intentional acts are directed at objects independently of the condition of the subject. That is how it is that human beings have a history. They can form wishes that go beyond the *conditio humana*. They can imagine a state of happiness such as Aristotle called 'happiness pure and simple', distinguished from human happiness.[8] They can dream of flying. But it was not their dreaming that led to their actually starting to fly one day. It was the human capacity

---

[8] Aristotle, *Nicomachean Ethics* 1101ª20.

to form a view of how the world is made, a view quite independent of any practical ambitions. Because this view is not a simple function 69 of their ambition but an independent variable, human beings can make unanticipated breakthroughs in discovering how the world is made, and from such discoveries there arose one day the possibility of flying. If worker bees were persons, they would have discovered long ago that they were all frustrated queens. But a revolution in their relationships would have led at once to the destruction of the affected communities. It is the mutual independence of practical and theoretical intention that enables the constant alteration in the conditions of life and action that is the hallmark of human history.

This independence is the reason we speak of persons as continuous acting-centres. The subject of a single kind of act would be no more than a function of the act itself. If acts of this kind formed a continuous sequence within a stream of consciousness, the subject of the acts, if capable of memory and anticipation, would have to be thought of as the subject of this stream of consciousness. But that would not be a 'subject' in the sense of a free, spontaneous beginning and origin, but only an integrating function. To be a free beginning, the subject would have to pursue things and exercise its will—precisely what our thought-experiment rules out. On the other hand, if the subject were only capable of willing, and had no power of theoretical reflection and theoretical intention, it would be even less like free spontaneity. It would be a blind 'drive', like the will in Schopenhauer. But one and the same subject thinks and wills. If a subject is capable of both theoretical and practical intentionality and (still more important) of a love that can rank intentions preferentially, and if these acts are independent variables, then the subject cannot be conceived as a mere function of acts but must have an independent standing. The subject must be seen as a spontaneous initiator, a being-in-itself, known by its acts but not to be identified with any of them. The subject can achieve a distance upon his or her own acts in a quite specific sense, by using one kind of act to relate itself to the others. The subject can realize that he or she wants 70 something, can view that wanting with approval or disapproval, and can come to realize it or avoid the realization.

In the Middle Ages there arose a long and unresolved debate about the priority of will over knowledge or vice versa, which was taken up again in modern philosophy. Scheler's argument for the priority of a basic intentionality of love, lying behind and providing the ground for theoretical acts as well as for purpose and will, has yet to be subjected to a thorough exploration and interrogation. It would appear, however, that Scheler's conception of a basic love provides a bridge between the fundamental condition that Heidegger describes as 'attunement' and the 'intentional acts' of Husserl's phenomenology.[9] It is the differentiation of different types of act, however, that makes personal existence possible. Persons exist by being present in each of their acts, but not so inseparably fused with any one of them as to disappear into it altogether.

---

[9] [On 'attunement' (*Stimmung*) see Ch. 4 n. 3 above.]

6

Transcendence

I

It is a truth about all higher life-forms that to understand their behaviour we must credit them with 'intentions', in the general sense of taking cognizance of states of affairs. The dog runs through the house to his bowl; it is evident not only that he wants to feed, but that he has a clear idea of where the bowl is. Animals can recognize likenesses and make practical generalizations; and that is a foreshadowing of conceptual generalization. The scope of animal experience incontestably includes experiencing the relations in which different things stand to one another.

The millennia-old description of man as the 'rational animal' is still useful as a zoological definition. Rational organization of life, separation of ends and means, speech and abstract conceptualization are all marks of *homo sapiens*. The most important difference, however, is that of *intentional acts*, as distinct from merely registering states of affairs, which is inextricably part and parcel with any ongoing activity. Intentional acts are different. Acts of practical and theoretical intention are separable from one another as independent variables, and because this is the case, we are forced to think of the subject of them not as a mere *factor* in each act, but as a self-identical and persistent *subject* of a multiplicity of acts. That means, however, that the person, while wholly present in each act, occupies a position at a distance from it, reflecting on the objectivity of its object and so transcending it.

'Transcendence' means, in the first place, a graduated enlargement of the horizon of intentionality by conceptual abstraction.

The highest level of abstraction is the type of thought we call 'philosophy', i.e. conceptual analysis. This explores the contents of intention back to their a priori conception, it explores the application of a priori schemata to experience, and their possible roots in experience. In conceptual analysis the word 'being' is the most 72 abstract of all conceptions, the most inclusive in scope and the most devoid of content. It means 'something in general', and includes everything that could possibly be the object of an intention. The rational animal is capable of this extreme level of abstraction, and capable even of subsuming itself under the general class of 'beings'.

The horizon of 'being', in this sense, is itself and in its own right the object of an intentional act that terminates in something that appears unbidden as a 'clear and distinct idea'. Descartes, a founding father of the philosophy of pure concept, was also the most clearsighted observer of its limits, and opened the way to a quite different understanding of transcendence. He became aware that even the unchallengeable self-evidence afforded by the *clara et distincta perceptio* might possibly be misleading. Anything that is self-evident, inevitably, is self-evident to *me*. Self-evidence is a state of *my* mind. To be sure, away from the self-evidence itself the mind has no path, however narrow, to follow. There are no alternative certainties; even a *reductio ad absurdum,* in which self-evidence collapses in on itself, cannot provide them. But where does that leave us?

What is it that we should be looking for, over and above the evidence of clear ideas uncontradictorily connected with each other and with all the data of experience? What is a doubt *about* if we cannot say how it might be overcome, since every conceivable means of overcoming it is put in doubt?[1] Descartes's doubt rested on a consideration that leapt beyond the rationality of *animal rationale,* the sphere of intention: that all our thoughts might be nothing more than thoughts; that all the contents of these thoughts might be nothing more than the contents of thoughts. *This* thought presumes that we are already conscious of a space that consciousness cannot occupy, a space in relation to which consciousness is 'nothing more than' consciousness. Descartes called this space 'the infinite'. It is

---

[1] For what follows see R. Spaemann: 'Das "sum" in "Cogito...sum"', *Zeitschrift für philosophische Forschung* 41 (1987), 373–82.

beyond all thoughts that are possible to us, all contents of our intentions. It is not simply that the contents of consciousness arise *within* this space without taking cognizance of the space itself; for in that case it would make no sense to worry about whether they were illusions. As the contents of my thinking, concepts are what they are. 73 The reaction of insects to their environmental conditions serves the survival of their species; in this there is no question of their being *mistaken.* There is no use for the word 'truth' in respect of these conditions. No beast reflects upon the fact that the world surrounding it is no more than *its* world, relative to its specific organization. No beast thinks beyond the scope of its own surrounding world to conceive itself as simply a feature of some other animal's world, a bearer of meanings that are meaningless to itself.

So, then, there is a second sense that the word 'being' has for persons, over and above the 'something in general' that it means for 'rational animals'. This second meaning is what makes Cartesian doubt a possibility. It would make no sense to worry about being mistaken with respect to 'something in general' lying within our field of consciousness. That is why Husserl's methodology implied leaving this second significance of 'being' and 'transcendence' out of account. To focus the intention on something beyond doubt, something unbidden and self-evident, one must set aside Descartes's ground for doubting the self-evident, his 'posit of Being'.

Descartes's suspicion of an all-embracing deviation supposes transcendence of this second kind: it engages with a space not coextensive with the space of consciousness, a space within which consciousness is an occurrence vulnerable to self-deception. It assumes a realist view of the psyche, for the psychological sphere is one of the things 'there are' in the world, and every intention that we form may be no more than a property of this psychological entity. This posit, too, is abandoned by Husserl. The phenomenologist's '*epochē*' means taking the transcendence of consciousness out of play, in order to explore what appears unbidden and self-evident purely on its own terms. To suspend transcendence in this way, however, did not simply make it disappear. The question of the ontological status of transcendent consciousness was bound to blow the phenomenological approach apart. To put the original transcendence of the person out of play could, after all, mean merely that the 'pure objectivity' thus achieved was no more than a 'deficient mode' of what was originally given. This was Heidegger's insight.   74

II

Descartes held that the disclosure of the absolute and infinite dimension of being was not only underived, but also irrefutable. Since it allows suspicion of the deviance of all our thought, we cannot regard this dimension as deviant itself. For Descartes it can be understood only as immediate presence, i.e. the presence of God. Hegel agrees, when in the Introduction to the *Phenomenology of Mind* he conceives of the Absolute as 'beside us' and 'wishing to be beside us', which conveys the underived and contingent character of this thought of the Absolute.[2]

It may seem at first as though this leap of consciousness into a sphere beyond its reach will prove no more than an empty reflection on the tautology that all objects of *consciousness* are *objects* of consciousness. The point of view from which this can be thought and known appears to be the point of view of no particular subject, a 'view from nowhere' that gets us precisely nowhere. Beyond thinking, there is nothing to be thought about; beyond seeing, there is nothing to be seen. 'We never really advance a step beyond ourselves', as Hume says.[3]

But if that were so, how could Descartes even have *thought* the whole intentional content of our consciousness might be illusion? *As what it is*, it simply *is*—and is therefore not illusion. Nothing can be illusion by virtue of what it is, only by virtue of what it suggests about itself that it is not. Objectivity-as-phenomenon suggests something lying behind it, something that bestows itself and persists in itself, revealing itself but not exhausted by its revelation. When I dream I have climbed a mountain with a friend and stopped over in

[2] G. W. F. Hegel, *Phenomenology of Mind*, tr. J. B. Baillie (San Francisco: Harper & Row, 1967), 132.

[3] David Hume, *Treatise of Human Nature* 1. 2. 6, ed. L. A. Selby-Bigge (Oxford: Clarendon Press, 1968), 67.

a mountain-lodge with a grey roof on which four ravens sit, I cannot be wrong about what I have *seen*. It would make no sense for someone to try to put me right: 'It wasn't this friend but a different one'; 'The roof was red'; 'There were six ravens not four'. I am the one who has had the dream, and no one can tell me about it. There is only one aspect of the scenario that I got wrong in my dream, and realized when I woke. I thought I was on a walk with my friend, *and* that this friend was on a walk with me. I thought that the landlord of the lodge where we stopped over figured in *two* visitors' experience. It is true that I heard the voice of my friend in my dream; but he did not say anything.

This is not a phenomenological distinction. It does not arise at the level of the intentional object. 'Being-in-itself' (*Selbstsein*), by definition, is not an object of intention. If, when I speak with my friend the next day, he assures me that he did not go for a walk with me, perhaps that, too, is only a dream, but I have absolutely no way of finding out, since no one can know whether it is so but my friend. Being-in-itself implies that being is radically plural. There is no continuum that leads from what I know to what you know, from the pain I experience to the pain you experience. Everybody knows this. Everybody knows that there is someone else, 'the other'. I know I am the other person's other person, yet am not exhaustively accounted by what the other knows of me. Nor is the way I appear to the other merely a modification of *his* state, something that I have brought about in him that can neither be false nor true as such. It is *I* who appear to him, *I* who am the measure of the adequacy of what he sees. The question whether he judges right or wrong when he says I am in pain is not settled by the coherence of his perceptions; it is settled solely by my pain, the pain I actually have. This is something we both know. Only I can finally confirm his judgement of my pain.

Kant's 'thing in itself' is no more than a symbol in a purely theoretical construction, a mathematical point generated by reflection on the objectivity of objects of consciousness. Only when we experience *ourselves* as Being-in-itself, situated at that mathematical point, does it afford a ground for metaphysical realism. The content Kant provides for the ontological mathematical point, the thing in itself, is the human experience of freedom. The mutual relation of persons, then, must be a metaphysically real relation. That the other person is real cannot be accounted for solely in terms of his objectivity to me or to himself. To me it is real that he is real to himself, just as it is real to him that I am real to myself.

III

Personality is the paradigm for being—not as 'something in general', but as transcendence of objectivity, 'being in itself'. That does not mean that everyone first understands his own being—solipsistically, as it were—and then somehow transfers this absolute self-experience to other objects of experience, to other human beings, to animals, and finally to other natural units. On the contrary, the experience of the other is co-original with the experience of self, and is already implied in the transition from *cogito* to *sum*. A solipsistic consciousness, encompassing the whole terrain of reality in itself, would not get so far as to understand itself as *being*. Its being, like everything else, would be no more than a thought. A solipsistic *cogito* would have to be expressed as 'I think that I think that I think...' For Descartes it takes the thought of another thinker, God or an evil demon, to bring this infinite series of reflections to an end.[4] The Other cannot mistake my thought for his own, for I am not merely his thought. But neither can he think—not truthfully, at any rate—that there is no thought but his own. He has to recognize that I am thinking, or else be wrong. So in relation to him my thought acquires the dignity of Being. We stand in relation to one another as existents. Descartes's *sum*, therefore, is neither mere inference from his *cogito*— a point he emphasizes especially—nor a tautology. The reason it is not a tautology is that there is more than one thinker, potentially at least, and 'he thinks I think' does not mean the same as 'I think I think'.

With the thought of Being there arises the thought that consciousness transcends its intentional content, i.e. transcends itself.

---

[4] 'Author's Replies to the Second Set of Objections', *The Philosophical Writings of Descartes II*, trans. J. Cottingham, R. Stoothoff, and D. Murdoch (Cambridge: Cambridge University Press, 1984), 93–120.

For Aristotle the *noēsis noēseōs,* the divine consciousness, must, as the solitary 'One', lie beyond being, like the Platonic good. To think of God as Absolute Being, by contrast, means to think that in himself he has what it is to be another—*another,* not *other!* That is to think of him as Trinity, an always-open sphere of mutual Letting-be.

Persons are beings who find themselves in just this position. They are beings to whom the thought of being occurs as beyond all material, substantive, or intentionally directed thought, since they are themselves beyond it, which is to say, they are free. Cartesian reflection implies the structure of 'having' decisive for personal being, which commands the totality of a person's attributes (*Sosein*). A person puts a distance between him- or herself as subject and the whole content of his or her consciousness. Doubt can drive a wedge between all these contents on the one side and the subject that has them on the other. To be sure, the subject cannot simply offload them all; that would be self-annihilation, since its being is quite simply its having of them. But the subject exists by *having* them, not by *being* them, and so stands outside all its own attributes—can even regard them all as misleading anomalies. True, that would be to make itself out a curious entity, hardly thinkable as a creature of God; yet as *this* thinker with a purely *lexical* identity, that is what it can maintain it is—which is the point of the Cartesian *cogito.*

As 'abstract' entities, persons comprise a space. They do not share personhood as a common attribute, in the way that human beings share humanity. 'Person' is not a classifier, but points to an *individuum vagum,* the unicity of an individual life. 'Person', therefore, is an analogical concept, like 'being'. Persons are called persons in the same way that members of a family bear the same family name. The name means something different for each member of the family, father, mother, daughter, son, brother. It is not a general concept that embraces them all regardless of their distinctive differences. The family name assigns a particular place in the family structure to each one who bears it. In the community of persons, similarly, each person has a place forever uniquely defined as his or hers. That person exists only with this place, and this place with that person. We are not talking of empty Newtonian space, *loci* indifferent to what occupies them. In this space there are no empty places, nothing like 'possible persons'. Persons do not belong to the sphere of 'ideal beings' *(Wesenheiten)* which may or may not actually exist, for there is no 'idea of' the person, but only actual persons. The man whom I met in my dream remains, when I wake, just what he was, a man. But it turns out that he never was a person.

In this case we might also say, 'he was never a *living* man'. Living is how animate things exist, and so it is also how human beings exist. Persons, therefore, are living human beings. There is no other way of being a person—e.g. thinking or having one or another kind of conscious state—than that of being a human. If there are no purely possible persons, existence is not something a person can either have or not have. Real thinking, to be sure, is different from the simulated thinking of machines in that it is *experienced* as thinking. Personal life consciously experienced is for us the paradigm of life in general. We can understand non-personal life only by analogy with personal life, i.e. by subtraction from it.

But we can also say of non-personal living things that they are not merely *instances* of a class. They, too, are more than mere 'cases of...' In place of 'instantiation', living things relate to their *genus* by the succession of generation, within which they have a definite place. Instantiation—being merely 'an instance of...' something— is appropriate only for non-living things. And this all poses two questions: (1) What distinguishes the community of persons, the personal space, from the space of generational relations of natural biological species, as in the primarily biological relations of mother, father, children, etc.? (2) If the being of persons is human living, what sense does it make to say that the man in my dream was a man, but not a living man? He was certainly not a dead man. The lion in the *Pathe News* is obviously alive, even if it is not real. Does life, too, not belong to the sphere of the phenomenal, and can we not distinguish possible life from actual?

Our reply to (1) is that personal relations can 'rise out of' biological relations. Just as the biological functions of a human being often become personal acts, e.g. sexual intercourse, eating, drinking, so it is with the basic relations of consanguinity and affinity. One can easily see this from the fact that these connections are lifelong, and it is irrelevant whether we welcome the fact or not. Mother will always be mother. This is not true in the same way of animals, among whom the relation comes to an end with the cessation of the biological function, and becomes indistinguishable from the relation to every other fellow-member of the species. The incest-taboo among humans makes the point especially clearly in protecting a variety of relation against loss of personal clarity. In many cultures, such as nineteenth-century Russia, it was impossible even for brothers- and sisters-in-law to marry, even though no consanguine relation existed between them. This is how the bond of procreation can be replaced, in respect of its personal meaning, by adoption. The personal relation is not as such genealogical. Persons cannot, like members of non-human species, be treated as twigs on a common tree. Rather, they are like abstract locations in a physical space, always there.

In reply to (2), on the other hand, living things are not always there. Are living things always alive, then? Is being alive simply the decisive *attribute* of a living thing as we encounter it, or is it, as Aristotle thought, 'the being of living things'?[5] Aristotle did not have our problem, because he had no concept of contingence or of the ontological difference between subject and attribute. The 'first substance', the individual thing, is, for Aristotle, simply 'that which is', *to on*. The form that is responsible for *what* it is is also responsible for the *fact* that it is. 'Form gives being,' as Thomas says.[6] Here, as in Plato, 'being' means being structured in accord with what one is, participating in the idea. The Platonic demiurge is not a creator, but a craftsman who imposes ordered forms upon chaos. That some particular thing, fully qualified as such and such a kind of thing, may stand in some *other* inner difference to its being, so that it can either be or not be: that is a thought that only becomes possible in the context of the biblical doctrine of creation out of nothing. The mastery of amorphous potential ('without form and void') by form and definiteness is a *second* step to creation itself. *Forma dat esse* is, so to speak, placed within brackets. For Thomas Aquinas the matter–form complex is ideal twice over: the ideal being (*Wesenheit*) is *individual*. Every individual possesses an ideal structure that may be realized or unrealized. Correspondingly, each individual being, for Thomas Aquinas, corresponds to a divine idea. Yet this is the idea of *a human being*, not the idea of *a person*; a human being is not called a 'person' unless he or she exists *outside* God's mind, *extra causam*.

---

5 Aristotle, *De anima* 415^{b}13.   6 Thomas Aquinas, *ST* 1. 30. 4.

Existence carries with it a moment of sheer facticity, which cannot be got round. And if we think of facticity as the work of a creator, we must, by implication, think of God as sheer freedom.

An answer to the question whether life counts among the attributes of living things or indicates the existence of which the attributes are predicated, will decide the truth of the statement, 'life is the way persons are'. It is this question that creates uncertainties about whether the lion in the dream or on the screen is a living lion. This is how these uncertainties arise: life as such is a once-for-all event, an occurrence, not a form that may or may not occur. Life is the heightened, or, better, original, paradigmatic existence. Being derives from life, and we achieve the concept of being by subtraction from the concept of life, in the same way that we achieve the concept of life by subtraction from that of the life we are conscious of living. Living consciously is the fullest being. 'To lack intelligence is to lack perfect life', we find Thomas saying.[7] Analogously we might say: 'to be without life is to lack perfect existence'. Yet life is the way living things are, only when a living thing has definite attributes. Everything that lives belongs to a kind, and has a form. Biological kinds are 'ways' of life, just as types of being in general, patterns of attributes, are forms of existence. These 'ways' can be separated notionally from their realization, can be thought of as ideal beings that may or may not be realized, just as musical 'ways' are separable from actual performance and may, for example, be committed to manuscript and copied. Ways of existence are possibilities; existence itself is actuality. An animal in a dream or in a film is a 'way of life', about which we can ask whether that life was actually lived. Life belongs to its concept, but we cannot infer from the concept that it was realized. Even a particular lion may, as a 'way of life', merely look as though it were alive. But life *as such* cannot equally well be or not be, for life *is* what it is to be.

IV

Personal is distinguished from non-personal life by the fact that we cannot describe it as a 'way' of living. Persons have their nature—

---

[7] In *Nic. Eth.* 9. 11. 1902: *Qui non intelligit, non perfecte vivit.*

human nature, for example—as their way of being. They are not, as Meister Eckhardt describes the godhead, 'wayless being'.[8] But their way is not what they *are*, but what they *relate to*: they take it on, they carry it through, or they refuse it. That is what we mean when we say that persons are not *something*, but *someone*. Either this someone exists, or there is no someone at all, only something. It belongs to the properties of the personal pronoun 'I' that no one can use it in direct speech to refer to an imaginary individual. It always has a reference. For a person, to be real is always to be alive. The relation of the person to him- or herself is the original paradigm for the thought of contingence, which the Islamic philosopher Avicenna was the first to articulate as a difference between 'quality' (*Sosein*) and 'existence' (*Dasein*). Persons are beings who experience this difference immediately. We have discussed this so far in terms of the distance between persons and *what* they are, their 'quality'. Quality is whatever they 'have', the 'way of being' in which they are not wholly immersed. But contingence is generally understood as an aspect of existence itself, in contrast to necessary ideal forms of being, which are what they are and have no need to exist. The personal experience of contingence operates on both fronts, in fact: in contented or discontented wonder at my attributes, and in astonishment at my own existence. Matthias Claudius expresses this twofold amazement in the verse:

> A child before the Christmas tree,
> My parent's gift I claim:
> I am! I am! and possess *thee*,
> Resplendent human frame![9]

Who is it that is so amazed at his own existence? Is this the experience of a kind of being that, to its great surprise, finds itself instantiated? But what would this kind *be*, before it actually *was*? Ought we to suppose that attributes exist before attribution in a kind of pre-existent existence? The conception of being as an act befalling an entity raises the logical difficulty that the entity is presumed to be

---

[8] Eckhardt, *Deutsche Predigten und Traktate*, ed. J. Quint (Munich: Carl Hanser, 1969³), 176 ff., cf. pp. 180, 334.

[9] 'Täglich zu singen', in Matthias Claudius, *Worauf es ankommt, Ausgewählte Werke*, (Gerlingen: Lambert Schneider, 1995), 429 f.

already *there* in some sense. So we come round to thinking of kinds of being as 'ways'. Finite being can only be a way of being: it is not the way that has being, but being that has the way.

Non-personal entities are so immersed in their 'way' that only we who stand outside them can think of them as contingent. Only persons can appreciate their own contingence, and only they, when they grasp the limits of their existence through the mediation of the world as a whole, can appreciate the world's contingence, too. But the position from which they can grasp this is neither that of attribute nor that of existence. A person is not a kind of being that is typically astonished to find itself existing. It is not a kind of being at all; it is a being that *relates* itself to its kind, i.e. its attributes. Precisely the constellation of attributes is experienced as contingent. But neither is a person *the* Being, expressing itself in finite ways of being. Persons are not the Absolute, since they only have being in the first place through having a kind of being (*Wesen*), a finite set of attributes, a nature. Their experience of contingence is a view from nowhere. Personality hovers at a point between being and kind, between absolute and finite.

This point of indifference we call 'freedom'. It is indeterminacy in respect of the sum total of *what* someone is, and therefore the possibility of achieving further distance on everything that has been the 'way' of one's being, one's total history. But this is not effected by one's store of energy or inner resources that harbour alternatives, possibly preferable, to what one's nature has made one. If this were the case, freedom would be just another kind of nature, a nature of nature, an attribute determined by decisions beyond one's own power. Freedom's point of indifference is the situation of the person from which it always appears in principle possible that one's thinking and willing might be one's own only anomalously. Transcendence can last only while this consciousness lasts, in a movement that reaches out to being beyond thought.

To think of Being-in-itself is to think of something beyond thought, something that connects our thought to its object. Since the thought of Being is itself a thought, it necessarily falls short of its object. The thought of something beyond thought is not itself beyond thought—that was Thomas's objection to Anselm's onto-logical argument for the existence of God. In a dream we may consciously reflect that what we are dreaming is real and not a dream, and may even experience what Scheler considered the proof of reality, resistance.[10] But we are mistaken; for when we wake, we must face the fact that we were deluded, and that even the resistance was a dream. As Hegel shows in the introduction to the *Phenomenology of Mind*, the difference between the immanence of thought and the thought of something beyond immanence, itself lies within the sphere of thought. That means that from the theoretical angle *this* thought cannot have a complement. Being is not an object of intention; the thought of being, accordingly, is never so complemented that being is disclosed as such. Disclosure would mean that it became the content of the vision or thought of the one to whom the disclosure was made. But how is what is conceived as beyond thought to become the content of thought? Approaching from a purely theoretical angle we are necessarily left in the realm of appearances—though these appearances point beyond themselves to something else, something that becomes visible and in the very moment of becoming visible is hidden.

V

Our theoretical angle is situated in a life context where we always have something to be concerned about, i.e. where we are in pursuit of something. What is it we are in pursuit of? What, in the last analysis, are we concerned about? What is the final object of our practical intentions? There must be something we want to have for real and not only in appearance. This is what Plato calls 'the good'. But might not the good be just another subjective condition, a certain state of the subject, which could be induced by a helpful appearance?

The first challenge that produced philosophy came from the sophists' answer to this question: the thing we want for real and

---

[10] Max Scheler, 'Die Stellung des Menschen im Kosmos', *Gesammelte Werke* (Berne: Frarcke, 1976), ix. 112; cf. 'Idealismus-Realismus', 214.

not only for appearance is pleasure, 'feeling good'. This answer is paradoxical. It can apply only to human beings, but if human beings understand themselves in this way, they lose touch with what distinguishes them as human, what makes them persons. An animal is always concerned with this or that, with forage, warmth, or sexual congress. But we who observe the animal can interpret its behaviour as concerned only with certain states of equilibrium. The ends it pursues are, unbeknownst to it, no more than means to achieve these states. The proof appears to lie in the fact that we can induce such states in animals without supplying the 'natural ends', and then the animals seem not to miss them. So what they are after for real and not only for appearance is apparently nothing more than feeling good, which, incidentally, is not the same as physical satisfaction. Certain species of animals know something like self-sacrifice. Birds feed their young to the point of exhaustion. In their case self-sacrifice is the condition for a state of equilibrium; such an animal does not feel good if it does not sacrifice itself. Again, the end that evokes its effort can be simulated. In this regard the distinction between reality and appearance is meaningless. If the simulation is successful, it has succeeded.

Only persons reflect explicitly on the gulf between 'how it appears to me' (*für mich*) and 'how it really is' (*an sich*). To think of 'how it appears to me' means that they have crossed the gulf and planted their feet on what is really there. They can, it is true, pull back deliberately. They can opt for appearance, for self-deception, for the pleasure of feeling good in place of joy, i.e. joy *at* something or other. But no one can do this consistently without surrendering humanity. Epicurus, who named pleasure as the highest and only good, showed this in an exemplary way. Without good friends, he writes, there can be no pleasure in life; but to have good friends one must be a good friend, and to be a good friend one must be ready to sacrifice one's life for friends if need arise.[11] That is the dialectic of hedonism. But someone who is not perverse wants *real* friends, is not content with the impression of having them. None of us would want to spend the whole of life in bed, maintained in a state of artificial euphoria.

---

[11] *Fragment* 590, in Diogenes Laertius 10. 121.

The anti-human Utopia of a complete 'virtual reality' comes threateningly closer, it is true, supported by an anti-philosophy that preys upon real philosophy. But in fact it will not be so easy to achieve the abolition of man. If someone on his deathbed is told that his children have just been rescued from shipwreck, he wants to know if it is true. How something seems *to me* can only be how it seems to me for as long as I can think that that is how it really is. To want to be deceived is always a mark of despair, expressing the sense that one isn't up to coping with reality. This is most obvious when someone accepts a transparent pretence of love. Real enjoyment of friendship begins when we know, or are persuaded, that the warmth shown to us conveys real feeling, and is not put on, even if it makes no difference to us in the end whether it is put on or not.

And the same applies in the case of one's own love. *Amor extasim facit.*[12] Love cannot have an object whose ontological status is in doubt; it is directed to 'the other'—not an object of intention 'given' in the world, but a 'self' that is more than is given. Objects of intention are defined by their attributes, qualitatively. The object of love, on the other hand, is identified indexically; there is no indeterminacy in love's reference. Suppose the place of someone we love were taken by a double—a perfect double, equipped with all necessary information about the memories we had in common. The deception might escape our notice, but as soon as we were told, as soon as we realized that this other person's past was not the one we shared with someone else, we would feel betrayed. The substitute would not be the person we loved. We might possibly come to love this person, too, but that would be a different love.

We understand what is meant by talk of love as 'ecstasy'. What we do not know is whether ecstatic love has a reality apart from the words we use to describe it. We feel alive in the fullest sense only when we love, but when we reflect on the character of love as ecstasy, we find we can love someone simply from loving love. Transcendence on its own could not be aware of itself in this way. A person becomes known to us only through the medium of a bundle of qualities that are by no means unique. Real love is not directed to these qualities, but to the unique particularity of the other, even when he or she

[12] Pseudo-Dionysius, *De divinis nominibus* 13.

alters in some way. Yet we do not have an unlimited ability to keep hold of an object of reference undergoing qualitative variation. It may be true that the lover cannot explain his love in terms of the specific characteristics of the beloved, but if there occurs a very radical shift in those characteristics, it is as though the beloved has disappeared. The reason for this may lie with the lover: while love was fresh, it seemed beyond question that love had reached the core of the beloved and must of its nature be unending, but if it does in fact end, the experience is as if he never did get through to the core of the other's being. It is like this with the ecstasy of the mystic who unites himself with the godhead and enters eternity, becoming one with what is unending in itself. But the moment of unity does indeed end, and the worshipper 'returns to himself'.

In retrospect, however, the state of mystical union is no illusion. For it accompanies the mystic back, and though no longer experienced directly, the reality he encountered is held firmly in his mind. At this point we speak of 'faith', *fides* in Latin, a synonym for 'trust'. Faith is the normal form of human transcendence: the other's being, though not immediately experienced, does not disappear. The form in which the reality of each self makes a claim on every other is 'recognition'. To be capable of recognizing others, one must have immediate experience of *one* other, which is to say, one must 87 have loved. After that, what remains is trust.

The elementary form of such absolute encounter with reality is the intersection of the other's gaze with mine. I find myself looked at. And if the other's gaze does not objectify me, inspect me, evaluate me, or merely crave for me, but reciprocates my own, there is constituted in the experience of both what we call 'personal existence'. 'Persons' exist only in the plural. It is true that the gaze of the other may in principle be simulated, for the other is never presented to us in the compelling immediacy of pure phenomenon. It is a free decision to treat the other as a real self, not a simulation. What that decision essentially consists in is a refusal to obey the innate tendency of all living things to overpower others. Positively expressed, we may call it 'letting-be'. Letting-be is the act of transcendence, the distinctive hallmark of personality. Persons are beings for whom the self-being of another is real, and whose own self has become real to another.

VI

There is a tendency in modern science to simulate life in order to understand its nature. But the only things that can be simulated are qualities and quantities. A qualitative identity can be either real or unreal. The indexical identity of the self cannot be simulated, for it is not available as the object of a theoretical intention. It is available only to recognition and to the faith that recognition implies. Only in this way can we refer with precision. 'Objects' are merely things I 'have', and an object of intention exists only in relation to the 'having' of some subject. The centre of being (*Selbstsein*) that evokes our transcendence, the other person, stands to us in a relation of reciprocity. I am a part of her world, as she is a part of mine. I exist for her as she exists for me. It is a reality for me that I exist for her and that she knows she exists for me. On this reciprocal relation is founded the metaphysical realism that is decisive for persons. It is 88 a necessary condition for intentionality, too, though not to be reduced to intentionality.

A centre of being can display itself only through certain publicly visible qualities. Every means of display is susceptible in principle of simulation; for qualities are phenomena, and phenomena may be simulated. Personality arises when we refuse to treat the other like a simulation or dream, as a mere 'something', existing for me without my existing equally for it. This refusal is implied by love and recognition, which are incompatible with doubt as to the other's reality. That means they are incompatible not only with solipsism, but also with treating realism as no more than a hypothesis. We can observe in Nietzsche how the loss of a relation to reality goes along with the dissolution of the person and the loss of personal unity. If I am not someone who can be 'meant' as who I am, I am not 'someone' at all, but only 'something'; I possess no necessary principle of inner unity. Not being someone else's 'Thou', I cannot be my own 'I', but only a succession of unowned states—'a longing to be no man's sleep under so many eyelids' (Rilke).

The 'metaphysical realism' that characterizes our relation to other persons is not simply that relation and nothing more. It is what distinguishes the human mode of being in the world from the animal in principle. It relates not only to persons but to everything there is, at least to all living things. For human beings there is no pure subject–object relation, and a situation *vis-à-vis* reality is always and at the same time a relation of 'coexistence'. Nietzsche demonstrated that our relations to things as substantial entities follows the paradigm of our relation to persons, and so stands or falls with it. That is immediately apparent in dealings with animals. Our spontaneous reaction to an animal in pain supposes that its pain is somehow real, not merely 'real for us'. Evidently, the pain is not a phenomenon for us. The phenomena permit us to infer that there is pain, since there are ways in which it resembles pain we experience as our own. But there is no lower threshold below which anything can exist for us only in an objective mode.

No particular theory of knowledge is specially favoured by metaphysical realism. No conclusions can be drawn from it about the relation of the 'thing in itself' to its 'appearance', or about the ontological status of our categories for understanding the world. It amounts simply to this: if we cannot transcend appearance and get through to the being that reveals and conceals itself, there can be no persons. For persons are themselves beings that reveal and conceal themselves. They are not simply subjects in a 'subject–object relation'; they are essentially subject and object at once. They are realities that can be met with in the world; in principle they are vulnerable to a methodical reduction to the status of mere object. This reduction can even be undertaken in their own interests, as in the case of a surgical operation, where the subject-character is temporarily eliminated by the anaesthesia; yet the personality is not eliminated, but remains present throughout the procedure. This is a particularly instructive example, because it shows that what makes contact personal cannot be captured in a snapshot, at a given moment or in a brief episode. Continuity of consciousness may be tied to actual consciousness at every moment; but continuity of person is tied to the continuity of an organism in the world, which others can identify as that of one person in particular.

The temporary suspension of subjective consciousness, undertaken to restore someone's physical wholeness, has a perverted mirror-image in the sadistic reduction of a person to an object, not by suspending subjectivity but by objectifying the subjectivity itself.

The point of this undertaking is to make the suffering person him- or herself experience objectification as a means to the satisfaction of someone else. Here we see once again the peculiar character of personal existence, in which subjectivity is only one moment. Personhood is a solitude that others may experience, and an experience of others' solitude. Since the body is the medium of existence-for-others, physicality belongs essentially to human personality. The body implies vulnerability to radical objectification. But it is the 90 hallmark of personality to see in another's body the disclosure and revelation of another centre of being, to accept displacement from the central position that is determinative for all non-personal life.

7

Fiction

I

'One cannot wear a mask for long. The fictive soon reverts to its natural state.' So Seneca wrote, using *persona* in the sense of 'mask'.[1] In Chapter 2 we traced the change of meaning that befell the pair of terms, 'nature' and 'person'. In the view of the ancients all human device and fabrication (*nomos*) was secondary to nature: it depended upon nature for its possibility, was measured against the standard of nature, and finally reverted to nature. Human activity, from this point of view, was no different from animal behaviour, such as the nest-building of birds or the ritual battles of bees for position in the social hierarchy. These belong to nature. 'Nature' is one of those concepts that include their own opposites. So, for example, it is 'natural' for humans to speak; but there is no 'natural language'.

It is characteristic of human nature that the 'fictive', or artificial, forms a separate and independent dimension of life, not integrated into the natural behaviour patterns of self- or species-preservation. Here we have a particularly clear instance of that non-identity with their nature that entitles us to call human beings 'persons'.

Animals, too, possess redundant forms of beauty and performances superfluous to the functional requirements of biological goals. Animals play. The biological function of birdsong could be discharged by various other sounds less charming to the ear. Similarly with visual displays: the surface markings of birds, fish,

---

[1] Seneca, *De clementia* 1. 1. 6: *Nemo potest personam diu ferre. Ficta cito in naturam suam recidunt.*

and reptiles with their refined colour-patterns are, of course, impressive to the females and so of service to selection, but in other animals there is no apparent causal connection between 92 advantageous characteristics serving survival or reproduction and beauty of decoration. Furthermore, and more importantly: to point to the advantages of surface patterns for selection, as Adolf Portmann underlined, merely transfers the problem; for we still have to explain why the females confer their favours on aesthetic grounds.[2] Obviously, it is nature that 'plays'. The patterns of life that she produces do not correspond with any strictness to the demands of biological functionality.

Certainly this playful excess of nature can itself be seen to have a function, at least when it gives rise to playful activity. It promotes training, quick reactions, and flexible adaptation to changing conditions, as well as experimental strategies of action. Human play, on the other hand, admits of no such explanation. Neither do human festivities. These are to such a degree their own ends that from a biological point of view festivals and games involve the expenditure of disproportionate and pointless amounts of strength, effort, material resources, and time. Play ultimately takes precedence over life.

Huizinga once posed the question of 'how far every ritual act falls within the category of play'.[3] The sacred resembles play in being set apart from the functional field of *bios*. Viewed from the sphere of the holy, conversely, ordinary behaviour can be understood as play. Such was Plato's innovative focus on the relation of play and seriousness. In setting out to contradict 'current theory' on that topic, he had in view something very different from what the modern European thinks, i.e. that play is subordinate to the serious business of life. The view Plato attacked was 'that we put up with serious things for the sake of play'. In antiquity the consensus was that the goal of seriousness was leisure, just as the goal of war was peace. Plato did not challenge this, but defined seriousness in a new way. Play *is* serious. The good life is not in the service of play; it must *be* play.

---

[2] Adolf Portmann, *Neue Wege der Biologie* (Munich: Piper, 1960), 166.
[3] Johan Huizinga, *Homo ludens: A Study of the Play Element in Culture* (London: Paladin, 1970), 38.

'I mean we should keep our seriousness for serious things and not waste it on trifles, and that, while God is the real goal of all beneficent serious endeavour, man, as we said before, has been constructed as a toy for God, and this is, in fact, the finest thing about him. All of us, then, men and women alike, must fall in with our role and spend life in making our play as perfect as possible—to the complete inversion of current theory.'[4]

The idea of life as a game was taken further by the Stoics in their teaching that life must be lived as an actor plays his part on the stage, with detachment. Advice from the Apostle Paul points in the same direction: 'Let those who have wives live as though they had none, and those who mourn as though they were not mourning, and those who rejoice as though they were not rejoicing, and those who buy as though they had no goods.'[5] At the far end of this road stands Felix Krull the confidence-man, with his confession to living 'symbolically' and his contempt for the 'grossly factual situation'. Living symbolically, for Felix Krull, is 'true freedom'.[6] Paul and the Stoics draw exactly the opposite conclusion. Grossly factual situations cannot detract from freedom if they themselves are treated as a symbol, that is, if life is treated as a role. We can read off what to do from natural inclinations, which declare the law of nature to us. But we differ from purely natural beings in that our inclinations contain no more than instructions for role-play. Hunger does not force me to eat, though in normal conditions it shows me that I ought to eat, and is a sufficient prima-facie reason for doing so.

With persons life itself belongs to the category of *mimesis*. It becomes its own imitation. I once heard a 5-year-old child say to his mother after a number of games of Let's Pretend: 'Do you know what we can play at now? You be mother and I'll be your child!' After working his way through a variety of roles, his normal life-relationships looked like just another one. Role-play and masks (animal and human) are a feature of every known human society. Dressing-up is a game that children play the whole world over.

---

[4] Plato, *Laws* 803c, tr. A. E. Taylor.
[5] 1 Cor. 7: 29 f.
[6] Thomas Mann, *The Confessions of Felix Krull, Confidence Man*, tr. Denver Lindley (New York: Knopf, 1955), 101.

To mimic identifiable personalities is one of the simplest means of giving entertainment and raising a laugh. And in such settings everyone is capable of 'double book-keeping', as it is called in connection with schizophrenia. We know that the mimic is only playing, and is actually someone else; but we suspend our knowledge. We know as though we were not knowing, and give ourselves over to the appearance. We expose ourselves voluntarily to emotions of fear and compassion. We enjoy shedding tears, because it is as though we 94 were not shedding them. The first person to go on record with astonishment at this was Augustine, recounting how he wept over the story of Dido in the Aeneid, 'because she killed herself for love'.[7] The audience of an artistic fiction must develop a non-identity parallel to that of the artist. It is not first taken in by the illusion and then disabused of it. Rather, it lets itself in for the play, and so lets itself in for treating the players as what they are made out to be, though it knows they really aren't that at all.

II

But are we ever just exactly what we are? The possibility of role-play depends on the fact that as persons we are always playing a role. Our identity is, on the one hand, simply the identity of a natural thing, an organism, and as such we can at any time be recognized by others as one and the same with ourselves. But this basic natural identity contains only a set of directions for the way, and on that way we must look for our identity—or construct it. The person is neither the product of this construction, nor the end-point on the way. The person is the way itself, the whole biography anchored in biological identity. Persons are not roles, but they are role-players, who *stylize* themselves in one or another manner.

Stylization takes place within a culturally determined framework. When this framework is weakened and tradition loses its hold, the need for 'self-discovery', 'self-affirmation', etc. can assert itself, together with a readiness to accommodate to forms of

---

[7] Augustine, *Confessions* 1. 13. 20–1.

totalitarianism, dictatorial or democratic. Even the individual tone of voice is only the personal variant of an inflection peculiar to a linguistic community, and we can only understand the one by familiarity with the other. Like handwriting, it is not the transparent result of a style deliberately assumed, but neither is it a direct expression of the speaker's 'nature'. It is both together.

Human beings know no immediacy, pure and simple, apart from occasional moments of unconscious spontaneity or states of deep depression, when nothing seems worthwhile and even the will for self-expression fails. Human nature is not what human beings *are*. The statement from the Psalm, 'All men are liars', cannot be refuted by examples of seemingly irreproachable uprightness.[8] Even Augustine's *Confessions*, let alone Rousseau's, are in the highest degree a product of self-stylization, though the intent may have been quite the opposite.

Augustine knows that his self-knowledge is not immediate. What he exposes is not his search for himself, but his search for God. He exposes himself only in reaction to experiences he has had of himself on this route to the Absolute, a route, as he understands it, that leads from habitual and constitutional self-deception into truth. Only absolute truth shows anyone his self-deception, and so shows him the truth about himself. The process of undeceiving leads back to oneself by way of radical distance, i.e. repentance. The point is not to be stripped of every role, but to take on the only true role that a human being can play—'putting on Christ'.[9] To expose oneself in a book thus involves a double refraction. One must allow the reader to listen while the author confesses what God has allowed him to see. The purpose is to lead the reader along the road the author has travelled. For the truth in whose light Augustine exposes himself is not *his* truth; it is the truth of the good, the 'truth in which we are all concerned', as Plato put it, before which we are all found liars.[10]

Rousseau's self-stylization, on the other hand, is paradoxical. He adopts the style of a poor savage who fetched up in an urban setting, the *homme naturel* who for a while tried unsuccessfully to play the game of social convention, then experimented with citizenship in

[8] Ps. 116: 11, cf. Rom. 3: 4. [9] Augustine, *Confessions* 8. 12. 29.
[10] Plato, *Gorgias* 505E.

the ancient Roman mould, and finally gave up and revealed himself
to the world as he really is, 'in every way true to nature'. 'Never
was deliberate wickedness further from my intention than at that
moment,' he writes, describing how he accused his employer's house-
maid of the theft he himself had committed, and saw her dismissed in
disgrace.[11] Rousseau's pathos is the pathos of innocence: 'I shall come
forward with this work in my hand to present myself before my
Sovereign Judge...I have displayed myself as I was...and may any
man who dares, say "I was a better man than he."'[12] He creates a role 96
out of refusing to play a role. Natural man he conceives, characteristically, as a speechless, artless hominid. Becoming a man amounts
to self-alienation, for with speech and the division of labour men lose
their transparency to one another and confront one another in roles.

The question we are left with is why Rousseau sets his *Confessions*
down in writing. Of course, 'poor Jean-Jacques' is a role like any
other—but it is a new role. This is the first time we encounter
a programmatic refusal of the self-stylization that characterizes personal being. Man 'in every way true to nature' is one for whom
personal being has become too demanding, and who makes a new
role out of that. Rousseau's epoch-making repudiation of the arts and
sciences is submitted for the prize of the Academy of Arts and Sciences.
And wins it—repudiation is just what the Academy was looking for!

Yet Rousseau's decision in favour of culture-criticism was not
made without a backward glance. One must either be a citizen
through and through, devoting oneself to Fatherland and affairs of
state from early years; or else, when 'there is neither country nor
patriot', nothing to command total allegiance, one must exist
on the level of civilization like a savage in the city, an *homme
naturel* at home only with oneself, not with the esteem of one's
fellow-citizens.[13] Rousseau's abhorrence of his contemporaries is an
abhorrence of '*l'homme double*', neither radically self-alienated nor
radically self-contented, but realizing an inward existence through
roles that are merely public show.

But that is what a person is. The person exists in appearance and
attempts to keep up with appearance, except when he or she lapses

---

[11] J.-J. Rousseau, *Confessions*, tr. J. M. Cohen (Harmondsworth: Penguin, 1953), 88.
[12] Ibid. 17.   [13] *Emile*, tr. P. D. Jimack (London: Dent, 1911), 8.

into cynicism—and that is a role, too, though one hostile to civilization. The humanity of a civilization can be measured by how much hypocrisy flourishes in it—'the homage that vice pays to virtue', as was said in the seventeenth century. In art the insubstantial pageant *is* a pageant, the play *is* the thing. Art suspends the control of reality over our construction of the world. It describes possible worlds, of which the real world is one among others and looks strange by comparison. So Montesquieu viewed the France of his day through the eyes of a Persian traveller, and taught us to find the self-evident rather odd.[14] This we can do only because we are 97 creatures that adopt the 'de-centred position'—Plessner's idea, so intricately connected with our theme, must have its proper name at last.[15] Art shows up what is true of persons all the time. 'Poetically man dwells', wrote Hölderlin, who had a word for it—and a poetic one, too![16]

III

We relate to the world through symbols. The world we inhabit is susceptible of explanation, and we constantly add new layers of explanation to it. Animals, too, live their lives in a world (*Welt*) that means something to them; we call it their 'environment' (*Umwelt*). But they do not rise above it to a point of self-possession where they can put it in perspective, i.e. think about its 'meaning'. The personality of human beings is evinced in their capacity to distinguish the world of signs from what is signified. In this way they win control of signification, which makes them freer than they could ever be in relation to things that exist independently of them.

It is not as though signs had a life of their own that could emerge from their semantic dimension. Words, at least, could never be like

---

[14] Charles Secondat, Baron de Montesquieu, *Lettres persanes*, ed. P. Vernière (Paris: Klincksieck, 1963).

[15] Cf. Ch. 1 n. 11.

[16] 'In lieblicher Bläue…': F. Hölderlin, *Sämtliche Werke*, ii/1 (Stuttgart: Kohlhammer, 1951), p. 372. [This phrase was the title of an essay by Martin Heidegger, in *Poetry, Language, Thought*, tr. Albert Hofstadter (New York: Harper & Row, 1971).]

this, and neither could the art of speech. Words are not moulds impressed upon shapeless reality. They are products of a symbiosis of world and person that we could never devise. The more saturated with experience they are, the richer their accumulation of connotation and association, the more fit they are for constructing a uniquely poetical world, in which metaphor displays its peculiar power of disclosure. The metaphorical use of words is not a secondary, off-duty use, *post eventum*, but matches the original function of speech. The metaphorical range of 'light', for example, in our talk of 'clarity', of intellectual 'enlightenment', of 'illumination', or of 'insight', would not be possible, and would not be understood immediately by every schoolchild, if the word 'light' actually referred to nothing more than a physical or optical phenomenon. What we call 'transferred' meanings of the word have nothing to do with the physical phenomenon, strictly understood, i.e. the phenomenon physics can describe. If 98 there is something common to the meanings of a word, that is because the word *always did* refer to this common something.[17] That is what makes it comprehensible that Genesis ascribes the words 'Let there be light!' to the first day of creation, while sun, moon, and stars are not created until the third day.[18] The poetic use of words is primary—more primitive than uses that employ definition to eliminate overtones and undertones for clarity. 'Poetically man dwells.' That means, the artistic play of words protects the freedom of a relation to the world that is genuinely historical and not bound to nature, a relation in which clarity is helpful only in cases of obscurity, where it is needed to assist the human mastery of nature.

There is one symbolic world that regularly dispenses with the semantic dimension of symbols and has no interest in reality, and that is music. Music can convey psychological occurrences expressively, but does not need to do so. In music we simply add something to the world, a succession of sounds that obeys neither physical laws nor chance, but is organized like language as a meaningful communication that means nothing other than itself. The construction of such

---

[17] Cf. Hans Lipps, *Untersuchungen zu einer hermeneutischen Logik* (Frankfurt: Klostermann, 1959²).
[18] Gen. 1: 3, 14–18.

worlds of pure meaning belongs at the end of a lengthy development reaching its culmination, broadly speaking, in European culture. Now it appears to be drawing to an end.

IV

What we now see emerging is a reversal of this cultural direction, requiring a highly dialectical account to do it justice. It affords a glimpse of the distinctive dangers to which the human animal is exposed by personal existence. Art and nature together compose the human world, and we cannot make a clean break between the way we construct ourselves and the way we really are. It is equally pointless to want to make a break between reality and our interpretation of it, for every attempt of this kind is doomed to be just another interpretation in the end. The reverse is equally true: the more economical, impersonal, and abstract the interpretative patterns we impose upon 99 the world, the less they show us of what is the case. In psychology scientific and confirmable experiment that screens out all the researcher's subjective factors may yield quite precise results, but will tell us very little about what anyone really is. The reality of a human person in all its depth and complexity is accessible only to someone who invests something of himself or herself in the encounter. It is not the most impersonal, but the most personal observation that reveals most of what reality is in itself. It is one of those persistent prejudices of modern thought to think that the less subjective something is, the more objective.

The subjective symbolic world of imaginative art conceals and reveals at one and the same time. Art instructs us how to see, hear, and understand reality. The way reality is for us, is not the way it is *simpliciter*. It is always something more, or something less. Either it is set in coloured light that falls on it from outside, from this angle or that, or else it lies shrouded in darkness. But personal transcendence has the special power of reaching beyond its own patterns of interpretation to what lies behind them. In reflecting on these patterns it frees itself from being tied down to the way they function. It constructs something like a realm of its own, where imagination rules unimpeded and interpretative patterns are open to variation. That is the condition for 'history'. It was no mistake on Plato's part to regard musical innovation as the most powerful force for change in the culture and constitution of the city.[19] Art anticipates what is dawning—in contrast to the retrospective reflection of philosophy. That is what art was like, at any rate, during its long period of development as free play of the imagination.

Yet this epoch seems to be drawing to a close, and something else replacing it. Human personality is apparently turning against human nature. Persons, we have seen, can press behind the objects of their intention in pursuit of how things really are. Transcendence enables us to reflect on the subjectivity of all our intentional objectivity. It is, so to speak, the reverse side of our reflection. But reflection can in turn, as it were, round upon transcendence and swallow it up in a merely subjective state. Even love can be viewed as a subjective feeling for chance interchangeable objects. 'Being' can be thought of as an empty word, or as the intentional object of a 'view of being'—though what *this* view has its eyes on is something we don't hold views about! The scope of reflection is proportioned to the scope of transcendence. When we think something, we may reflect on the fact that it is thought; when we see something, we may reflect on the fact that it is seen, and so on— always understanding reality itself as a kind of picture. Modern thought has persisted in this direction with increasing radicality. Heidegger spoke of an 'age of the world-picture' and saw it as a development that had its roots in Plato.[20]

The so-called 'naturalist epistemology' claims to have uncovered the mechanisms and biological function of this pictorial function— a claim that demonstrates a peculiar lack of self-awareness. For brains, too are 'pictures', obviously enough, and so cannot be an explanation for pictorializing. Naturalist epistemology deals entirely in pictures—it is merely that they are not pictures *of* anything or anyone. For our purposes, what it amounts to is simply this: finite persons, capable of distinguishing the 'way I see it' from what is

---

[19] Plato, *Laws* 797A.

[20] Martin Heidegger, 'The Age of the World-Picture', in *The Question Concerning Technology and Other Essays*, tr. William Lovitt (New York: Harper & Row, 1977).

'really there', can systematically adopt the policy of isolating the way I see it as the sole object of interest. Greek philosophy from Protagoras to Epicurus went some distance with this project. But it took modern technique and the means to simulate consciousness to put us in a position to reconstruct reality entirely as a picture. The now-common expression for this is 'virtual reality'. This is no longer a matter of conscious play, not even of conceiving the whole of life as play. On the contrary, play has been so perfectly orchestrated that it has—for us—taken over as reality. Leibniz's vision of monads without windows has become a technological reality: everyone left alone in a world of imaginations and depictions, cut off from everyone else. And the simulation is so good that nobody feels that anything is missing.

For Leibniz the world that appears to the subject could neither be constructed or manipulated. It had to be the exact representation of the real world, for which it was dependent on a pre-established harmony of things guaranteed by God. Nowadays the real world has been reduced to a wholesale warehouse of information for chips and images for cameras, so that everyone can see the world-picture that he wants or deserves, not excluding 'Cybersex' to stimulate feelings without the need of people to be involved with or of efforts and frustrations that are part of every real human relationship.

Most of this, of course, is science fiction. It is not quite so easy to achieve the abolition of man. All our present knowledge confirms that children will not become normal human beings without real human beings to communicate with. And if adults can perhaps content themselves with simulated women and men as 'playmates', or even prefer them, like Rousseau, for whom imaginary women were better than real lovers, they would be hard put to extend the principle to food and drink, which requires real people to put it on the table. 'Virtual reality' cannot actually replace reality. But what it can replace is art, the fiction of alternative reality experienced *as* fictive. Art can be supplanted by simulation that is bound to be felt as real, since reality, and with it life itself, has long since been understood technologically as simulation. The new form of fiction understands human beings in a radically objective way, which is to say, understands them as animals not living in an *open* world but at the centre of their own self-referential environment.

We think that as transcendent beings we are always one step ahead of the game; but this kind of self-mutilation merely confirms that we human beings are what we are, i.e. capable of resisting what we are. In other words, we are persons.

8

Religion

I

The balance between transcendence and reflection is not a stable one.
Each of these two movements projects the other as its necessary
complement. To go behind the given to the giver, beyond
the objective to the self-disclosing self-concealing, requires that the
object-character of the given, how it appears to us, becomes a matter
of reflection. Each of the two movements, however, tends to assert
itself against its complement by posing as the more fundamental
ontologically. And by incorporating the other as an element of
itself, it disposes of it.

So it may seem that transcendence is the truth undergirding
reflection. Reflection on how the given appears to us proceeds on
the formal assumption of Being. Unless our consciousness can
occupy a sphere that it has not itself defined and circumscribed,
reflection on how any object appears to us is tautological, trivial,
and empty of meaning; for without a reality beyond appearance,
everything is precisely as it is seen to be, and reflection is contentless.
But we *do* reflect on the object-character of the given, and that
means we have gone beyond it already and occupied this uncircum-
scribed sphere.

On the other hand, it may seem that transcendence is a contentless
and purely formal moment *within* reflection, always liable to be
overtaken by further reflection. Every thought about what lies
beyond thought is itself a thought. Hegel made this overtaking
process the constructive principle of the *Phenomenology of Mind*.
He thought he could show how the dialectic of 'how it appears to

me' (*für-mich*) and 'how it really is' (*an-sich*) reaches an absolute point of rest in a 'real self-appearance' (*an-und-für-sich*).

The Hegelian dialectic can be thought of as putting the notion 'person' into motion. In 'having' himself, the person appropriates what he is already. The end of this process is the emergence of a Speculative Thought, in which both transcendence and reflection are assigned a subordinate role. Consciousness has no need to rise above 103 itself to reach the truth about itself. Simply by being present to itself, it is present to the Absolute, too—but only because the Absolute always *was* the truth of consciousness, and the process of searching for the Absolute always *was* the original form of the Absolute's presence. 'If it were not in its very nature, and did it not wish to be beside us from the start...', Hegel writes, the Absolute 'would scorn the trick' of our trying to master it 'like a bird with a limestick'.[1]

Already present, and already known to be present, the Absolute is encountered in the form of *religion*. We are not concerned with whether it is possible for thought to catch up with the presence of the Absolute and bridge the gap between thinking of Being and Being itself, nor whether Hegel accomplished this. As early as Schelling, it is well known, there was an attempt to show that such a bridge can only undermine the object of thinking of Being, and transcendence with it, by reducing it to a mere escapade of thought. Being is always 'unanticipated' (*unvordenklich*). Yet the unanticipated is present to us in the conception of God. And Descartes, the first to base his whole philosophy on subjective reflection, could only assure himself that subjectivity was real by way of the conception of God he found there, i.e. in religion. In art subjectivity devises its own stage on which the insubstantial pageant is reflected without melting into the thin dialectical air of Being; in religion, correspondingly, and only in religion, subjectivity asserts its own reality and substance without reneging on its standing as subjectivity. (This may not be true for every religion; I take Christianity as the model here.) In conceiving of God and of its own creation, reflection comes to a standstill, confronted with itself as Being, but not in the way naturalist

[1] G. W. F. Hegel, *Phenomenology of Mind*, tr. J. B. Baillie (San Francisco: Harper, 1967), 132.

monism does when it tells us that our understanding of ourselves is a misunderstanding, a second and supervenient phenomenon quite easily explained by evolution. From this point of view transcendence with its posit of Being is but an impotent reduplication, constantly overtaken by reflection on its conditions, while reflection itself is merely a natural phenomenon. A religious understanding of subjectivity can treat it *as a person*, i.e. an existent that was 'meant to be' subjective and could not exist otherwise. Thought, with its aspiration 104 to truth and to the disclosure of Being, is doomed to frustration at the unanticipated nature of being, except on one condition: it must think of the Unanticipated itself as subjective personality.

At an earlier stage in the dialectic of spiritualism and naturalism there arose certain habits of speech that have been decisive for our epoch: one could speak of reflection without transcendence and of transcendence without reflection, of subjectivity which disowned its nature and of nature without spiritual dimension. Religion is undialectic by comparison! There the original unity of being and thought, of power and meaning, is not so much thought as worshipped. It is what we are not, the presupposition of what, as subjects, we are. Thought can dissolve this unity, and necessarily does so; but then our thinking falls into unconscious oblivion of itself, forgetting the presupposition of its own activity. This forgetfulness can be sustained only by an incessant flight forward towards Utopia. Thoroughgoing materialism is as utopian as thoroughgoing idealism; what each amounts to is the abolition of man and the disappearance of the person. Thoroughgoing idealisms have been tried; and such trials have been possible because idealism is realized in the medium of pure thought. Their refutation has been that they never achieved the compelling intersubjective position that they thought themselves entitled to; each successive thinker busied himself with 'overcoming' what had seemed impossible to overcome, and the collapse of idealism as a whole was actually the result of its determined implementation. Materialist monism, on the other hand, is genuinely incapable of determined implementation, and on its own account of itself is, in Popper's phrase, 'promissory materialism'.[2] We have to forget it while we are speaking to one another. Indeed, materialist theories

---

[2] Karl Popper and J. Eccles, *The Self and its Brain* (Berlin: Springer, 1977), 96–8.

assume we can forget them while we study them, since on their own terms they can have no significance.

II

From conviction or antipathy, persons can be irreligious. Yet it is constitutive for human personality that religion lies within the range of human possibilities. A person has a nature, nature does not have a person. Human activity is not prescribed by the system of human instincts. Precisely for this reason nature as such has no normative significance for human beings. Textbooks in evolutionary biology are wont to conclude with urgent appeals that we should take responsibility for the survival of species; but those appeals have no logical connection with the contents of the textbooks. After we have been taught how evolutionary selection shapes the behaviour of natural kinds to fulfil the functions necessary for survival, we are suddenly told that this is no longer unproblematically the case with *human* behaviour, so we must make a point of adopting survival as a principle of conduct. In nature there is not the slightest trace of a reason for doing any such thing. If man is 'Nature's liberated captive', why should he willingly deliver himself up to captivity at the hands of this same Nature?[3]

Religion gives one answer to this question: nature is not the last horizon, but something we 'have'. Taken as a whole, nature is 'creation', and its teleological structures allow us to discern the creator's will for humankind. Nothing less than a personal will can be the source of normative 'natural right' for persons. 'If God does not exist, everything is allowed,' asserted Dostoevsky, a saying that Wittgenstein adapted.[4] That is no less true if we acquire the elements of morality independently of religious belief, for apart from religious belief it is still unintelligible *why* we should do what we think best

[3] Johann Gottfried von Herder, *Reflections on the Philosophy of the History of Mankind* 1, in *Sämtliche Werke*, ed. B. Suphan (Berlin: 1887–   ), xiii. 146.

[4] Ludwig Wittgenstein, *Notebooks 1914–16*, ed. and tr. G. H. von Wright and G. E. M. Anscombe (Oxford: Blackwell, 1961), 91: 'If suicide is allowed then everything is allowed.'

overall in the teeth of weighty private interests. It is even unintelligible what it could *mean* that we 'should' do something. One may recognize a value, but a person is not compelled to be governed by it.

We are creatures that 'have' our nature, and control both our own nature and nature in general. Having nature is our existence; controlling nature, we control ourselves. The question is, can there be any standard for how we exercise control? Is there such a thing as responsibility for oneself? The idea seems unthinkable without 106 something to be responsible *to*. If we are all responsible to ourselves, we can absolve ourselves from responsibility whenever we want. And if the responsible agent and the one who holds the agent responsible are one and the same, the agent is free to make and remake the terms and conditions, which amounts to the same thing.

III

Unless it is a religious idea, responsibility for oneself is vacuous. But if it is a religious idea, there is something *to whom*, not merely something *for which*, we are responsible. In which case the shape of responsible action is no longer arbitrary, and such terms as 'natural morality' and 'natural law' acquire a rational meaning. For if personality means to have one's nature, the integrity of one's nature is of essential significance for a person.

There is a forgetfulness of persons that can arise in a specifically personal context, and this takes two forms, leading to apparently opposite extremes. The acosmic personalist, on the one hand, recognizing no obligation to his own or any other nature, is faced with the question of where to find objects for his will, purposes for which to set about mastering nature. The only available answer is: they spring up naturally. Precisely by refusing the normative implications of nature, his will and action themselves become subject to natural explanation. The very thought of arbitrary, unrestricted control of nature makes the human subject a purely natural phenomenon. It is, indeed, a mark of living things in general that everything they encounter is reduced to a function of their self-direction. Living things are prone to expand their reach, checked only by their physiological structure and the natural balance of powers. If humans think of themselves as no more than natural phenomena, there is no imaginable standard by which they can limit themselves in relation to the balance of powers. Only by understanding themselves as *more* and *other* than nature, can they recollect nature as a standard for their conduct. Nature sets no obligatory limits, only religion does. 107 But the limits religion sets are what *would* be natural limits, *if* there were natural limits for persons. Nature has no numinous influence on men and women as nature, only as God's creation.

'Act as if the maxim of your action were to become by your will a universal law of nature,' runs Kant's formulation for the categorical imperative.[5] We cannot wish this were actually the case, for that would be the end of freedom and of every imperative, too. But we can ask ourselves whether we could conceive or desire a nature in which everything occurred in conformity with the practical maxims that we happened presently to entertain. In moral action we imagine ourselves the creators of nature, but we do not actually conduct ourselves as such. Moral action, rather, is the attempt to see ourselves from the creator's perspective and to ask what he must have willed that we should will. Such a question is susceptible of an answer only in a categorical structure that allows some answers to be right and some wrong, and this kind of structure emerges only among living creatures. In the physical regularities of inanimate nature without relation to living creatures, no such thing as right and wrong, no such thing as good and evil, is to be found. But once we have to do with teleological structures, we encounter 'malfunction', the failure to accomplish ends, and from that point on nature is in principle relevant to morality: a sphere for the exercise of responsibility, 'a book who runs may read', containing directions by which persons may govern their conduct.

The impulse to pick up a beetle lying on its back and set it on its feet is quite spontaneous. But there are actions and impulses that we approve or disapprove, think well-intentioned or mischievous, irrespective of whether we have the impulse to do them.

---

[5] Immanuel Kant, *Groundwork of the Metaphysics of Morals*, AA iv. 421 (*Practical Philosophy*, ed. and tr. Mary J. Gregor (Cambridge: Cambridge University Press, 1996), 73).

These epithets can be appropriate only because there *are* natural tendencies in the first place: our own, which we acknowledge, and other people's, with which we try to identify ourselves. The exercise of personal will does not spring out of nothing, but comprises the acknowledgement, rejection, or transformation of natural impulses. Religion enables human beings to see themselves as creatures of nature without having to abrogate their personhood. In other words, it enables them to understand themselves as subjects without disowning their status in nature as 'things indifferent'.

Responsible action can happen only if at the same time we are 108 *relieved* of responsibility. Being responsible for absolutely everything undermines the very idea of responsibility. We lack both knowledge and criteria to calculate a future course of world events and weigh it against alternatives. Limited responsibility—for a definite sphere of activity over a definite period of time—does not entitle us to sacrifice the rest of the world to whatever we may happen to be responsible for. But it does entitle us to focus our attention and distinguish intended from unintended consequences. This is required in any and every act. Action differs from mere occurrence precisely in that certain consequences are singled out as ends-of-action, while others are sidelined as unintended. That is the meaning of the phrase 'end-of-action'. The selection of ends that makes an act possible is incompatible with having responsibility for absolutely everything. Such selection is common to humans and other animals. Yet human beings, as rational creatures, are placed before a universal horizon that seems to make it illegitimate. Utilitarianism frowns on partiality in the ordering of our loves as a moral failure. It demands that we deny our natural creaturehood in the service of radical universality, yet at the same time viewing those affected by our actions as wholly creatures of nature as far as their pursuit of their subjective welfare goes. If personality means having a nature and a corresponding relation-to-self, then neither the utilitarian agent nor those affected by that agent's actions could qualify as persons.

The idea of universal responsibility not only destroys the conditions for action; it is also, in a strict sense, Utopian. A comparison of possible alternative worlds would be an impossibility, and once we had compared them we would have no criteria for evaluating them. At the very least we should have to assume that beneficial short- or medium-term consequences allowed us to anticipate a desirable longer-term course of events. G. E. Moore demonstrated both the necessity and the utter implausibility of this assumption.[6] But if we are not entitled to assume that limiting responsibility to what we can foresee is serviceable to the longer-term good as a whole—or at least not destructive of it—there can be no moral action at all. This assumption, too, in fact, is a religious one. That is why Fichte spoke of 'faith in divine providence' as a condition for moral action.[7] 'Do the right in thine own sphere, The rest will of itself come clear.'[8] If *that* advice is badly misleading, we can never know what it would be prudent to do. Moral responsibility must be relieved of the weight of universal responsibility, and the relief is called 'religion'.

109

IV

There is another way in which religion relieves us and enables us to act. Under conditions that vary from one religion to another, it brings *forgiveness* into view, lifting the burden of objective guilt and despair. The consciousness of guilt can be so great that all hope drains away of doing anything to restore a positive balance to our life as a whole. We have already observed that the idea of an overall balance implies an objective view on one's life, without total personal immersion in each moment and each action. It is what has gone wrong in a life, its guilt, that locks us into situations that deprive us of personal freedom to engage, as it were, freely and immediately. Only the consciousness of forgiveness unlocks these situations, 'so that your youth is renewed like the eagle's'.[9] That is to say, it permits

---

[6] G. E. Moore, *Principia Ethica* (Cambridge: Cambridge University Press, 1903), 108: 'The arguments...are all more or less vitiated by the assumption that what appear to be necessary conditions for the attainment of most pleasure in the near future, will always continue so to be. And, even with this vicious assumption, they only succeed in making out a highly problematical case.'

[7] Johann Gottlieb Fichte, 'Über den Grund unseres Glaubens an eine göttliche Weltregierung', *Werke* (AA 5), 347–57.

[8] Johann Wolfgang von Goethe, 'Sprüche', 61. *Werke,* i (Hamburg: Wegner, 1948), 314.

[9] Ps. 103: 5.

the person once again to make a creative destination of her acts without hindrance from the past. Repentance cannot achieve liberation on its own, for guilt is an objectively imprisoning complex of circumstances that cannot be overcome by the guilty subject unilaterally. The idea of such a complex is not itself a religious one, whether as interpreted by Anaximander, for whom everything 'pays the price for its injustice' by passing from the scene,[10] or in the Indian idea of Karma. Religion is involved in the belief that weeping is heard and sins are forgiven. The certainty of such forgiveness can only be mediated through a particular religious tradition. But the religious possibility, the possibility of forgiveness, is indispensible for persons as such, because it also makes it possible to keep continuity with oneself as a person over time. Forgiveness is the force that resists entropy. Religion is the hope that the Second Law of Thermodynamics does not have the last word on reality.

---

[10] Diels, *Fragmente der Vorsokratiker*, frag.1.

9

Time

I

'I think...I am.' The first part of Descartes's famous utterance says something about the structure of consciousness. Lichtenberg thought the primary certainties of consciousness could be better expressed by the formula, 'It is thought...'[1] Avicenna had anticipated that opinion: a man suspended in space, blind and immobile, could in the absence of sensory experience think only, 'cogitatur'.[2] Descartes assumes that consciousness is already *self*-consciousness, a kind of familiarity with oneself. But it is anything but clear what that hyphenated 'self' means. It certainly does not mean that consciousness implies knowing which individual it belongs to. The 'I' of the Cartesian *cogito* starts out as a merely formal 'I'. Unlike most living European languages, Latin does not express the subject of a verb in the first person, but leaves it to be understood from the verbal ending. And if consciousness arose from a single type of intentional act, or indeed from a single act, it would remain with this purely formal structure. It would be conscious of itself as consciousness, and there would be no point in postulating such a thing as a subject. But the 'self' becomes more definite when we are conscious of ourselves as feeling, thinking, and striving, when we realize that the same 'I' that am hungry also recognize the hunger as my own and

---

[1] Georg Christoph Lichtenberg, *Aphorisms*, tr. R. J. Hollingdale (Harmondsworth: Penguin, 1990), 168: 'We should say *it thinks*, just as we say *it lightens*. To say *cogito* is already to say too much as soon as we translate it *I think*. To assume, to postulate the I is a practical requirement.'

[2] Avicenna, *De anima* 1. 1.

want to eat to satisfy it. Then subjectivity must be conceived as more than a structural moment in intentional acts. It must be independent, apart from its acts.

But a further step is required, as we have shown, if we are to move from 'I think' to 'I am', from establishing the subject of acts as a self to affirming its being. When I have the thought, 'I am', I have left behind the way it appears to me (*für mich*), simply by having that dimension 112 explicitly in my mind. Having it in my mind means that I distinguish how it appears to me from how it really is (*an sich*), simply by virtue of the formal implication, '*it is the case that* it is how it appears to me'. The gap between what appears to me and what really is, opens up with the possibility of my being seen by others. But I can only appear to others if I am more than a consciousness, if I have an *outer aspect*, a nature that the other encounters as a 'something'. This nature must be such as to reveal my subjectivity. If it were not, it would not be me that the other perceived. Actually to *assert* my 'I', the other would have to *be* me; but there is a symbolic representation in which 'someone' can be *visible* to someone else. This possibility is decisive, not for subjectivity in the sense of immediate familiarity with oneself, but for identifying oneself, for the consciousness that one *is* a self. It is decisive, therefore, for personality.

The person, then, not only *is* a consciousness, but *has* a nature. Persons are not merely subjects of consciousness; they are subjects of consciousness that know they are natural objects in the world, even if they do not always know what their nature is. Persons are such things as—for example—human beings. Subjectivity merely abstracts a moment of reflection characteristic of persons. Since persons reflect on themselves as subjects, they are *eo ipso* more than subjects. Non-human animals have purely subjective experiences. They live wholly in the inner world that determines the meaning of everything they meet in their environment. Accordingly, they have no inkling that their inner world *is* an inner world, just as they have no inkling of their own being, or of any being. Persons command a view of the inner–outer difference because they know about it.

The reason that they know about it is their *temporality*. It is temporality that allows this difference to emerge within subjectivity, temporality through which the personal relation-to-self is constituted. Subjectivity as such is punctiliar and instantaneous. 'I think' is powerfully and immediately self-evident, but only in the present tense. The past and the future, 'I thought' and 'I will think', never occur to us immediately, but only as 'ecstasies' of the present, as survival and anticipation. Memory stretching beyond the reson- ance of the immediate past is mediated knowledge, and may deceive 113 us. Yet it is I, and not anything else, whose sensibility, experience, thought, and will occur to me through the medium of memory. Everything else I remember is available to memory only as some- thing I experienced, observed, or thought. The intention we concen- trate upon objects directly (*intentio recta*) is only indirect (*intentio obliqua*) when we remember them. When I recall my experience of something, it is the *experience* I recall—together with its object, or even ahead of it.

For Descartes the contents of memory are *cogitatum* not *cogitatio*, object rather than subject. Their reality may in principle be doubted, and they are guaranteed only by the consistency of God. Subjectivity is in the present tense, and that is the sole reason it can be so sure of itself. Since Descartes's theme is not personality but subjectivity, he does not reflect on the fact that *cogitatio* itself turns into *cogitatum*. The contents of memory, though mediated and uncertainly real, do not belong to the outer world. They are consciousness and lived experience—*my* consciousness, indeed, and *my* lived experience. It is not the case that my own experience of living is always immediately self-evident to me. The greater part of my experience, which I remember, is not so. My subjectivity has in the course of time become increasingly remote from me, yet without ceasing to be mine. It is just because it is mine that I remember it.

Locke proposed to define the identity of persons by continuity of memory. I can claim as my own and be held responsible only for what I remember.[3] This proposal runs into the sands of self-contradiction. Hume abandoned it, and with it he abandoned

---

[3] John Locke, *Essay Concerning Human Understanding* 2. 27. 16, ed. P. H. Niddich (Oxford: Clarendon Press, 1975), 340–1: 'Whatever has the consciousness of present and past Actions, is the same Person to whom they both belong... For as to this point of being the same *self*, it matters not whether this present *self* be made up of the same or other Substances, I being a much concern'd, and as justly accountable for any Action was done a thousand Years since, appropriated to me now by this self- consciousness, as I am, for what I did the last moment.'

the idea of a personal continuity altogether. Locke departs from Descartes in taking the question of personal identity further than the immediate presence of actual consciousness. But then he collapses this trans-temporal identity back into the immediacy of experience, i.e. of memory. So memory is presented as the form of immediate self-identity, which it certainly is not. Memory supposes the explication of subjectivity, the turning of the inward outward. The memory 'recovers', as we say, the past self, and fuses itself with it. 114

This fusion is not a new immediacy. The identity of the person is still a mediated one. The toothache of memory, mine though it was and mine though the memory still is, is not a toothache I have now. It doesn't hurt the same. And that is why I can either imagine past pain or forget it. If I imagine it, that doesn't make it painful, though imagined present pain is real pain. If I forget about it, that does not make it any less the pain that I once had. If I suppress it, there may be present effects more far-reaching than those of the pain I recall, which is present and distant at once. The identity of consciousness is not, as Locke assumed, the same as the consciousness of identity. Memory is not knowledge, but opinion. My memory lapses can often be corrected by others' memories, even when they concern me directly.

II

The constitution of personal identity is inseparable from the process of self-externalizing, disowning oneself in the course of time. Self-disowning is not inconsistent with being a subject originally at one with oneself. Immediate familiarity with oneself is not the same as *possessing* oneself; it is not self-consciousness. Self-consciousness arises only through externalization, for I can only possess what is separate from me, just as I can only surrender what I possess. The subject that becomes certain of itself by reflection and so realizes its personal being, can do so only by recalling its past self into the present. This way of putting it, however, is misleading, beginning from an initial, immediately self-present self, which then proceeds to externalize itself through time and become a person. Beginning with

the subject in this way has the effect of reconstructing a complex 115
reality that was actually there behind subjectivity from the first.
The instantaneous *cogito* is an abstraction. The abstraction is possible
because it is, as we have seen, the hallmark of persons that they have
a perfectly clear numerical identity that cannot be pinned down in
terms of qualitative attributes, so that identification is never a matter
of description. We may be tempted to give this abstract identity
distinct from substantive qualifications the status of an entity, and
call it a 'self'. But if the self were an entity with a causal relation to the
brain, it would have to be a 'something' with its own distinctive
qualities after all. A self would then possess a 'nature' which would
need another self to 'have' it. The thought of the self arises simply
from the fact that human nature is something someone 'has'. But
what has it? Not an independent entity, but the very same human
being. He or she is a whole not only greater than the *sum* of its parts,
like any other organism, but greater than the *organization* of its parts.
The human being is 'someone'.

The self as a point of numerical identity is an empty conception,
yielding no way of distinguishing one individual from another nor of
conceiving subjects other than as events of consciousness, vanishing,
atomic, and momentary. Even if memory draws these events together
into a biographical whole, that, too, is a momentary event of consciousness, another part of the process which the subject can never
view in its totality. I, the subject, am always situated somewhere
within the process, not outside it. I have no viewing platform to
look out on the process from start to finish. The viewing platform is
for everyone else. It is by anticipating *their* view, then, that I can get
beyond the abstract idea of myself as a discarnate subjectivity. Here
the person comes fully into view, or better, the human being comes
into view *as* a person.

Yet to other people, as to ourselves, we are accessible as persons
only through a 'nature'. The person is not a self beyond its nature, an
entity without description. What it is, is the having of its nature at its 116
command. The qualitative attributes are what make the 'stream of
consciousness' possible, and this excludes the possibility that all
its immediate, momentary points of consciousness could collapse
indiscriminately into a homogeneous 'now' without dimensions.

The condition, then, for personal intersubjectivity is that subjectivity externalizes itself in time. The problem with intersubjectivity is that other people's inwardness is accessible only through symbolic representation in the form of natural features. We do not know it *as* subjectivity. The only thing someone else can present to me is an exterior surface. This gulf would be unbridgeable if finite subjects existed only as momentary and discrete events of consciousness, which could have no exterior surfaces. Exterior and interior would then be contradictory alternatives, and our talk of 'representation' only a meaningless noise to cover up the unbridgeable gulf. Subjectivity would be no more than *my* consciousness *of* myself *for* myself, or else it would cease to be subjectivity. Since no one has my pain, no one could know what I have when I am in pain.

Existence in time, however, means that subjectivity is in pursuit, reaching out to become what it has not yet become; by persisting in time it becomes its own past and its own outside. This outside is not like other objects with no subjects, but is an *inside turned out,* an outward inwardness. The hunger I recall when I speak of it to myself and others is and remains *my* hunger, though by the time I recall it I am no longer hungry. The objectification of past subjectivity makes it possible for subjects to be objectively accessible to others *as* subjects. That is, it is what makes them persons.

Inner subjectivity on its own does not suggest such a thing as time. Indeed, it is based on *abstraction* from time. But when subjects think of themselves as existents, possible objects for another subject, it presumes they have become objectified to themselves, have become an outside taken back inside again. This is what we mean by memory. Only the sidelong glance of memory makes the experience of something in particular a particular experience. We gaze on ourselves as subjects, and we look to ourselves like this or that. That is how we can be this or that to others without losing our status as subjects. Memory, in making us objective subjectivity to ourselves, makes it possible for us to be so for other people, too.

It is memory that really reveals us to ourselves. Momentary subjectivity is merely a limit-concept. Only the godhead, as Augustine saw, occupies the perennial Now, because only the godhead is thought as infinite particularity, such that its relations *ad extra* constitute its inner being. The godhead subsists as three persons. According to Thomas the godhead cannot have *real* relations *ad extra,* relations to the creation, because that would be inconsistent with infinity. Its relation to the creation is a virtual relation, upheld in the Father's relation to the Son: 'In that same word which is the Son the Father utters both himself and the creation.'[4]

Finite subjectivity is not the same as infinite particularity. It is deficiency of being, or quest for being. Time unfolds as subjectivity appropriates being, as subjects 'become' what by nature they 'are'. Persons cannot simply 'be' their nature without further ado: they must persist in the task of 'having' it. In the depths of depression we may sense this as so overwhelming a task that we have no energy left for the quest for being. The person may even rid itself of the being that it has as its nature. But having its nature is what its being is, getting rid of the nature means getting rid of itself. The person does not continue when the human being is gone.

Self-consciousness is consciousness of what we have already appropriated, i.e. of our past. For a person to be 'a being' is to be a 'has been'. The Aristotelian definition of a being contains a significant reference to the past: 'being what was'. 'Subjects' can relate to one another only on this basis: they must be what they were, must possess a *natura naturata,* a developed phenotype that identifies them a second or third time round. This ontological origin of time makes time irreversible. A line, on which one may go to and fro, is hardly, Bergson noted, a fitting metaphor for time.[5] The drawing of a line is not itself a line. Leibniz imagined time as the drawing of a parabola, the formula for which was the monad as pure subjectivity: the monad is the point that contains the formula like a cell containing the whole genetic programme of an organism. But the formula cannot be established without constructing the parabola, which means drawing the line, for the line has no reality until it is drawn. Persons are *real* subjects that *are there* for each other, and that is why they are not *merely* subjects.

---

[4] Thomas Aquinas, *De potentia* 9. 9 ad 13: *eodem verbo sc. filio pater dicit se et creaturam*; cf. *ST* I. 34. 2, I. 37. 2.
[5] Henri Bergson, *Time and Free Will: An Essay on the Immediate Data of Consciousness,* tr. F. L. Pogson (London: Sonnenschein, 1910), 99–104.

III

Time, and our own involvement in it, always were a matter for wonder to mankind, inviting efforts to understand why things are as they are. Augustine's remark is well known: he knew what time was if he was not asked; when he was asked, he could not tell.[6] Whatever we may mean by calling time the form of our existence, it cannot be that time is unobservable. It cannot remain hidden from thinking beings, because they are also living beings, and as such always have time as their adversary. Their being is a quest for being, made necessary by the fact that being incessantly slips away from them. The thought of substantial beings whose *actual* existence is a sufficient cause of their *future* existence is an abstraction worthy of Democritus's conception of non-contingent blocks of reality. Time is the perpetual ground for lamenting the *conditio humana*—as though we could imagine some other way of existing! We have seen that time is the condition for objectivizing inwardness, and so also for finite personality. But this objectivizing of inwardness means, at the same time, that time is unreal. Past, present, and future are not equal in ontological status. What has been is no more; and the future is not yet. What is, is the present; and since the present as such incessantly passes away, it pursues future being. The verb *vergehen*, 'to pass', means 'to cease being'; the past (*das Vergangene*) is what has ceased to be. What the objectivizing of inwardness amounts to is an unrealizing, and this is expressed in the Greek proverb, 'Count no man happy before he is dead.'[7] If *eudaimonia* means the objective success of life as a whole, it follows that the only happy life is one that has come to an end. A building can be judged only when it is completed; but in the case of buildings completion is not the same as being over and done with, because a building is only *objectively* real.

What temporality means for persons is that inwardness becomes objective in the sense of passing away. Passing, however, is the inner experience of a living being only while that being pursues being,

---

[6] Augustine, *Confessions* 11. 14. 17: *si nemo ex me quaerat, scio; si quaerenti explicare velim, nescio.*

[7] Aristotle, *EN* 1100A.

reaching out for the being that comes towards it. Aristotle interpreted living things' pursuit of being as a striving for participation in the eternal.[8] That interpretation takes the point of view of reason, for which reflection on time is bound up with the experience of frustration. If the objective success of life, our 'happiness', is tied to the condition of being past, then the experience of happiness can never be more than incomplete. But happiness over and done with is yet more incomplete, because no longer experienced. So Aristotle speaks of 'merely human happiness', distinguishing it from 'happiness pure and simple' that presents itself inescapably before our eyes as a model, but from which we are barred simply because we are men.[9] The idea of a real, timeless unity of the person within and without is an idea human beings are never free of. It forms the background against which our awareness of time's peculiarly 'annihilating' character stands out in relief.

Plato thinks of timelessness wholly from the starting point of the objective form. Ideas are timeless, and the finite is real to the extent that it participates in ideas. But because the finite in itself is nothingness, its participation passes away perpetually, and is real only as it continually aspires to participate. The particular as such is not ideal, and therefore not an object of knowledge. True statements about contingent facts are not timelessly true. According to Aristotle not only can one not know anything about tomorrow's low tide, but nothing one says about it today can be either true or false.[10] In most modern logic, which has eliminated tenses from predicates, the position looks very different. It does not use the words 'is', 'was', and 'will be', but makes do with a timeless 'is', which suffers no loss of truth through the passage of time because the predicate has a temporal indication incorporated in it. The statement 'I am in pain' can be true today and false tomorrow, but the statement 'Jürgen Klinsmann is in pain on 28 March 1996' seems to be timeless. But this is an illusion, because the date means nothing in the last analysis unless it bears a relation to the 'now' in which the speaker stands. Only by assuming a timeless knower with a knowledge extending to temporal and contingent events can we attribute atemporality to the knowledge of contingents. But that means thinking of the absolute as

---

[8] *De anima* 415ᵃ26 ff.   [9] *EN* 1101ᵃ20.   [10] *De interpretatione* 19ᵃ30.

personal. If God always knows how tomorrow's tide will ebb because he has no tomorrow, we can say that the truth about this ebb-tide is a timeless truth, and propositions about it true irrespective of when they are formulated.

But to think of a personal God, which is to say, a three-personal God, is to think of an inwardness that does not incessantly slip away to become objective, but has inward being precisely in self-utterance, looking on himself, and looked on, through 'another of himself'. This thought is what transforms the idea of timelessness from indifference into eternity, which Augustine called a 'permanent now'. In place of indifference to time we have contemporaneity with every lived present of finite beings, and so with their actual inwardness. This is not something God has to actualize by self-objectification, but is, in a strong sense, an inward knowledge of self-consciousness, because— as Augustine says again—'God is more inward to us than we to ourselves.'[11] A subjectivity that really knows in this way, not superseding its knowledge as it passes away, is the transcendent ideal of the striving for knowledge that Paul expresses in the lapidary formula: 'then shall I know as I am known'.[12]

IV

Such thoughts—that there is a timeless consciousness of temporal things, and that eternity is contemporary with every moment— have far-reaching consequences for our understanding of time. Inevitably, time loses its ontological reality. Boethius points out that to speak of God's 'foreseeing' is a metaphor that draws God improperly into time: it is not that God knows today what will happen tomorrow, but that everything is equally present to him. Boethius himself, however, uses no less misleading an illustration: travellers cannot see the road before them, though that road is visible from a tower.[13] This is an example of the 'spatialization' of time that Bergson cautioned against.[14] If past and future are equally present *sub specie Dei*,

---

11 Augustine, *Confessions* 3. 6. 11: *Deus interior intimo meo.*
12 1 Cor. 13: 12.   13 Boethius, *Philosophiae consolatio* 5 prosa 6.
14 Bergson, *Time and Free Will*, 99–104.

coming-to-be and passing-away are simply the mode in which finite persons live out their being. What is, in an absolute sense, is simply the Absolute. That each moment is contemporary with the 'permanent now' means that there is only a relative difference between one moment and the next. It is an aspect of what it means to experience the world as finite persons.

But the difference between one moment and the next would be empty, and time would be pure 'slippage of being', if each new present moment were not full. It is not time that flies, but experience, crammed full with variation of mood and content. Persons are not condemned to reach out for a stream of being that glides away out of their grasp; they relate successive moments of experience to one another, so that *time assumes a form*. Empty time, the infinite and infinitely divisible stream, is a mere abstraction. Experiences of varying duration are what make up the reality. As they connect their different experiences to one another, persons themselves are formed in time.

The paradigm case of temporal form is music. The constituent elements of a piece of music are not the individual notes, but small clusters short enough to be retained in the memory immediately, something like an extended moment. The form of the whole piece is then realized by conscious recollection and comparison of its elements. Often we have to hear a piece several times to grasp it; we may even need a programme note. The realization of a piece of music in time is entirely 'ideal'; it is a timeless something that we cannot think of without time. For temporal form is constructed on the fact that individual moments are neither simultaneous nor indistinguishable.

There is a paradox in this situation. The more indistinguishable the moments, the more inconsequential their difference, so much the more relentless is the annihilating passage of time. To 'kill time' means to give oneself up to time's killing effects. To take time seriously, to use time, to wait, to recognize a moment, to see when something is 'on time': this is to overcome time by making it a material for form. Even our complaints about our own transitoriness may assume a form, and that form is already an answer to our complaints. As persons, we are suspended between awareness of time's annihilating effects and awareness of time's own annihilation against the backdrop of the eternal present. Laid out flatly alongside one another like that, these two ideas cancel each other out without the contradiction giving rise to anything sensible. But Plato's answer both to Heraclitus's 'Everything is in flux' and to Parmenides's 'Everything is one' was the discovery of the *idea,* the form that maintains itself in the flux of not-being, a form to which we relate through the act of knowing. To think of a person is to think of one's own existence as a form—not a form that maintains itself through time as an unfluctuating object of timeless knowledge, but a form that is itself a formation of time, a 'temporal form'.

10

Death and the Future Perfect Tense

I

'By man came death.' Only persons die.

Epicurus tried the following reflection to argue death out of existence, unsuccessfully: there is no such thing as death, for while we live, we are not dead, and when we are dead, 'we' are no more. Being dead is a property no one has.[1] But we cannot banish the knowledge that one day we *shall not be*, but *shall have been*; and this is the knowledge that makes death real. We foresee a retrospective view on ourselves—someone else's view, not our own.

There is another use of the future perfect tense, distinct from the knowledge of death. That is the use that imposes temporality on our personal consciousness. We become an object to ourselves each moment, and foresee that each moment 'will have been'. Yet we never stop owning our past as ours. Things that cease to have the meaning for us they once did acquire new meanings in new contexts.[2] But knowing about our death is different. Here we foresee a *radical* objectification that removes all prospect of integration through a sustained continuity of meaning. In Christianity, as in other ancient mystery-religions, conversion and baptism are fittingly described as a kind of death, 'dying with Christ'. The point of the

---

[1] Epicurus, *Epistula ad Menoeceum*, 125: ὅταν μὲν ἡμεῖς ὦμεν, ὁ θάνατος οὐ πάρεστιν· ὅταν δ' ὁ θάνατος παρῇ, τόθ' ἡμεῖς οὐκ ἐσμέν.

[2] [In this chapter the author develops an extended contrast between *Bedeutsamkeit* and *Sinn*. English offers no pair of words that easily captures the contrast intended here between immediate relevance and ultimate importance. I have opted for 'meaning' and 'significance', with 'pointless' for *sinnlos*, though the reader will be conscious that these are used here as terms of art.]

comparison lies in the radical discontinuity of meaning. It is as though the former life belonged to someone else.

The death of others impinges on non-personal creatures, too, making a difference to their lives, whether of loss or liberation. Life itself goes on. They know the fear of whatever poses an objective threat to their lives. Such threats are part of animals' experience, making them either run away or stand and fight. But none of these instinctive reactions implies a knowledge of their own end. Danger-signals disturb the homoeostasis and release the appropriate pattern of behaviour to restore it—as a rule, the pattern designed to ensure survival. The first priority of this programming is the survival of the kind either through their own descendants or through their herd or troop. At the moment of danger the bee stings and the drone fertilizes the queen, though in doing so they perish. What animals are out to do is to maintain, achieve, or alter certain states.

Only for persons does the question of their own existence or non-existence arise. They look back and forward, and know that there was, and will be, a world of which they themselves were not, and will not be, a part—another change of state, but a change of the world's state, not of their own. To be able to think like this means thinking of ourselves as an element in others' worlds, and so conceiving the world as a process that goes on without us, undeterred and only slightly altered. This is the 'view from nowhere', the viewpoint of intelligence. From this perspective there is no more significance in one individual life than in another. One's own death is an 'accidental' event, simply another instance of the general rule that human beings die.

But personality means, as we have seen, that the intelligent individual is more than another 'instance of' something, and knows it. It means that the intelligent individual is something more than a living being with one more property besides life, namely intelligence. Intelligence is the 'form' of our living. Personal life is not, like other life, centred on itself. It is not defined by the imperative of self- and species-preservation. Its essential distinguishing mark is self-transcendence, the highest form of which is called love. Intelligent individuality is itself universal, and the universal has concrete reality in a plurality of individual persons. In conjunction with this the thought that 'life goes on' is an escapist self-deception: what our own death amounts to is the end of the world. For the world has to be *someone's* world, and as *my* world it comes to an end. There are, of course, other people's worlds, but they end too. There is no continuity that just 'goes on'. With the idea of the person, death takes on an aspect that puts in doubt everything in our lives that gives them meaning.

II

Knowledge of our own death is not just one more piece of knowledge like others, not an item of information to be slotted into the framework of understanding that permits us to conduct our lives rationally. Knowledge of death is incommensurable with every other knowledge that we have. If we think of 'planning for life' on the same lines as planning for some specific endeavour, and pursue our plan by means of the same kind of rationality, we evade the personal character of life's demand. Specific endeavours form the web and the woof of day-to-day practical rationality. They have precise ends, which may sometimes surpass the limits of our individual ambition or life-span; and in pursuit of these ends there are rational choices of means.

Such practical rationality involves a rational assessment of the time at our disposal for any endeavour, and this may sometimes be in terms of a more or less probable life expectancy. The point of confusion—the illusory 'flight to the universal'—arises where we view life itself as an endeavour of this sort, upon which it is up to us to impose a meaningful shape. That would require points of reference for cost–benefit calculations in relation to life as such. The so-called 'calculated suicide' is an example of this train of thought, and it is actually an easy conclusion to reach if one imagines that after a certain age the cost of staying alive, as measured by rational indices, grows steeper and steeper and is subject to the law of diminishing returns.

But the idea of a cost–benefit spreadsheet is an illusion, resting on the fantastic notion that there are criteria to measure the value of living as such—as though we could somehow stand outside the life we were actually living and weigh it up. This fantasy is one that only persons could entertain, yet it is precisely the personal character of life that it misrepresents. It is true that a person 'has' his or her life, and having it, can give it up. But *what* is given up is simply oneself. The being of the person is the having of the life, not some entity over and beyond the life. There is and can be no criterion to settle decisively whether living is a sensible thing to do or not. The effect 126 of the fantasy is to rip the intelligence's 'view from nowhere' out of the life of the individual—as though the two were unrelated!

Just such a flight from the logic of personal existence is implied in the application of probability-calculus to one's own life expectancy. This can be a sensible thing to do if, and only if, one is deliberating a particular project and wants to know whether, given the probable span of time remaining to one, it is a reasonable endeavour to embark upon. Of course, we know that the improbable can happen; but since not doing one thing implies doing another, and since the other thing we may do will also depend on calculated probabilities for its rationality, it is more reasonable, given the alternative, to proceed from probable than from improbable assumptions. The same goes, *mutatis mutandis,* for consent to undergo medical procedures; it is not irrational in that kind of decision to ask about the probability of predicted outcomes.

But that is as far as we can go down this road. When it comes to life as a whole, the persistent calculation of probabilities is no longer a rationally defensible procedure. The closer we get to understanding our lives as a whole, the less significant probability becomes. Probability is a statistical concept. Its 'cash-value' (to use William James's phrase) lies in repetition; it has to do with frequency-distribution. To apply it to one's own life is to treat one's life as one among others, which is to adopt the standpoint of pure reason, for which life always goes on. But where we are personally concerned with our life, probability calculations about its length have no meaning. For we have only the one life, and we usually have no definite knowledge of its length. It can only have the one length that it will in fact have, whether it is probable or improbable statistically. Unique happenings are not susceptible to probabilities.

Animals cannot compare their lives with any alternative state of affairs. As long as they live, they stay at the centre of their world with 127 no inkling that one day they will not be alive. From the standpoint of reason, on the other hand, one's own life appears commensurable with other lives. Yet what the discovery of the person amounts to is that every personal life, not only one's own, is actually incommensurable. Where probability calculation has no purchase, ignorance of the time of our death is total. But that means that the knowledge of one's own death 'colours' each moment of life to the same extent. Its meaning can only be meaning *here and now*. Life's completion is not a rounding-off conceived from some external vantage-point; it occurs in the midst of living, while the person still has a relation of some definite kind to his or her own life. Rousseau wrote that we should never force children to adopt a way of living that would be pointless if the child failed to reach a certain age.[3] We do not know when the child will die. We must make it possible for the child to die at any point without being compelled to say that it died too soon. No one dies 'too soon'. Talk of 'premature' death in humans springs from a false analogy between life and undertakings that do not have their end in themselves.

III

The presence of death in life—'in the midst of life we are in death'—cannot, we have said, be fitted into our existing structure of meaning; on the contrary, it raises doubts in our minds about all meaning of that kind. In the face of the knowledge of death, of course, the vital impulses keep going, and for as long as we surrender ourselves to them they give meaning to whatever affects our vitality; but they cannot stand up to reflective interrogation. The drone finds it worth the effort to fertilize the queen, because he is ignorant of the fact that it costs his life. But reflection on death relativizes all the meaning we derive from vital impulses. Only life make vital goals meaningful; so they cannot make life meaningful. Self-preservation is a natural impulse, but interest in self-preservation is relative to an existing life striving to preserve itself. If it fails, the striving

[3] Rousseau, *Émile*, tr. Jimack, 126.

ceases, so that nothing, it seems, is lost. Within the context of life we 128
are engaged with things, but, as Heidegger demonstrated, we are not
engaged with life itself.[4] Schopenhauer was the first to highlight the
specific experience of pointlessness that results from this discovery.
Clinging to life, like the pursuit of sexual fulfilment or any other
impulsive tendency, struck him as a bondage to absurdity character-
izing all life.

But beyond this complex of vital meanings, which seems to have
nothing to do with anything, a further horizon comes into view. This
we may call the 'complex of significance', and it can be a factor only
for the kind of life that, knowing about death, has discovered the
finitude of finite things. For what can it *mean* that the complex of
vital meanings strikes us as absurd? It means that it is predicated on
the assumption of life itself; it has no way of engaging with life as
a totality, of affording any importance to life itself derived from the
vital impulses. That is a logically compelling insight. But what is this
'sense of absurdity' that piggybacks on it? It doesn't need to. If we are
not looking for significance, we don't miss what we don't find. The
idea of absurdity occupies a quite different dimension from that of
'vital meaning'. It is not derived from it, and not derived even from
the event of its frustration. Deliverance from impulse, in creating the
conditions for the vital-meaning complex to capsize, also creates
the conditions for the other complex to emerge from its shadow.
The sense of absurdity belongs to this second complex, which we are
calling 'significance'. What Schopenhauer did not realize is that it can
include the complex of vital meaning within its scope.

'Significance' is meaning 'toughened' by the consciousness
of finitude—by which is understood that it asserts itself in the
face of death, and is thus emancipated from time. To enjoy
the company of a friend over an evening meal with a glass of wine
in the midst of beautiful scenery satisfies a number of elementary
needs: entertainment for the eyes and palate, the presence of a trusted
companion, the free flow of thought. The meaning of what satisfies 129
needs is, in the first instance, relative to those needs and therefore

---

4 ['Engagement' translates *Bewandtnis*, which Macquarrie and Robinson, in their
translation of Heidegger, render 'involvement'. See their note on p. 115 of *Being and
Time*.]

radically contingent. Now let us assume that this is a farewell meal in the expectation of death. Life has come to an end, and with it all that makes such an occasion meaningful. Soon everything will be as though it never was, and no memory will endure. One could say that the whole thing hardly repays the effort. The occasion is robbed of its meaning in advance by our awareness of the imminent destruction of all that gives it meaning. The meal before hanging sticks in the throat—though such is the power of instinct that one may find one has an appetite at the end, the absurdity of it notwithstanding.

But an alternative response is possible. A different feeling might surface in the course of that last encounter, a sense of preciousness that lifts the occasion out of its contingency: 'It is good so!' Such a feeling would not be threatened by the imminent end of life and of the meanings that derive from life, but would actually be awakened by it. 'It is good so!' does not mean, 'It is good for me right now, but the good will disappear when I do.' It means, 'It is, and will remain, good that this fleeting moment occurred and that its significance is unveiled.' Meaning, together with the feelings it engenders, is pulled out of the contingent and relocated in the timelessness of 'significance'. If the friends savour their food and wine, it is not because instinctual needs are satisfied, but because the whole complex of need and satisfaction has been lifted out of its relativity. It is not simply that something 'good for me' is 'good as such'. The event in its totality, with its two contrasting aspects, appears as something of which it can be said—both now and always—that it is good that it occurred. The nothingness of what succumbs to time is converted into preciousness.

What happens in this example has a logical equivalent when expressions for past, present, and future are replaced by atemporal expressions with temporal indicators attached. A true sentence containing the words 'now' and 'is' will be untrue tomorrow. If we replace 'now' with '10 a.m. on 14 March 1996', the truth or falsity of what we then go on to say is timeless. But we also have a temporal means of expressing the participation of our 'now' in timelessness, without abstracting ourselves from our own time. This we do by means of the future perfect tense. If it has ever been true that something 'now is', it is forever true that that something 'will have been so.'

Grasping the significance of things is associated not only with the satisfaction of vital impulses, but with their frustration. From the point of view of vital meaning, it is absurd if someone loses his own life in a fruitless attempt to save someone else's. The failure of the action robs it of the positive value it might have had as serving someone's good. In the event nobody's interest was served. If we celebrate this deed all the same, and honour its memory, that is because there is significance in the very fact that it occurred. It was a fine deed, one such as serves to justify the world. It will always be good that it occurred. The leap from vital meaning to significance corresponds to the leap from present tense to future perfect. The future perfect is the form that eternalizes things. Since everything present is also about to have been—for ever and ever—it belongs already to the dimension of the timeless. What *was* future *became* present; what *is* present *becomes* past; but past it *will* remain for all futurity. An event of which we had to say when it was present that it would cease one day *to have been*, would be unreal, even while it was present. Meaning, taken on its own, is finite. Something that has meaning for us now will one day lose its meaning; and when it does, it will cease to *have had* any meaning. For 'having meaning' is not something with an ontic standing of its own; it is purely relative to something else that does have ontic standing. When the relation disappears, the meaning leaves no trace of 'has been' behind it, other than the 'has been' of the relation. If the relation has become meaningless, its meaning has evaporated. If, on the other hand, we can find *significance* in a past relation, that significance will always be there, and so therefore, will its original meaning, now preserved indirectly as a constituent element of its significance.

With the anticipation of death the whole of life is shifted into the timeless dimension of the future perfect tense. It will forever 'have been', and that is how such predicates as 'significant' and 'absurd' come into play. Life becomes something more than the stubborn persistance of a blind urge to survive, the expression of an instinct. Consciousness of finitude delivers life from inherent absurdity, and supplies the condition for finding it precious. Persons exist by having 131 their lives as a significant, and therefore precious, possession. Anticipation of the end penetrates life to its innermost core. It confers on us an experience of the significance of things which the 'bad infinite' of temporal immortality would shatter, since if nothing were precious, nothing could be significant. If anything done once could be repeated endlessly, indefinite anticipation would suffocate every human relation from the word go, for our relations are those of finite beings. There could be no promising 'forever'; there could be no promising at all, in fact, to engage our whole existence and bring our freedom to its height, if 'forever' did not mean 'till death'. Anticipating death puts us in the position to relate to our lives as a whole, the position in which we *have* our life. And that is how persons exist.

IV

Only a life *had* can be surrendered. Death as the surrender of life is the quintessentially personal act. It is not granted to everyone in a literal sense. The forms of extreme artificial life prolongation which have become standard in our times make death more usually 'succumbing'. Yet the act of death is still with us, as it always was. How it is interpreted by the dying person depends to a large extent on the convictions which he or she has formed in the course of life. But, leaving phenomenal description aside, the wish so often voiced these days for a quick death stands in contradiction to the wish for death as a personal act, as found in the old Christian prayer, 'from sudden death, good Lord, deliver us'. Religious rites and the *meditatio mortis* as a practice for death, assume that human beings approach the end of life not as extinction but a last duty laid upon them to perform. The paradox in this is the clearest possible illustration of what being a person is. Every motion, including life itself, is subject to Aristotle's demonstration that the end of a motion is not a part of the motion. That was the basis on which Epicurus explained death away. If, by contrast, the end of a human life is understood as a human act, that is because the person has adopted a position in relation to his or her own life. The end of the motion is not part of the motion, but the ending of a motion by the mover is very definitely an act.

One form of dying in which one takes an active role as mover in performing it is suicide. Yet this is definitely not the model for a truly personal death. Here actor and victim are one, though the two roles are in contradiction. To kill is not to die, to be killed is not to kill. Suicide is the most extreme form of non-identity. Thus Wittgenstein understood it as a sin, assuming that it is done freely and with forethought.[5] In suicide one does not surrender life; one 'takes' one's life. In personal death activity and passivity are not violently opposed in this way, but passivity and suffering *are* what is performed as an action.

Suffering is an act; this structure of death corresponds to the specific structure of personal life. Human beings 'have' their life, but they have it as recipients who were not asked whether they wanted it. They only exist as those who have received life. 'Life is the being of living things.' But for human beings being is itself something that confronts them, something they must make a go of. Their own being confronts them with the task of reaching out for being. In death suffering is the deed demanded, while in life the demand for a deed is, in a sense, suffered—in that wholly neutral sense of suffering which includes grateful acceptance. But it is not only the demand for a deed that we experience through living in time. Life in time is already a kind of dying, in the sense of having to surrender. For time continually steals the world and our own selves from us. Saying goodbye is a ground-rule for the self-aware life, a life not founded ultimately on forgetfulness. Life that has become self-absorbed, life that does not possess itself, cannot possess its own past either. Persons 'have' a past life, but they have it 'as though they had it not'. Stolen from them, it is their possession *as* something stolen, and as such can never be stolen from them again.

But in dying it is not only our present life we must give up, which we have always had to do and have rehearsed, but also our past, the past that will now persist only in the memory of those who survive us and will gradually be absorbed into the collective memory of the community. If surrender is the true proof of possession, dying is the supremely human act. Anticipation of death, knowledge of inevitable surrender to come, makes our life personal by penetrating and structuring it. Only the affirmation of the future perfect makes the present tense fully real.

[5] Ludwig Wittgenstein, *Notebooks 1914–16*, ed. and tr. G. H. von Wright and G. E. M. Anscombe (Oxford: Blackwell, 1961), 91.

11

Independence of Context

I

Everything we experience is set in a context; there is a system of categories covering all possible objects of experience. Everything we experience resembles something else in some respect. There is some kind of connection. Everything has its meaning, even if it is impenetrable or uninteresting. There are no 'brute facts' with no relevance at all. If we knew the number of atoms in the universe, even that would have a kind of relevance, affecting the way physicists depicted the universe. The distance between a given pebble on the surface of the moon and the key-ring in my trouser-pocket, on the other hand, is not a distinct fact at all—not, that is, until I give it meaning by picking it out as an example of something wholly uninteresting. In *naming* what we come across we strive to fit things into the context of the world we know, we build on relevant points of resemblance to make everything identifiable. For nothing can be identified except *as a such-and-such*, which is to say, by virtue of a description that accommodates it alongside other things.

But there is a sense in which living things resist accommodation to context. To live is to be a self, irreducible to objective appearance. Living things have a 'drive' that constitutes them as monadic centres, important not for the meaning they *have*, but for the meaning they *confer*. When I recognize that something is alive, I recognize it as a fellow-existent, not exhaustively accounted for by what it is for me. The recognition, however, requires something more of me than that I should have a life of my own or be a centre in myself. It requires that I should *transcend* the living centre that I am. And that is what persons do: they recognize themselves as living centres of inwardness alongside other centres, each constituting its own context of experience.

The contexts of these others are closed to us. We cannot know what it is like to be a bat. The inwardness of beasts presents us with a riddle—not the kind of riddle that can be solved, but a definitive ontological hiddenness. To know what it is like to feel something, one must feel it; it cannot be known from outside. But since we can objectify our own inner states by converting lived experience into memory, we can observe resemblances between one experience and another, and so liken our own experiences to those of another being. When we predicate the words 'suffering' and 'joy' of other animals, these are not bare equivocations. They give a firmer purchase to our understanding of those creatures' situations than any other words could.

The reason one experience can resemble another is that every living thing is situated alongside others within the all-embracing genealogical scheme. One thing separates itself from another in perpetual self-differentiation from the stream of life. This is the effect of 'drive'; yet, in the form of sexual drive, it feeds right back into the stream of life again. Indeed, we can view self-differentiation as an especially efficient way of sustaining the stream of life. Seen in this light, the subjective aspect of experience could be taken for no more than an epiphenomenon, and the objective function for the real thing. But the objective function affords us no decisive reason to adopt its goals as our own when we act. Animals make connections among other things, but they do not connect with themselves. They have no idea that their drive serves an objective function. This connection has no significance for them.

That is how it is that we can include the lower animals in our own lives by setting them to work and exploiting their behaviour for our own ends. If in so doing we accord their lives a respect that restricts what we do to them, that has nothing to do with the animals' instincts, which are simply those of self- and species-preservation. An animal's *inwardness-as-drive* does not make its life a focus of significance, for the goal of the drive is precisely not a goal that the animal itself, lacking reflection, has subjectively determined. It cannot anticipate the possibility of its own non-existence; it knows nothing of Being. The drive is extinguished when the animal is extinguished, and then the meaning of the animal's environment is extinguished, too. The fact that the subjectivity of animals is proof against absorption by our own contexts of meaning is not a matter of the animal's witholding *itself* from being made use of. Rather, our responsibility to a particular animal is due to its *inwardness-as-existence*. We have a responsibility for the quality of its subjective 136 experience. Preventing suffering is the single moral issue in relation to non-personal living creatures. And in this there is a proper place for hedonistic calculus; we can sensibly decide to put a suffering animal down to bring its suffering to an end. We may even dispose of its life for ulterior ends, since the wider meaning-context is not objectively excluded from our calculations; it is not all transmuted into 'significance'. That is why non-personal life can provide material for new contexts of meaning, 'blind' to the original context. The ends that bees or guide-dogs serve have nothing to do with the ends these animals pursue, though one set of ends makes use of the other. These animals are not self-transcendent; to them there can be owed no debt of truthfulness; but the debt we do owe them, while they are in our power, is care for their subjective welfare.

With the human countenance of a person it is all quite different. Here the incommensurable breaks in. In whatever contexts we have to do with human beings, and however we may use them as means to our ends, we may never, as Kant says, 'use humanity... merely as a means'.[1] That is to say, the other remains, as him- or herself, essentially outside all contexts available for our intepretation of events, outside 'the conditions of possible empirical knowledge'.[2] Lévinas's formula is, *au delà de l'essence,* but this is potentially misleading.[3] It translates Plato's *epekeina tēs ousias,* 'beyond being', which means, 'beyond categorically structured reality'.[4] But if we think of Being not as the the most abstract being, as 'something in general', but as 'absolute posit' (Kant again), the *actus essendi*

---

[1] Kant, *Groundwork of the Metaphysics of Morals, AA* iv. 429 (*Practical Philosophy,* ed. and tr. Gregor, 80).

[2] *Critique of Pure Reason,* A 600/ B628, tr. Paul Guyer and Allen W. Wood (Cambridge: Cambridge University Press, 1998), 567–8.

[3] E. Lévinas, *Otherwise than Being, or Beyond Essence* (The Hague: tr. Alfonso Lingis Nijhoff, 1981).

[4] Plato, *Republic* 509ʙ.

preceding every possible objective attribute, then 'Being' means precisely the same as Lévinas's 'beyond being'.[5]

The incommensurability of the person is simply the incommensurability of 'absolute posit'. Personal identity, as Being-in-itself, cannot be equated with any qualitative specification; it eludes every possible definition in terms of context. And so, Lévinas writes, the command 'Thou shalt not kill' stares out imperiously from the face of every human being, without context, without condition, subject to no calculus of optimal outcomes, no weighing up of rival goods.[6] This limit imposed by this unconditionedness is actually a negative one; it describes a boundary that circumscribes responsibility and the possibilities of action. All *positive* activity must be conditioned. 'The unconditioned', Goethe said, 'bankrupts us in the end.'[7]

Where saving human lives is in question, or meeting murderous assaults from other humans, we are bound to make context-relative decisions, weighing up the quantitative and qualitative gains for human life. As human beings we are naturally parts of wholes. But by consciously shaping our acts in relation to a whole greater than ourselves, we leave the subjective and vital elements of 'meaning' behind, and come to define ourselves at the higher level of 'significance', the social level. And then we cease to be mere 'parts' and become a 'whole' of our own, not integratable into wider contexts. We act as a person. Because the being of the person is the having of its life, no human being has the power to dispose of another; no human being may be treated merely as an element in a context by which one could not define oneself, or be supposed, as a rational being, to define oneself. So the saving of lives may justify the sacrifice of one's own life, but it cannot justify the intentional killing of an innocent. The unconditional value of the person limits the responsibility we bear for any larger whole.

---

[5] Kant, *The Only Possible Argument in Support of a Demonstration of the Existence of God*, AA 2: 74, (*Theoretical Philosophy 1755–1770*, tr. D. Walford and R. Meerbote (Cambridge: Cambridge University Press, 1992), 119).

[6] Lévinas, *Totality and Infinity*, tr. Alfonso Lingis (Pittsburgh: Duquesne University Press, 1969).

[7] Goethe, *Maxims und Reflections*, 1081.

II

The peculiar independence of context that is part and parcel of personal presence in every context, is equally apparent in the structure and significance of self-expression in word and deed. The truth-value of human speech and the moral quality of human action possess just this same independence, and that is how they represent the speaking and acting person without intermediary.

Human speech, of course, is always set in some context, and we need to know the context if we are to grasp its semantic and performative significance. Contexts in general are not always unambiguous, and overlap. One and the same expression may be understood in different senses, used with different intentions; and even more extended reports may be fundamentally misunderstood if they are incomplete, or if attention flags. Nevertheless, human speech has the property of being made up of discrete statements, the truth value of which is generally independent from that of other statements. The statement, 'Caesar was killed by Brutus on the Ides of March,' requires a good deal of filling in linguistically and historically if we are to understand it. The sense once clarified, however, it is either true or false; its truth-value is invariable in relation to varying contexts in which it may be uttered. If true, it remains true, when-and wherever spoken; if false, it remains false, and falsifies any statement of which it forms an element. We can only start making true statements again when we have finished with the statement that contains a false statement in itself.

Nor can false statements be made true by advancing them in support of true statements. If a murder suspect gives false information about his whereabouts at the time, he can hardly argue, when challenged with the false testimony, that his statement was taken out of context, since the alibi was only *meant* to establish the point that in fact he did not commit the murder. On the contrary, as far as the truth of the alibi is concerned, it is decisively damaging that the information served *only* the purpose of the context and was useless in any other. False statements are heavily context-dependent, and anyone who sets out to maintain a falsehood must keep the context clearly in mind to avoid self-contradiction. One needs a sharp intelligence to lie, and a quick presence of mind; but truth-telling requires nothing of this order, since every true statement is compatible with every other. Biblical scholars sometimes appeal to what they call 'narrative-function': the 'function' served by the reports of the empty tomb in the New Testament is, evidently enough, to support the credibility of the message of Jesus's resurrection. Yet if the reports are defined solely by their narrative-purpose and are not true in every other context too, they are in the same position as the fabricated alibi. Their purpose is tainted with the untrustworthiness of the story supposed to support it. Strong context-dependence is at home only in literary compositions, where such truth as there is resides in the whole, individual statements having a strictly functional status.

Speech that has to do with reality must be true or false independently of context. That is as much a matter of the nature of the world as of the nature of the person. The world is of its nature structured so as to make all particular utterances about what is the case either true or false. Coherence theories of truth can work only when coherence is understood sufficiently broadly to allow falsification by empirical data. Yet persons, too, are in a position to present themselves as truthful or untruthful in each utterance they make. If speech were an open-ended continuum of utterances with no independent significations, and no meaning was communicated until it was finally signed off as a whole with nothing to add, persons could not be wholly present in their speech, and so could not be present at all. Just as each statement is 'connected' by its sense-content, as Frege puts it, either to 'the true' or 'the false', so in every completed element of speech the person is present as capable of truth and connected to it. To each statement there corresponds a unique intentional act, in which the person is present as a whole.

This 'parcelling up' of signification is the condition of personal intersubjectivity, the condition of truth-serving speech. Speech is possible only when no one has literally to 'talk themselves out' in order to say something true. Otherwise we would have to observe the end of others' lives before we could decide whether what they said was true or not. There would be no communication of truth at all. But communicating truth is something each person does, and that is why the capacity for truth in speech must be parcelled up.

The smallest unit of truth is the statement. When the truth of 140 particular statements is uncontroversial, we can expect people to attend to a succession of statements in order to grasp the shape of the speaker's thought. But if at a certain point a speaker asserts something false, the listener has the right to break in, since everything the speaker may construct upon that premise will be false. The speaker has no right to insist on being allowed to finish to make his meaning clear, for that assertion had a meaning of its own, independent of its context. Only on these terms is it possible to communicate the truth.

III

Moral action, too, is composed of independent wholes. As human speech is made up of statements, so human conduct is not a single extended continuum to be judged only at the end, but consists of discrete actions with their own significance.

The old saying, 'call no man happy before he is dead', is about what we have called the 'success of a life', *eudaimonia* to the Greeks. This aspect of our action has to do with the course of life as a whole, in relation to which the importance of particular acts is not fixed once and for all, but is a function of a context that remains open until it comes to an end. The end of the context is not even imposed by death. For if someone devotes a life to some great undertaking that involves many others, when the next generation asks if that life was a 'success', i.e. 'happy' in the classical sense, it will have to consider the success of the undertaking and the long-term consequences of the life.

But it is quite different with the specifically personal, what we call the 'moral' (*sittlich*) aspect of action. Moral evaluation is concerned 141 from first to last with particular acts, and can be done without any reference to the wider context, except where it is a factor in the agent's motivation. It is true that acts once performed may be elements of new action-contexts subsequently, even assuming a moral function quite remote from their original moral character. Repenting a wrong action can have a transforming power. In the

New Testament it is said that there is more joy among the angels of heaven over one sinner who repents than over ninety-nine righteous people who need no repentance.[8] Alternatively, truly virtuous acts may subsequently be a matter of self-satisfied recollection, with ambiguous, or wholly negative, implications for the moral character of the person. But these developments make no difference to the moral quality of the original act, just as it makes no difference to the truth of a true statement if somebody asserts it as a confidence-winning measure to lead his listeners up the garden path.

For the moral act as such it matters supremely that the whole person should be present in it. Just as every statement that incorporates a false assertion is false, so an action is wrong if one of its constituent elements is not right: a wrong place, a wrong time, a failure to consider circumstances, an immoral motive, or, indeed, a type of action wrong in itself such that no context could right it. A sentence of Pseudo-Dionysius which Thomas Aquinas quoted more than fifty times sums the point up exactly: 'good arises from a consistent cause, evil from any kind of fault'.[9] There is an asymmetry between good and evil action-types. To say that an act is good 'as such', i.e. by virtue of its action-type, is not to say that it cannot be vitiated by its context; for an appropriate or inappropriate context is an element in the agent's motivation, reflecting the care the agent has or has not taken. Only as a factor on the inside of action can a context affect the moral quality of the act. But an action that is wrong 'as such', by virtue of its action-type, cannot be made good by any context, motive, or circumstance. It is unfitted to represent the moral person. It vitiates the internal context which gives rise to action in the first place.

Because an act incorporates every morally relevant contextual feature as an element of itself, its moral quality cannot be made a means to any external context. Morally it can be judged only in and for itself, apart from context. There are other, non-moral criteria

---

[8] Luke 15: 7.

[9] *Bonum ex integra causa, malum ex quocumque defectu*, quoted by Thomas from Dionysius, *On the Divine Names* 4. 30. See e.g. *ST* I-II. 18. 4 ad 3; I-II. 18. 11; I-II. 19. 7 ad 3. I have commented further on this in my Introduction to R. Schönberger's German translation and commentary of I-II. 18–21, *Über die Sittlichkeit der Handlung* (Weinheim: VCH, 1990).

for judging acts, it is true; but these can never override the moral point of view to give precedence to a contextual demand. Either the context is morally relevant, so that it is a question of moral motivation whether it is given due weight or not, or it has no weight to offset the moral demand. The moral point of view tolerates no relativity that might affect deliberation. We may, of course, reflect subsequently on the beneficial consequences of immoral actions, but that is something different. The agent can be treated as means to an end retrospectively, and this is legitimate since it does not 'use' the agent, in Kant's phrase, but merely reflects. That is why a philosophy of history such as Hegel's is amoral—but not immoral, so long as it confines itself to retrospect and never slides into deliberation. It simply locates individuals in their contexts, in which they are merely parts of a whole and serve as means. But this approach abstracts from personality, which is the essential ground on which they are not susceptible to being treated as means. 'Though we might tolerate the idea', Hegel wrote in the Introduction to his *Philosophy of History*, 'that individuals, their desires and the gratification of them, are thus sacrificed and their happiness given up to the empire of chance, to which it belongs; and that as a general rule individuals come under the category of means to an ulterior end—there is one aspect of human individuality which we should hesitate to regard in that subordinate light, even in relation to the highest; since it is absolutely no subordinate element, but exists in those individuals as inherently eternal and divine. I mean, morality, ethics, religion.'[10]

'This inner focus,' he continues, 'this simple region of the claims of subjective freedom, the home of volition, resolution and action, the abstract sphere of conscience, that which comprises the responsibility and moral value of the individual, remains untouched; and is quite shut out from the noisy din of the World's History, including not merely external and temporal changes, but also those entailed by the absolute necessity inseparable from the realization of the Idea of Freedom itself.'[11] That means, the region of personality is not 143 defined by the context that surrounds it, and cannot be robbed of

[10] G. W. F. Hegel, *The Philosophy of History*, tr. J. Sibree (New York: Dover 1956), 33.
[11] Ibid. 37.

its unconditional claim. We might rather say that it is *itself* a context for a recognition transcending time and history, an a priori context, in principle infinite, where every person, known or unknown, has a place. And to this context the criteria of truth and goodness belong. Not themselves defined by finite contexts, they define true statements and good actions for all imaginable contexts. No finite context can invalidate them. Statements and acts, on the other hand, that are wholly determined by their function in a given context, lose the property of being transportable to other contexts without change to their personal meaning.

12

Subjects

I

Persons have faces, by which they are known to one another. Persons exist *for* each other, and therefore exist only in the plural. They are persons by virtue of 'having' what they are, that is to say, their nature. This involves their recognizing what they have been, and so is inescapably bound up with temporality. The 'nature' of which the person is the 'subsistence' is the nature of an organically living being. Persons are living beings. And persons foresee their own deaths.

With the modern refoundation of philosophy by Descartes all these statements became, at one stroke, incomprehensible. They had to be 'reconstructed'. Persons are human beings; but Descartes needed laboriously to reconstruct human beings. Actually he never speaks of human beings, but only of subjects and objects, which he understands as different, even incommensurable, substances. The subject, the 'thinking thing', is defined by its consciousness. It has no face. Whether there is more than one subject depends on whether the possibility of others is a necessary condition for a subject to think, 'I am!' But in any case the *cogito* has no temporal extension. It is momentary self-consciousness. Whatever it knows of itself can relate only to the past it remembers, which is not its immediate being, but something it has. In this way Descartes divided the subject from itself. What happens, or may happen to it, what it remembers, above all what it is like—all this is set at a distance from its own relation to itself. The aim of all this is *certainty*, the securing of the subject as distinct from everything not identical with it. It seeks to gain possession of non-identity on a permanent basis, and so make human subjects 'the lords and masters of nature'.[1]

Descartes thus sets apart from subjectivity the whole range of qualities, everything that one 'is' by 'having'. This shows up the decisive feature of personal existence, but only to throw it back into obscurity directly. What Descartes actually says at this point is in tension with what he demonstrates by saying it. The having of one's nature he calls 'mastery'. The goal of the separation is to secure the masterful and self-certain subject on the one hand and its mastery over nature on the other. In this way consciousness becomes a substance apart, not *somebody's* consciousness. Personal being is having a nature; it could therefore never *want* the self-contained security that formed the leading idea of the Cartesian philosophy, as of Stoicism before it. Leibniz wrote penetratingly that the *cogito* was not a new beginning on its own terms, but the fruit of retrospective reflection trading on an earlier discovery: 'various things occupy my thoughts'.[2]

The nature over which we have mastery includes our own nature, physical and psychological. This human nature is as much a part of the external world as the tools by which we master nature. My body itself is my first instrument of mastery, and to keep this instrument intact is the most important human concern. 'The preservation of health has always been the principal end of my studies,' wrote Descartes in 1645 to the Marquess of Newcastle.[3] Connected with this is the replacement of the idea of *eudaimonia,* the success of life, by that of 'contentment'. Contentment, as distinct from happiness, is what makes us independent of every circumstance which we do not control. That 'life' which may succeed or fail is not an aspect of subjectivity, in Descartes's view, for subjectivity is all about self-sufficiency; it is an aspect of the objective world. So the concept of happiness, *beatitudo,* is also relegated to the external world,

---

[1] Discourse on the Method 6, in *The Philosophical Writings of Descartes,* tr. J. Cottingham, R. Stoothoff, and D. Murdoch (Cambridge: Cambridge University Press, 1985), i. 142–3.

[2] G. W. Leibniz, *Animadversiones,* in *Philosophische Schriften,* ed. Gerhardt, iv. 357: *varia a me cogitantur.*

[3] *The Philosophical Writings of Descartes,* tr. J. Cottingham, R. Stoothoff, D. Murdoch, and A. Kenny (Cambridge: Cambridge University Press, 1991), iii. 275.

transformed into a Utopian ideal of human welfare. It is, according to its new definition, 'all the perfections of which human nature is capable'.[4] The only contribution an individual can make towards it is to pursue knowledge, which yields self-contentment. All that remains of the person is the objectively rational pursuit of ends on the one side, self-sufficiency on the other. All that is left to it is to live the life its nature indicates as well as possible, situated alongside others, and to find a significance in this that transcends biological goals.

Cartesian dualism precipitates the crisis in the concept of person, because it is impossible within its terms to think of *life*. Since Plato, and in particular since neo-Platonism, the ontological trinity of being, life, and thought, had had a foundational role. In this trinity life was the effective paradigm. Life, Aristotle wrote, was 'the being of living things'.[5] We can think of inanimate being only by analogy with our own, but our own is life. Thought is life enhanced and fulfilled. 'Life without understanding is imperfect life, life halved.'[6] But life as the mediating term between being and thought falls victim to the Cartesian judgement that it is not a clear and distinct idea. In order to live one has to stop thinking, Descartes told the Princess Elizabeth.[7] The story of how the person was demolished is the story of the demolition of life—which, again, is all one with the demolition of natural teleology.

The inspiration for this came from Christian theology. The argument we have seen developed by many twentieth-century authors: orientation to an end means anticipation, but anticipation implies consciousness. The aim was not the arrow's but the marksman's. Whenever we meet the phenomenon of something aimed, we must look out for what aimed it. That there are structures of final causation in the world is the premise for a proof of God's existence, not a proof like Aristotle's where God is the final term of aspiration, the ultimate *telos*, but one in which God is the marksman, or perhaps the engineer who sets up machines to achieve their ends.

---

[4] To Princess Elizabeth, 18 August 1645, *Philosophical Writings*, iii. 261.
[5] Aristotle, *De anima* 415ᵇ13: τὸ δὲ ζῆν τοῖς ζῶσι τὸ εἶναί ἐστιν.
[6] Thomas Aquinas, *In Nic. Eth.* 9. 11. 1902.
[7] Descartes, Letter to Princess Elizabeth, 28 June 1643, *Philosophical Writings*, iii. 226–9.

To think of the inherent ends of animals as 'ends in themselves' was dismissed, from Sturmius in the fifteenth to Malebranche in the eighteenth century, as heretical idolatry.

Thomas Aquinas understood the illustration of the arrow with a grain of salt, as an analogy. Creation is something rather different from the construction of a machine. God, unlike *homo faber*, confers upon his creature a *telos* of its own. That means, God can create life as being-in-itself. But this, too, seems an obscure thought to later thinkers. What is it that God creates, when he creates life? Does he create things that anticipate future states and act appropriately? In that case it is *thinking*-beings we have to deal with. Or does he create things whose behaviour serves ends they are unconscious of? But that can only mean that they are machines. Aristotle had used an illustration of a flute-player who plays without having to think about it. How did the art of playing get into the flute-player? He had to practise, it would seem, which is a deliberate course of action. But nature, says Aristotle, is like a flute-player who doesn't need to practise. Does that not make us all automatons again? If life is just conscious life with consciousness removed, what is left? We are back where we started.

And yet we are not, for conscious life is conscious of itself *as life*, first of all, not as consciousness. That means, it is present as a drive before it is consciously present; its consciousness—*of itself*, that is— comes later. Naturally, we have no idea what it is like to be hungry without being conscious of it; yet when we do become conscious of hunger, we know that the hunger was already there unconsciously in some degree.

For Descartes this gulf cannot be got over. As *conscious*, the drive of life belongs to *res cogitans*. As *unconscious*, it is merely an inadmissible interpretation of a mechanical process. There is no continuity between the one and the other. But a great deal stands or falls with this continuity, as Leibniz saw, since with it is tied up what we call 'the person'. If life is unthinkable, so is the person, for persons are living beings. The identity of the person is a function of the identity of a living thing. And where consciousness and matter are defined independently and opposed as incommensurables, we end up with quite different criteria for the identity of human beings and of persons.

II

That was what John Locke saw, whose pioneering exploration beat
the path for many others. Recent discussions of the person in English,
associated with the names of Derek Parfit and *mutatis mutandis* Peter
Singer, follow the lines of Locke's thinking closely. One can only
marvel at the long incubation period! Kant, apparently, was the great
delayer.

Locke treated the subject in the seventeenth chapter of his *Essay
Concerning Human Understanding*, where he expounded the sources
of the ideas of identity and diversity. By 'identity' he did not mean
what logicians mean by the term, the tautology A = A, but the
question of how an entity may be identified as the same over a period
of time. Things occurring at the same time in different places are
different things. Things occurring at different times in different
places may either be different things or identical things. Things are
identical when they have a single 'beginning', held in common
with no other things.[8] But can 'something' not so alter over time
that it is no longer the same entity, its unique beginning notwithstanding? One could reply that in that case the two resulting entities
do not have the same beginning at all, for when one replaces another,
we have to think in terms of a new beginning. But this reply fails. We
can only decide whether we have a new beginning when we already
know we have a new entity. We cannot resolve the question whether
the entity or entities are the same by reference to a new or a common
beginning.

In fact, however, Locke does not think of identity as persisting
through time. The empiricist principle that only atomic sense-data
are ontologically basic, and that synthesis is a constructive attribution, rules out the idea of identity as the unity of a process. Locke
writes: 'Only as to things whose Existence is in succession, such as are
the Actions of finite Beings, *v.g. Motion* and *Thought*, both which
consist in a continued train of Succession, concerning their Diversity
there can be no question: Because each perishing the moment it

---

[8] Locke, *Essay Concerning Human Understanding*, 2. 27. 1, ed. P. H. Nidditch,
(Oxford: Clarendon Press, 1975), 328.

begins, they cannot exist in different times, or in different places, as permanent Beings can at different times exist in distant places; and therefore no motion or thought considered as at different times can be the same, each part thereof having a different beginning of Existence.'[9] When Locke writes that every motion ends in the moment it began, he is not thinking of motion in Aristotle's sense, as the 'actualisation of possibility'.[10] Rather, he conceives it in mathematical terms, as a construction by infinitesimal calculus, which is to say, he does not think of it *as* motion at all, but as a succession of infinitely short discrete events, each occurring at a certain definite moment in a certain definite place. Motion as motion is, as Aristotle knew, not susceptible to mathematical treatment. Even Leibniz, who discovered this way of treating it, knew as much. Motion can be grasped only with the help of such concepts as potentiality and anticipation, which belong to the realm of action. To think of something in motion we must leave its precise location at a precise point of time undefined. Locke got it the wrong way round. Instead of thinking of motion in terms of action, he thought of action in terms of motion—conceived from the fictional standpoint of objective discrete sense-data. So he dissolved its unity into an infinite sequence of instantaneous events. Something in motion, therefore, could only be identical with itself if it were *not* in motion, which is to say, not susceptible to change. Atoms are the only example of this that Locke could recognize, on the ground of their absolute simplicity.

With this step the mode of being that characterizes living things disappears from view. To live is to be in motion—'in motion', that is, in the way we are when we act. Life as the mode of being characteristic of living things does not exist if there are only discrete states of organisms. Life is not *these organisms'* way of being. Their identity is constituted by an invariable structure unaffected by the replacement of its material elements. Machines have that kind of structure. What makes animals different from machines, on this account, is merely that the machine must be set up and ready before it can be put in motion, whereas 'in an Animal the fitness of the Organisation and the Motion wherein Life consists, begin together'.[11] It makes

[9] Ibid. 2. 27. 2, p. 329.   [10] Aristotle, *Physics* 201ª11–12.
[11] Locke, *Essay* 2. 27. 5, p. 331.

no difference for the concept of the person, Locke writes, whether we understand its unity as that of a machine or that of an animal.

These philosphical assumptions must be kept in view if we are to understand the novelty of Locke's new concept of the person. If life is not the mode in which living things have their being, the being of the person is not identical with a human life. '*Person, Man,* and *Substance,* are three Names standing for three different Ideas.'[12] The conditions for identity are not the same in humans and in persons. The definition that Locke gives of the person has, at first sight, nothing particularly striking about it, but seems simply to repeat the traditional definition of Boethius: 'We must consider what *Person* stands for; which, I think, is a thinking intelligent Being, that has reason and reflection, and can consider itself as itself, the same thinking thing in different times and places.'[13] It is, he continues, *consciousness* that makes one what he calls 'himself' and by which he marks the difference between himself and all other thinking beings. Personal identity is the self-equivalence of a thinking being.

The break with the classical understanding of the person is evident when we notice the change made to two of its premises. First, there is the atomizing of motion, which implies the atomizing of life and thought. Life can no longer be the way that living things have being, and thought cannot be life's coming to itself. The second alteration is the abandonment of the idea of potency. If persons are thinking beings, they must at any moment be *actually* thinking entities. They cannot be human beings asleep or unconscious, and so cannot—the main point—be *all* human beings, all members of a species whose normal adult specimens have consciousness and self-consciousness. What happens in actual self-consciousness on this new account is not that a living thing becomes aware of its identity; what happens is that its identity is then and there *created,* 'the same consciousness uniting those distant Actions in to the same *Person*.'[14] All actions united in a single consciousness are actions of a single person; but *only* those are. 'As far as this consciousness can be extended backwards to any past Action or Thought, so far reaches the Identity of that *Person*.'[15] For Locke, as we have seen, actions in

150

---

[12] Locke, *Essay* 2. 27. 7, p. 332.   [13] Ibid. 2. 27. 9, p. 335.
[14] Ibid. 2. 27. 10, p. 336.   [15] Ibid. 2. 27. 9, p. 335.

themselves are no more than a chain of discrete instantaneous events. Persons, too, are instantaneous events, namely, instantaneous states of consciousness that have the distinctive feature of taking previous states of consciousness as their content, i.e. of remembering them, and indeed remembering them as their own conscious states, with which their present state connects to make a single person. 'So that whatever has the consciousness of present and past Actions, is the same Person to whom they both belong.'[16] Identity of consciousness, then, is completely interchangeable with consciousness of identity.

Thomas Reid had already pointed out the counter-intuitive implications of this train of thought.[17] He proposed the story of a general celebrated for a feat of war: he remembers the feat, naturally enough, but does not remember an earlier event, a humiliation suffered as a child, which the deed was undertaken to blot out. Reid asks how the general can be the same person that suffered the humiliation that was compensated for by the deed. Call the three stages on this man's career A, B, and C. As C he remembers the man at B, and feels himself identical to him. As B he remembered himself at A, and was conscious of identity to him. But how can C be identical to B, if he is not identical to what B was identical to by virtue of his memory, namely A? There is continuity of consciousness, clearly, but continuity of consciousness does not amount to consciousness of continuity. The partial overlapping can only be observed from outside; it is not itself conscious. There must be a thread to hold things together with the character of a self-identical entity, something more than simple consciousness. My personal identity implies the continuing existence of this individual thing that I call myself. Whatever this self may be, it is something that thinks, reflects, decides, acts, and suffers. I am not a thought, I am not an act, I am not a feeling. I am something that thinks, acts, and feels.

The link between defining personality in terms of consciousness and the loss of the idea of life was something Leibniz remarked on immediately after reading Locke's *Essay*. 'If a man could be a mere

---

[16] Ibid. 2. 27. 16, p. 340.
[17] Reid, *Essays on the Powers of the Human Mind*, 3. 6 (Edinburgh, 1819), i. 466. A similar argument had been advanced in George Berkeley's *Alciphron* (1732).

machine and still possess consciousness,' he wrote in his *New Essays*, 'I would have to agree with you, sir; but I hold that that state of affairs is not possible.'[18] He laid decisive weight on a question Locke had set to one side as irrelevant: if consciousness is a coming-to-self on the part of a being with real identity (a living being, necessarily), to what 'self' does self-consciousness relate? It cannot be another consciousness, but can only be the living being itself. So there is continuity between this being's unconscious perceptions and the conscious apperception of it.

Leibniz can here be thought of as the discoverer of the Unconscious. By 'unconscious' we mean those processes in an animal of which, though not conscious, it could become conscious—and not by external verification, as when we feel the pulse in the wrist with the fingers of the other hand, but by their entering the consciousness immediately. Continuity between the conscious and the unconscious is what guarantees the continuity of the living individual, the person. It is one and the same person perceived both by himself and by others, and perceived *as* a person in both cases. Leibniz argues this by pointing to the objectivity of the juristic sphere, of property especially. Property is essentially personal, as opposed to mere possession, which animals too may have. It is an intellectual relation commanding mutual recognition, and so independent of the actual consciousness at any moment of the owner, who may forget, or may need to be shown, from a deed of sale or a land-registry entry for example, that something belongs to him.

If personality were consciousness, the person's memory could not be prompted or corrected by others. Praise and reproof, reward and punishment, would have no relevance to the living individual, but only to the consciousness aware of guilt or merit. Locke argued that only consciousness is motivated by rewards and punishments. The prospect of pain would excite no fear if only our organism were to be affected; for though the organism is one with ourself at present, it might not be so in the future. It would take a connection between present and future consciousness to make the pain ours. To vary the thought a little, put the case that we are informed that the human

---

[18] Leibniz, *New Essays on Human Understanding*, 27. 236, tr. P. Remnant and J. Bennett (Cambridge: Cambridge University Press, 1981).

being to which we are now identical will endure dreadful agonies under surgery; but that anaesthesia will interrupt the continuity of consciousness, expunging the memory of the agonies after coming to. Would this information worry us? Derek Parfit, whose speculations along these lines are carried to fantastic lengths, is prepared to accept that in fact we would be worried, but undertakes to demonstrate, as a faithful disciple of Locke, that our worry is unfounded and irrational. It is simply not the same person, he writes, who suffers first and cannot recall the suffering later.[19] Locke wrote in a similar vein: 'If the same Socrates waking and sleeping do not partake of the same consciousness, Socrates waking and sleeping is not the same Person.'[20] Our fear of going mad one day is quite unfounded, too: tomorrow's lunatic will not be the same person that took fright today.

III

David Hume drew out the implications of Locke's conception. The chapter 'Of the immateriality of the soul' in the *Treatise of Human Nature* is followed directly by a chapter 'Of personal identity', which takes up Locke's discussion. In the chapter on the soul Hume rejects Descartes's idea of a *res cogitans,* a soul-substance. Not only is it superfluous; it is incomprehensible, because the idea of even a material substance is incomprehensible. There are no sense-impressions corresponding to it. Our perceptions are 'all really different and . . . distinguishable from each another'.[21] We connect them synchronically and diachronically, and on the basis of our observations arrive at the knowledge of constant conjunctions. There is no reason to think of these conjunctions as terminating in substances in which several perceptions inhere. But who is this 'we'

[19] Derek Parfit, *Reasons and Persons* (Oxford: Oxford University Press, 1985). See pp. 165–8 for speculations on forgotten pain, pp. 204–17 for an elaboration of Locke's thesis and a statement of the overall position.

[20] Locke, *Essay* 2. 27. 19, p. 342.

[21] Hume, *Treatise of Human Nature,* ed. L. A. Selby-Bigge (Oxford: Clarendon Press, 1888), 245.

that Hume says does the connecting? Even if we can do without
a substance that properties inhere in, we cannot do without a subject
to connect impressions. Must I not say that the impressions *I* connect
are *my* impressions, and so different from other people's, which
I cannot connect because they are inaccessible to me? But what can 154
be meant by 'my' impressions? That is the question Hume then
pursues in the section on personal identity.

Is there an impression corresponding to the 'self', that may be
thought to persist alongside all our perceptions? No, Hume replies,
the perceptions are all there is, and the self is not another one. Apart
from 'some metaphysicians', such as one who 'thinks he has a different notion of *himself*', 'the rest of mankind ... are nothing but
a bundle or collection of different perceptions, which succeed each
other with an inconceivable rapidity'.[22] Even a single moment of
consciousness is a complex of different perceptions. Identity is an
impression arising from three kinds of relation: resemblance,
contiguity, and causation.[23] Now, relations are not real things; there
are no perceptions corresponding to them. And so there are no
relations between perceptions either, only the impression of
a relation that arises when we reflect on the perceptions. The person
is just such a relation imagined in the mind, and the site of the
relation is memory. For Hume as for Locke, memory is the 'spring
from which flows personal identity'.

This weak concept of identity permits Hume, nevertheless, to
extend identity further than Locke, and go beyond the limits of
memory by way of causal inference. Causal relations, of course, are
simply fictions like other relations. But these fictions help us reconstruct a past which we do not actually remember. We can include
what others have told us of ourselves in our own self-understanding.
So having shown that the person is a fiction, Hume can hand the idea
over to common sense. Personal identity is as much a matter of
convention as the identity of Theseus' ship, every plank of which
was replaced in the course of time. To disagree about numerical
identity, Hume concludes, is just to disagree about words, and
disagreements about personal identity are 'to be regarded rather as
grammatical than as philosophical difficulties'.[24]

[22] Ibid. 252.   [23] Ibid. 260.   [24] Ibid. 262.

With characteristic frankness he later added a short *retractatio* to the *Treatise*, which gave a more radical turn to the scepticism of his conclusions and confessed bewilderment in the face of this question. What does it mean to 'connect impressions'? Impressions of distinct objects can have their own distinctness; but we could never recognize real connections between distinct impressions. Impressions contain 155 no internal cross-referencing system, so they come to us as foreign as external objects. Any account we give of them is a retrospective supplement, not the way they are in themselves. That they should be *my* impressions supposes some account of the word 'my', and supposes, too, that the impressions stand in some relation to one who 'has' them; but these suppositions would simply explode the basis of empiricism. For personal identity to be real to the empiricist, it must be a perception; but that leaves us with the question how this perception is connected with others. If connections themselves were distinct entities, it would leave us with the question of how connections relate to things connected, and so *ad infinitum*. If the being of the person is not a *having* but a something one *has*, a 'perception', we are really left in the dark.

In speaking of these entities, of course, Hume cannot get away without the impression of a subject-of-impressions, one that connects impressions and interprets them. He speaks in this case of 'the mind'; or else he employs the picture of a theatre on which impressions are staged. But these conceptions are all, to use Wittgenstein's metaphor, ladders kicked away after use. Even this famous metaphor, however, raises a difficulty: in thought there is nothing but the ladder to distinguish above from below. If one kicks the ladder away, the distinction of above from below disappears, and one finds oneself at the bottom again. Hume's last word, then, is a capitulation: 'This difficulty is too hard for my understanding.'[25]

Unless one is prepared to abandon Hume's premises, the difficulty is not 'too hard', but by definition insoluble. The central premise is that perceptions and impressions exist independently, and are connected subsequently only on the basis of resemblance, contiguity, and causation. Causality assumes resemblance: if a similar sequence recurs often, we call the anterior member 'cause' and the posterior

[25] 'Appendix', ibid. 636.

'effect'. But what do 'anterior' and 'posterior' mean in this context? And what is a 'sequence'? These terms assume a temporal connection, but how is the impression of time constructed? By the experi- 156 ence of change, Hume tells us; but how, then, is change experienced, if all there is are isolated impressions? The experience of time trades on memory; but memory, for Hume, is the weaker reproduction of earlier impressions, known to be earlier by the fact that they are weaker. The claim in itself is dubious, since transitory impressions in the present can be weaker than strong impressions recollected. The important point, however, is that priority is not *definable* as weakness, for that would entail that present impressions are weaker than future impressions that will follow them, a conclusion clearly inconsistent with Hume's principles.

In reality the experience of change has nothing to do with differential intensity. The decisive thing for memory is that earlier impressions are reproduced *as* earlier. Without this no difference between one impression and another could be understood as change. If it is to be memory that constitutes a person, then the person is constituted by emancipation from time, the order of 'before' and 'after'. But this order, as we have seen, is the condition of the unity of self-distance and self-ownership that defines the person, and lies at the foundation of all subsequent syntheses. It is not just one among our atomic perceptions; temporal sequence frames the presentation of our perceptions from the outset. When recalling ourselves we relate ourselves to past impressions, we have already transcended ourselves. The recollection of past impressions insists on being something other than a present impression of impressions. It is an impression of impressions that once were real.

We 'entrust ourselves' to memory, rightly or wrongly. Evidently we cannot claim immediate certainty for the reliability of our memory. But the very thought that memory can deceive proves that it is more than a bare impression of impressions, which could never deceive but could only be just what it was. To recollect ourselves and recognize ourselves as persons, we must 'let ourselves go'. And this too, Hume tells us, is impossible. 'We never really advance a step beyond ourselves.'[26]

---

[26] Ibid. 67.

Hume penned that observation in connection with the question of 157 realism, the existence of things in the outer world. He searches for an 'idea' of this existence, and cannot find it. As Kant will say later, existence is 'not a real (i.e. material) predicate'.[27] To understand what we mean by affirming existence, we must do precisely what Hume says we cannot do, and advance beyond ourselves. The only resort left to Hume is that the idea of something's existing beyond our perception is simply a kind of intensification of the idea of the thing. To distinguish past impressions which we really had from imaginary memories, is to distinguish more intensive from less intensive impressions. All the reality of past impressions amounts to, in any case, is the momentary present consciousness of a kind of 'pastness'. Hume does not consider such facts as that someone else may report a past impression that I formerly reported to him. Solipsism is always 'momentarism'. A refusal to think of transcending the subject implies a refusal of the reality of time, and makes it impossible to conceive of personal identity as self-objectification.

What all this amounts to is that personal identity is incompatible with the Cartesian ideal of an immediate self-presence that is wholly certain. Truth, in a far from trivial sense, depends upon a willingness to entrust oneself—to something, someone, or even to oneself. The person is a being which, because it 'has' itself, is free to risk itself. It is no accident that Leibniz, who defended the concept of the person against Locke, thought the ideal of certainty the decisive error of Cartesian philosophy. And at a later date Hegel spoke of what 'while calling itself fear of error, makes itself known rather as fear of truth'.[28]

[27] *The Only Possible Argument*, AA ii. 73.
[28] *Phenomenology of Mind*, tr. J. B. Baillie (San Francisco: Harper & Row, 1967), 133.

13

Souls

I

Talk about 'persons' is common enough; talk about 'souls' has come to be discreditable. Materialism, in reductionist and non-reductionist versions, attempts to eliminate the soul without remainder and to account for its states and activities physiologically. Christian theology has more or less declined to put up a defence. Unwilling, for one thing, to accept ontological commitments at variance with those of its contemporaries—for theology more than ever today leans towards pastoral opportunism at the cost of intellectual and religious substance—neither does it want to obscure the biblical message of bodily resurrection with a philosophical doctrine of the soul's immortality. Yet how we are to think of our earthly and risen bodies as identical without a soul to provide for their continuity, is a question rather seldom asked.

Responsibility for the soul's precarious philosophical status rests chiefly with Descartes, who hypostatized it as an independent soul-substance, united obscurely with a material-substance to compose a human being by their combination. Kant brought weighty arguments to bear against the soul-substance theory, which he accused of 'paralogism'. This and Hume's argument from imperceptibility deprived the soul-substance of its philosophical credit. In its place there entered, with Kant, the 'transcendental apperception': 'The *I think* must be able to accompany all my representations.'[1] The self is indispensible for the constitution of consciousness, but its

---

[1] Kant, *Critique of Pure Reason* B131, tr. Paul Guyer and Allen W. Wood (Cambridge: Cambridge University Press, 1998), 246.

transcendental function does not require the underpinning of a separate ontological status. A system-theoretical account will do quite as well as ontology: the I-consciousness establishes in the most exact way the inner–outer difference that constitutes a system.

The most exact way, however, is not necessarily the most secure. It is vulnerable to dialectical reversal, characteristic of the logic of extremes. To mark the border between inner and outer is not a task that waits on self-consciousness. It happens much earlier, through what we call 'drive'. Drive breaks up the material continuity that could submerge the inner–outer difference, and guarantees the system its ontological identity, that of an Aristotelian 'substance'. Once constituted by drive, a system is no mere observer's interpretation or outsider's projection.

The I-consciousness, on the other hand, though seeming to secure the inner–outer difference by reflecting on it, actually contributes to its undoing. That is because it transcends it. Consciousness participates in a linguistically and intersubjectively mediated structure bigger than any individual. The content of intentional acts is not relative to one particular subject, but to what we may think of as 'consciousness in general'. Nothing in *what* we think makes our thoughts 'inward', only the fact *that* thought is anchored in the life-structure of a thinker. When we reflect on thoughts that were thought, it hardly seems to matter who thought them. The intentionality that constitutes the world attaches, for both Kant and Husserl, to a 'transcendental ego', not an individual person. To express it more precisely: the pure 'I' without any qualitative feature cannot be distinguished in the way we refer to it from any other 'I'. When a person comes to the point of expressing nothing but his or her own individuality, what is said does not belong to that individual exclusively. It is merely 'I', which, like other indexical terms, distinguishes one thing from another only in the context of intersubjective discourse.

The inexpressible sense that in saying 'I' we refer to something unique, but inexpressible and incommunicable in its uniqueness, is one of the most powerful sources of religion. Every name by which a person may be called refers simply to that individual; but the name cannot say what it refers to. No name is actually unique, on the one hand, and on the other, our approach to a person is always mediated through that person's qualitative characteristics. Despite the clarity of our intention, we do not actually know someone; we only know 'someone like that', i.e. someone we could in principle exchange with someone else. The conviction of a reality that cannot present itself to anyone objectively is a *religious* conviction, the conviction of a God 'who sees in secret'.[2] That 'the point of the soul touches God' is 160 a perception variously interpreted in various religions, corresponding to varieties of subjective experience. One experience is of immediate identity with the ground of being, implying that at this 'point' the self, our individuality, disappears 'like a drop in the ocean'. This is expressed in Buddhist mysticism and in thinkers such as Schopenhauer who have drawn on it. In Meister Eckhardt we read: 'There is that in the soul which, if the soul were wholly comprised of it, would mean that the soul was God.'[3] That is the cautious expression of a mystic who was Christian without being distinctively so. The distinctively Christian interpretation of the experience turns in another direction, finding in the religio-metaphysical depth of the I-experience the final confirmation of the uniqueness of each person. What we 'touch' when in our I-consciousness we touch the godhead is not a sea in which we disappear as individuals, but the site at which *this* irreplaceable human being is known *as* this human being. This is expressed in the biblical metaphor of a name which only one person bears and God alone knows.[4] This personalist interpretation is connected, naturally, with the understanding of the Absolute itself as trinitarian personal communion.

The spirit or mind (*Geist*) that we experience as the subject of intentional acts, the self 'beyond being' and beyond all qualitative specification, is not what we mean by 'the soul'. That Descartes identified his *res cogitans* with soul was enormously consequential for how the soul was understood subsequently. In fact Descartes had no use for the classical concept of the soul. The Aristotelian tradition had treated soul as 'form', the principle of living organisms. Descartes knew of no such principle, because for him living organisms were 161 machines. The term 'soul' was now going begging, so he put it to

---

[2] Matt. 6: 6.
[3] Eckhardt, *Sermon* 14, in *Deutsche Predigten und Traktate* 221.
[4] Cf. Rev. 2: 17.

work for the consciousness which, in some way very difficult to grasp, exists 'within' the machine, and thus the soul became an independent entity.

II

Behind this there lay a history. Aristotle had made a radical onto-logical break between 'soul' and 'spirit'. God, for him, is pure spirit, and the being of spirit is life; soul, on the other hand, is the principle of a lower form of life, the life of material bodies.[5] There is a class of ensouled beings that also possesses spirit; that is the class of human beings, but the human spirit cannot be understood as a property of the human soul. Soul is the essentially egocentric, teleologically driven principle of life that constitutes a substance separate from other reality. Spirit, on the other hand, stands above the inner–outer difference that the soul has constituted, since it can think this differ-ence in the light of the universal and eternal. Spirit participates in the divine, yet at the same time it is the principle that directs our life. Soul must be appropriately disposed to spirit, a disposition to act in intelligent ways that is called 'virtue'. But where intelligence is in its element, 'superior to the human level', it leaves virtue behind.[6] Here we are reminded of Meister Eckhardt's statement, quoted above.

Under Christian influence the opposition of soul and spirit disappeared. Human life itself must be 'divinized'. Two consider-ations led in this direction, both connected with the 'discovery of the person' and with the concept of 'the heart' that was decisive for it. By definition spirit is the power and presence of truth, participation in the divine. The egocentrically driven tendency opposing spirit is called, in the language of the New Testament, 'flesh'. The site of decision between spirit and flesh is the heart. There it is resolved whether spirit will remain opposed to flesh or become the defining reality of human existence. The act of the heart that opens itself 162

---

[5] Aristotle, *De anima*, 412ª20. ἀναγκαῖον ἄρα τὴν ψυχὴν οὐσίαν εἶναι ὡς εἶδος σώματος φυσικοῦ δυνάμει ζωὴν ἔχοντος.

[6] *Nicomachean Ethics* 1177ᵇ26, tr. T. Irwin (Indianapolis: Hackett, 1999).

to 'the light' (i.e. spirit) is called 'love'. The first command of Christianity, as of Judaism, is: 'Thou shalt love the Lord thy God with all thy heart, with all thy mind, and with all thy strength.'[7] The whole heart, mind, and strength, naturally, mean a conversion of experience, feeling and will, i.e. of the 'soul'. The heart is what makes the human soul 'spiritual'. Love is the distinctive act of the spiritual soul, which is the personal soul. In medieval Aristotelianism, therefore, there was talk of a human soul which, in fulfilling vegetative, animal, and intellectual (i.e. immaterial) functions, *is* spirit.[8]

The second reason for resolving the opposition of soul and spirit was an interest in the individuality of spirit and the spirituality and immortality of individual souls. For the Aristotelian tradition the principle of individuation of form was matter, and, consequently, space and time. If the human spirit is immaterial, that means it is not individual on its own. And indeed the contents of mental (*geistige*) acts are not related to the point of view of any given living creature with its particular interests. That was why the Arabian Aristotelian Averroes taught that a spirit immortal of its own nature could not be an individual spirit. The human individual dies, he thought, like every other ensouled animal. The spirit, released at once from matter and from individuation, returns to unity with the spirit of all other human beings. There is only one single human spirit.

This suggestion excited an uncharacteristically passionate response from Christian Aristotelians, especially Thomas Aquinas, arguing that the human spirit is *individually* immortal. The individual human soul, though given its individuality by matter, is not a kind of animal soul below the spiritual level. What makes human beings human is precisely spirit. The human soul is essentially spiritual, which is to say it is a spirit that is the principle of material life and differentiates animal and vegetative functions from itself. So the whole human soul shares in the immortality of spirit. When separate from the body, its 163 material functions of nourishment and sensory perception are, as it were, 'latent', awaiting the resurrection of the flesh.[9]

---

[7] Luke 10: 27, parallels at Matt. 22: 37, Mark 12: 30; cf. Deuteronomy 6: 5, Leviticus 19: 18. [The author has quoted the members in the order of the Mark text, omitting 'soul'.]

[8] Aquinas, *ST* I. 42. 2.

[9] *De unitate intellectus.*

A related concern had prompted the Council of Chalcedon to insist on the unity of soul and spirit. The context was its repudiation of the doctrine that though Jesus' soul was human, his spirit was not human but was the Spirit of God himself.[10] The Council saw in this a threat to faith in Jesus not only as truly God, but also as truly man in all respects. A man, so their argument went, is only a man if he has a human spirit, for the spirit is constitutive for the specific humanity of the human soul. If reason enters man, as Aristotle claimed, 'from outside', it follows that reason is not a vital function of the soul.[11] If it is part of the soul, however, it makes human existence rational in its totality. This passage of intellectual history would probably have disappeared from the educated consciousness long since, had not Rudolf Steiner dignified it as a decisive moment in 'the abolition of spirit'.[12] In the context of the problem the council faced, however, we can see it in exactly the opposite light: it was concerned to define the human soul by reference to the spirit.

The fusion of the ideas of spirit and life was encouraged by the biblical conception of God, always closely connected with life, especially in the New Testament. It is said of the Word in John's Gospel: 'In him was life, and the life was the light of men.'[13] 'Eternal life' is the essence of what Christ brought, though life is thought of in spiritual terms: 'This is eternal life, that they know thee, the only true God.'[14] As life is true being, so knowledge is true life. In the trinitarian conception of God the Aristotelian *noēsis noēseōs*, thought thinking itself, is conceived as a real sphere of inner motion, at the centre of which is *pneuma*, 'breath'. The Absolute is thought of as Spirit knowing itself as Spirit, willing to be thought of as subjectivity. But subjectivity is inseparable from life. Soul cannot be conceived as 164 spirit without spirit's being thought of as life. The Greek language

---

[10] This doctrine ('Apollinarianism') had been condemned at the Council of Rome in 382 in the previous century. Cf. *Tome of Damasus* 7 (DS 65).

[11] Aristotle, *De generatione animalium* 736^b27–9: λείπεται δὴ τὸν νοῦν μόνον θύραθεν ἐπεισιέναι καὶ θεῖον εἶναι μόνον· οὐθὲν γὰρ αὐτοῦ τῇ ἐνεργείᾳ κοινωνεῖ ἡ σωματικὴ ἐνέργεια.

[12] See e.g. Steiner, *Wie wirkt man für den Impuls der Dreigliederung des sozialen Organismus?* (Dornach: Steiner Veslag, 1986), 289.

[13] John 1: 4.

[14] John 17: 3.

was easily accommodated to this train of thought, having more than one word available for 'life', not only *bios*, but also *zōē*.

The conciliar decision was highly consequential, as it turned out, but in quite the opposite way to what Rudolf Steiner supposed. Viewed historically, what it anticipated was not the abolition of spirit but the abolition of the soul. The soul found itself caught in a kind of pincer-movement. From one side came all the weight the Christian tradition laid on the spirituality and immortality of the soul; talk about animal souls looked like equivocation, where for Aristotle soul had been the common factor linking man and beast. From the other side, the new natural science and philosophy of the sixteenth century dismissed belief in animal souls as heterodoxy. The functioning of living organisms, it was asserted, could be understood without the Aristotelian form-principle. Organisms must be conceived and explained as machines. Only humans had souls, and even they had them not as the formal power of their organic constitution, but as the substratum of consciousness, as *res cogitans*.

III

To understand the older classical idea of the soul we must understand how a system is a unity in itself, not merely to the observer. This is the case, at any rate, when the system is constituted by the experience of 'drive'. Such a system, we say, is 'alive'. Living systems are self-generating and self-organizing. But self-organization may seem to imply a logical contradiction: to organize 'itself', there must be, we suppose, something that organizes. If it is not yet a 'something', it can only be organized by a power that belongs to something else, for what could 'its own' power be, if there were nothing for the possessive pronoun to attach to? When Aristotle called the soul the 'form' of living beings, he meant by 'form' whatever makes a thing what it is, whatever makes it identifiable as *this* kind of thing, and so determines its way of behaving. But the word 'make' is used in a peculiar sense in this context. Something that 'makes' something is usually one independent entity that is the cause of another. And that is how Driesch understood the soul, 'the entelechy', as an agent effecting organic processes, while Popper and Eccles thought of 'the self' in the same way.[15] But the Aristotelian formal cause does not 'make' things in this way. It 'makes' in an analogous sense, as when we ask, 'What *makes* this song unforgettable?'—asking not about the poet or composer, but about a structural feature of the verse or tune. The Aristotelian 'form' is not supervenient; it does not add anything to an existing entity or plurality of entities, bringing them together into a higher unity like members of an association. It is the structural principle of a living unity, an elementary reality whose parts are no more than parts, virtual entities that become real entities only when the living unity dissolves and the soul disappears.

The 'form' of anything is not an *explanation*, whether in a scientific sense or in the terms of everyday speech. If someone asks, 'Why do you think the bird hovering in the air can see the mouse in the field?' there is a rational answer: 'the bird is a falcon, and falcons see mice moving from a distance'. In most cases this answer goes far enough. But the questioner may persist, demanding to be told why falcons can see so far. Then one must talk about a falcon's powers of sight, which almost always carries the explanation far enough. But exceptionally someone wants to know yet more: why do falcons have eyes of that kind?—which is tantamount to asking why there are falcons at all. The only available reply is a hypothetical story about how falcons emerged in evolution—and even this could elicit further 166 questioning, of course. What distinguishes the first answer—'falcons can see so far'—from all the subsequent answers, and why is it normally sufficient? Because a natural creature is not a mere step in a continuum of processes where each step links the accumulated antecedent conditions to the next step. A natural creature is 'something'. It has emancipated itself from its conditions of emergence to be something 'in itself', which supposes that it is a thing of such and such a *kind*, belonging to a species. For our ordinary dealings with the world we are content to know just so much about natural species as equips us to know how a creature will behave when we know what species it belongs to.

That goes for artefacts, too. If I know this is an aeroplane, I know it is likely to take off from the ground and fly through the air. Artefacts

[15] Eccles and Popper, *The Self and its Brain*, 96–8.

are treated as entities like natural objects, emancipated from the conditions of their production. Objects are dignified as 'something' on the ground that their specific accumulation of materials presents a 'type'; and the type is determined by a construction corresponding to a typical 'end'. If the object cannot be viewed in relation to its typical end, it ceases to be an object. A car may need an oil-change or repair job; but that is something we can say only while we continue to treat this heap of metal as a car, and so relate it to human ends. But when we say, 'This person, or this dog, needs something to drink,' we do not mean that they need it only while we continue to treat them as a man or dog. They need it *anyway*, whether or not we notice what they are. Their need arises within themselves and for themselves; it is their thirst.

The phenomenon that Aristotle's term 'substantial form' identifies is simply this: 'something' is *some thing*: it is a thing in itself and a thing of a certain kind. But when this something is a self-maintaining system, when its inner–outer difference arises in and for itself, not merely in relation to an external user, then we say it is 'alive', and we call its substantial form a 'soul'. The soul is a teleological structure, a 'plan of construction', which is not, as in the case of artefacts, a function of the observer who discovers it or the user who invents it. It is the soul 167 that makes the thing the centre of its own environment, creating meaning in other things relative to itself. If something is hungry, it has a soul.

At this point we do not need to settle the question whether the soul explains any feature of behaviour that is not explained well enough without it. Anyone who is dissatisfied at being told that the reason the dog runs to its bowl is that it is hungry, embarks on a long voyage of explanation—an infinite voyage in both Aristotle's and Kant's view, and therefore not a true voyage of *explanation* at all. That voyage is precisely what science is. In principle there is nothing inaccessible to its explanation, apart from the actual subjective reality of experience. But this cannot be explained scientifically. It is susceptible, no doubt, of a functional evolutionary account, but this explains no more than its selection on the basis of usefulness to survival, and suggests no reason for its appearance in the first place. Expressions such as 'fulguration' and 'emergence' are cyphers for what defies explanation in principle. And they obscure the point at issue, which is that the category-shift from object- to subject-language is *demanded* by the phenomenon, not physically *caused* by it. If we retreat from that category-shift, we are not prevented from talking about any object whatever localized in space. It is simply that we cannot talk about ourselves, our joys and sorrows, our pleasure and pain, as part of the world as a whole. And with this we cease to view living things other than ourselves as real, i.e. as entities identical with themselves.

It is lonely being the subjects that we are, but the loneliness is self-induced. The necessity of recognizing beings as ensouled is something like a moral necessity, an 'ought' that imposes itself not as a physical compulsion, or even a psychological one, but a demand of our freedom, revealing that there is something physically and even psychologically possible that is 'rationally', i.e. morally, impossible all the same. This necessity is like the moral demand that persons make on us, but is not identical with it. It is a different kind of claim, yet not entirely remote from a moral claim; so that to find a vocabulary to describe what 'life' means, we are driven to subtraction and 168 analogy based on our own conscious experience, the life of persons. What it means to be alive is something we know from experience. We know what it means that living creatures are the source of their movements, because we move ourselves. What movement is in general, we have not the first idea. If we try to think of physical motion as such, we either strip it of its character as movement and break it down into a series of infinitesimally short-lived stationary positions that we can measure, or else we draw on an analogy with the pursuits of living things, using words such as 'impulse', anticipating future situations in descriptions of present ones, and so on. The very last moment in a motion is when the moved object is not moved any more, just like the very last moment in our lives, when we are dead. The soul gone, the structure remaining is no more than a form viewed from outside, a corpse. The processes that set in at that point are not those of self-constitution but of formal decomposition.

We experience what it is to live by experiencing life as our being, the being of persons. Life is our being by virtue of our having life, and to have life is what it is to be a person. But since to be a person is to have an ensouled body, the person is extinguished along with the extinction of this body. Putting one's life at risk, having the power to sacrifice it for some goal, is the most important mark of personality, and the highest personal recognition is won by doing so. To be able to 'abstract from' one's own life is to be a 'lord', as Hegel showed in his famous chapter on 'Lord and Bondsman', while to hang on to life is to be a bondsman.[16] Since being a person means having, and having means being able to let go, only one who can let life go can really have it. But that means persons are 'above' being, unlike impersonal living creatures. They pursue being in the same way, but with them that is not the whole story. The pursuit of being is itself something that they 'have', something they can take up a position on. They are not simply *what* they experience, but the *subjects* of their experience. A relation to oneself is a relation to a subjective experience, intersubjectively mediated.

IV

As for the origin of the self-relationship, we are presented today, in 169 effect, with two schools of opinion. One starts from the fact of intersubjectivity, and proposes to treat subjectivity as a secondary phenomenon deriving from it. The other rejects that as impossible, since conscious subjectivity is the indispensible condition for every kind of interpersonal relation; and so it attempts a starting-point from self-consciousness conceived in solipsistic terms. The disagreement can only be overcome, it seems to me, if we make the distinction between *immediate* inner experience of the self on the one hand and *reflexive* awareness of the self on the other. Only, that is, if we realize that life and consciousness form a continuum.

Original inwardness, with its world of vitally important things opening out all round it, is not constituted intersubjectively. This inner 'self' is not the same as 'self-consciousness'. By 'self-consciousness' we mean the centripetal turning of the subject back on itself, which begins when we learn to see ourselves as others see us. Before children learn to say 'I', they speak of themselves in the third person; and this turning-back is more elementary than speaking of

---

[16] *Phenomenology of Mind*, tr. Baillie, 228–40.

ourselves as 'I'. With it the human subject abandons the simple systemic schematization of me at the centre of my world, steps out of the commanding central position, and for the first time takes note of him- or herself as one being among others. Only at that point can there be a relation-to-self.

But how do we learn to identify the being we first call by the name others use with the being whose experience is immediately ours, i.e. with ourself? Each speaker applies the personal pronoun 'I' to a different person. How does one learn to apply *that* pronoun to *this* being? The child has the experience of being looked at, and encounters speech directed at him, speech in which a personal name, or the personal pronoun 'you', recurs just where it impinges on that complex of experience received as his own. Or, better: the complex of experience is received as his own at the point where he is called by a personal name or a personal pronoun. In this way the child learns to understand his experience as his own and himself as the subject of that experience. He encounters himself as a recognizable and identifiable somebody in the same way that he recognizes and identifies human beings and things. And the experience with which he has hitherto been identical now becomes *his*. For only by ceasing to be identical with experience can one become identical with oneself. Only as I cease to be merely 'ensouled' does this soul of mine achieve inner unity, the unity of *my* experience, the unity of *my* soul.

V

The 'having' that constitutes personal being counts the soul among its objects, since the soul is something human beings 'have'. In ancient texts we often encounter people speaking to their souls. Who is it, in that case, that does the speaking? Not a third entity beyond body and soul, but the human being as such, relating to what he or she is. The contrary is also true: the person's mental acts are experiences, i.e. happenings of the soul. Intentional acts are timeless as such, while as psychological acts they are happenings in time.

The idea of the soul's immortality rests upon two phenomena. In the first place, the soul is not *only* the structure of the bodily organism that establishes its identity, though each and every soul is that. The identity of the soul is the identity of its subjective experience over and beyond an immanent or logical connection with material processes. Experience, it is true, may be induced causally by material processes; but *what* we induce or screen out in this way is of a different category from the means of inducing it. Today there is still no hint of any research that would throw light on the connection, and such research would appear doomed to frustration a priori, on logical grounds.

The second phenomenon, a corollary of the first, is the soul's experience of intentional acts. An act such as a discovery in history or mathematics is not only independent of physical events logically (apart from any that may be its object), but it cannot be thought of as 171 a *consequence* of physical events. There is, in fact, no state of the brain that could correspond unambiguously to an intentional act. Yet since we know nothing about the possibility of intentional acts arising without brain activity, it is possible to think that with the extinction of organic life such events, though timeless in themselves, can no longer be experienced, so that the human soul, like that of other organic beings, dies with its ensouled body.

For finite persons, as we saw in Chapter 10, ending, i.e. death, is the condition for transtemporal meaning. There is no contradiction in this, since it is not necessary for the the human person to be conceived as eternal in order that its significance should be transtemporal. It is enough that the Absolute, God, is conceived as the locus where this meaning is sustained. There are religions, that of the Old Testament among them, that are content to know that God exists. One could say that the postulate of immortality would be more compelling for some kinds of non-nihilistic atheism than for religion. For if meaning depends on subjective consciousness, the total obliteration of consciousness would amount to the obliteration of the past, and so of the future perfect tense. But we cannot think of such a thing. If we try to think that what is happening now will one day not have happened, we simply deny the reality of the present. The idea of the soul's immortality, then, is that transcendence, the participation of the finite in meaning, though of no functional use in itself for biological survival, does not hit the buffers when the struggle for survival does. As transcendent beings, persons necessarily think of themselves as mortal; yet they cannot think that they, or others who present themselves as 'undeniable Thou', are simply abolished at their ending in time. For their reality was not 'in time'. It is impossible to speak with someone one loves and exchange glances, all the time thinking, 'Soon you will be no more.'

It is because we know that the intentionality with which we conduct our lives is not a function of our organic survival-mechanism, that we can think of its continuance after death. Our nature as materially structured outwardness separates itself from the soul that structures it and falls victim to entropy. Sensory perception 172 without a material perceiver is unthinkable—as unthinkable, to borrow Aristotle's example, as a snub-nosed person without a nose.[17] It must situate itself, so to speak, on a level with what it perceives. Intentionality, on the other hand, is pure structure. Earlier we defined persons as identical subjects of differential kinds of intentionality. Such subjects cannot merely be structural moments in intentional acts, because they carry out a variety of different acts of their own. The contingent character of the link between activity and neuronal substratum does not allow us to say anything scientific, positive or negative, about separation from this structure and the immortality of the soul. Science is, by definition, research into states of affairs, and the emancipation of an existent from the conditions of its production is not a matter science can talk about. So it is incapable either of reaching or refuting the idea of the soul's immortality. If it is rejected, it is rejected on the basis of a would-be common sense that derives its picture of the world broadly from science and does not believe in anything that is not capable of scientific treatment. From the anthropological point of view this scientistic common sense is a deviance, and those governed by it drive a wedge between themselves and the history of the human race. For humanity has been marked from its beginnings by belief in survival of death and communication with the dead.

If the thought of another person's ceasing to be is inconceivable, that is not because of the intentional structure of the personal life of the soul, which can establish no more than the *possibility* of immortality. To postulate that this possibility is realized requires

[17] *De anima* 429^{b}19.

the transcendence of the person and the communicative personal existence that that implies. The 'position' of each person in this communicative space is plotted, as we have seen, in an a priori relation to every other position. Each person assumes a position defined by him- or herself for ever. Theoretically it would be conceivable that 'past' human beings constitute such a position 173 only for as long as their memory lives on. But just as it is not existing persons who assign their place to new arrivals, so with past persons: their place is not kept clear by others who remember them. The complex of mutual recognition demands that everyone assumes a place in the universal community of persons simply by virtue of his or her own existing. Piety to the dead is not a supererogatory work of mercy; it is the meeting of a claim. And if there is a claim, how can the one who makes the claim no longer exist?

The elementary form of relation between persons is recognition; but at a more 'personal' level these relations are those of *love*. Love is existential self-transcendence in which spirit and soul, universality, and concrete experience are one. Even experience itself is transformed by transcendence: in love the soul, no longer defined by the vital functions of survival, becomes the reality of spirit. Love is essentially infinite; the absolute affirmation of the other can never, while true to its conception, come to an end. No amount of empirical contradiction can reduce lovers' vows to silence. Death catches up inescapably with lover and beloved alike, and without the finitude it imposes there could be no human love at all. But the finitude of man is not the finitude of love. That the lover cannot accept the beloved's death as the end may be written off as weakness. But inability to think, and unwillingness to accept, the end of one's *love* is not weakness. It fits the reality of self-transcendence. In a manner it carries death within itself as an inner moment of its experience. So the Song of Songs calls love 'strong as death', and in what is called his 'hymn to love' the Apostle Paul says, 'love never faileth'.[18]

The immortality of the soul, then, is not only a postulate *of* love, but a postulate *about* love, refusing to think of it as ending because it cannot end without contradicting its own idea. As old as mankind itself, this postulate is not open to decisive philosophical

[18] Song 8: 6, 1 Cor. 13: 8.

demonstration. Philosophy can only clarify its meaning and refute the suggestion that it is impossible. Philosophy can liberate us from 174 the scientistic common sense that rests on no scientific argument, and in this it has the weight of universal human tradition on its side. One must add, however, that the idea gains in consistency and plausibility when associated with the resurrection of the dead. For then the soul as empty form is related to the person summoned back into existence. Life persisting as pure intentionality is restored to its multidimensional mode, though no longer under the iron rod of anxiety for survival, no longer subject to the reductive explanations of system-theory: to *zōē* rather than to *bios*.

When the Areopagites heard the Apostle Paul on this subject, they complimented him politely, observing, 'We will hear you again about this.'[19] The philosopher must be content with the immortality of the soul as a postulate, and can only say, with Socrates, that it is 'a venture fitting and worth while for a man to make. The venture is a glorious one, and he ought to charm himself with spells like these.'[20]

[19] Acts 17: 33.
[20] *Phaedo* 114D, tr. R. W. Livingstone (Oxford: Oxford University Press, 1938).

14

Conscience

I

We call human beings 'persons', because they are unlike all other living beings in the *way* they are *what* they are. *What* they are is an ensemble of properties which they share with others for the most part. The individual combination of these properties will apparently always be distinctive; but what makes persons persons is not their distinctiveness, but their uniqueness. Uniqueness is not merely distinctiveness extended to the point where, by and large, only reference to particular space-time coordinates will suffice to pin it down. On the contrary, persons are the Archimedean points *from which* alone it is possible to identify positions in space and time, for it is they that give meaning to the expressions 'here' and 'now'. Only persons have a 'here' and a 'now'—only, that is, living beings that constitute a centre of vitality with its own horizon, in the first place, and are aware, in the second place, of having such a horizon, so that they know that their centre is a merely relative one, and speak of 'here' as opposed to somewhere else, of 'now' as distinct from earlier or later.

Human action, too, is determined by a horizon. To be sure, it constitutes an element in the parallelogram of forces generating the world-process; but this is not how it appears to the agent, whose horizon is limited. Agents act towards ends; and ends are selections made from within the agent's horizon of an infinite number of future events that the action will contribute to shaping. The agent singles out *these* events as the 'ends' of his action, assigning a lesser status to *those* as 'collateral consequences'. This abstraction presumes the isolation of his own activity, as 'cause', from factors of secondary importance as mere 'conditions'. This twofold abstraction from a horizon is decisive for constituting action. Animals make abstractions of a similar kind from the horizon of their vital interests; but human beings, as a rule, *know* that they abstract, and we ascribe responsibility only to those who so act as to let it be known that they 176 know it.

This knowledge permits agents to adopt the horizon of other interests than their own present interests, or they may restrict themselves in pursuit of their own present ends to make them compatible with other ends. These other ends may be long-term ends of their own, competing with their short-term ends, or they may be other people's interests that conflict with their own. Apart from all these, there may be an interest only to be understood in the light of the distinctive character of personhood as *responsibility for him- or herself*, i.e. an interest in self-realization, in the sense of making an objective success of life.

Making an objective success of life is not the same as having a subjective sense of satisfaction—whether immediately or in the long term. Responsibility for one's life supposes that persons 'have' a life to live; but 'having' does not imply that the person exists as an entity independently of having life. They cannot, then, be responsible *to themselves*. Actually, there could be no such thing as a responsibility to self, for if there were, one could always excuse oneself from it. The success of my life may, of course, mean nothing to me. A mood of indifference or *ennui* may often be an expression of impotence, which may have pathological aspects, though it may also be a mood to which humans succumb freely. As such it is recognized in the classical spiritual tradition of Christianity as one of the deadly sins, *accedia*. The reason for this is that a human being is not only bound to answer to others for the pursuit of his or her interests, not only constrained by practical considerations in devising means to those long-term interests, but must justify them at a higher level in terms of an objective responsibility for him- or herself, a responsibility for 'right living'. Criteria for right living may be derived from the study of human nature or the laws of human society, or alternatively from obligations sanctified by tradition. But the sense of obligation is not itself an inference drawn from any of these. One may, with reflection, adopt a critical distance on them all; none of them is instinctively irresistible. The irresistible obligation is something we create for 177 ourselves when we give up our critical distance and accept responsibility for ourselves. To conceive of being responsible for oneself is the paradigm self-expression of the person. Of course, giving up the reflective critical distance does not mean slipping back into natural immediacy; one takes up a *new* immediacy such as is possible only when one has first achieved a distance on every interest that makes immediate demands, whether one's own or other people's. That is what it means to be responsible for one's life as a whole, including one's interests and impulses to action.

Even reflection is initially concerned with criteria set by one's interests. Only when viewed as 'right living' do we take responsibility for our interests themselves. Then they lose their immediacy. 'I am what I am' is not an argument-stopper any more. I become responsible for being what I am. No longer immediate, interests cease to afford the criteria with which reflection is concerned. The 'voice' that causes this initial interest-focused reflection to take a step backwards, the voice we customarily call 'conscience', contributes nothing new in the way of content, no additional interest to compete with the others. That would be the 'naturalistic fallacy' with a vengeance! It is a 'voice from nowhere', corresponding to the 'view from nowhere' characteristic of the person. What it says may be fed from a variety of sources; its own origins may lie in the psychologists' 'superego'. But we can speak of 'conscience' only when the demands of the superego are associated with the posture of self-distance and acceptance of the need for justification and answerability. Answerability cannot be 'due to myself'. That is merely a manner of speaking, which, taken literally could only mean that I made myself responsible to some picture that I had sketched of myself, a picture I could always redraw. And where might such a picture come from? Interests, unrecognized even by myself, might prompt me to produce it. And if, perhaps under the stress of passion, I were to break free from my self-designed picture, that could actually be a moment of self-awakening. Responsibility for my life as a whole cannot be owed to any *part* of that life, not to an interest, not to a passion, not to another human being, nor even to an ideal self.

II

Conscience is independent as a phenomenon of all its metaphysical 178 explanations; but those explanations may correspond more or less adequately to the phenomenon. They may therefore be either true or false. And an explanation that does not correspond to the phenomenon may feed back into it, and so sap the effectiveness of conscience.

It is the most unambiguous mark of a person to have a conscience. The conscience affords a radical unity to the human subject, while at the same time extricating the subject from egocentric individualism. It affords a radical point of unity, because it subordinates the subject's ties and obligations, responsibilities and loyalties, to responsibility for self. The idea that human beings are responsible above all for themselves has been attacked as Pharisaism and moral egoism. What this charge fails to take into account is that the idea is inescapable, on the one hand, and purely formal on the other.

It is *inescapable* because it is simply the practical side of reflection on reflection, which delivers us from the immediate impact of the material content of reflection, 'values' included. Max Scheler taught that happiness could never be intended directly. It was one of his few great mistakes to assume that this applied to morality, too, which could consist, as he thought, only in immediate value-judgements carried through in self-forgetfulness. Scheler failed to see the difference between primary, natural immediacy, the cultivation of which, since it has slipped from our grasp already, always leads to bad faith, and the second immediacy which, in Kleist's expression, 'has passed through infinity'—the immediacy of reflection suspended by conscience.[1] Here each person has to do with him- or herself, but not in a manner that could be labelled as 'moral egoism', but as responsibility for self, which means the end of all egoism, particularly the egoism that veils itself in the apparent innocence of natural self-forgetfulness.

In his posthumous *Cahiers pour une morale*[2] Jean-Paul Sartre drew attention to the fact that the refusal to incur guilt for the sake of

[1] H. von Kleist, *On a Theatre of Marionettes*, tr. G. Wilford (London: Acorn Press, 1989).

[2] J.-P. Sartre, *Notebooks for an Ethics*, tr. D. Pellauer (Chicago: University of Chicago Press, 1992).

bettering the world is not moral egoism if it springs from the idea of responsibility for oneself. For then it is not a matter of some 179 private interest of one's own, not even an interest in self-satisfaction, but of living one's life 'finely', displaying the glory of the creator. For the believer, Sartre holds, care for one's soul is not egoistical. Only the atheist is bound, as a matter of duty, to be a utilitarian, since there is no God to relieve him of responsibility for the world. On atheistic assumptions, as Sartre holds, a fundamental responsibility for oneself has no meaning, for there is no one to whom such a responsibility may be owed, no one to impose obligations and relieve us of them.

The *formal* character of conscience means that it is not an oracle, which could influence or prejudice moral judgement one way or the other by its particular deliveries. Conscience does not *influence* moral judgement at all; it *is* moral judgement. Conscience summons us back from our inclinations, and summons us back from the imaginary responsibilities among which we try to escape responsibility for ourselves. The radical unification of the person though the kind of self-encounter we call 'conscience' reaches as far as the criteria of good and evil, right and wrong, from which responsibility takes its bearings. These criteria must in the last instance be the responsibility of the person him- or herself, and a decision about them part of the life he or she has to take responsibility for. But that seems to create a vicious circle. We appear to need a further criterion for *this* decision, and so *ad infinitum*; or else the decision is blind and arbitrary, so that everything that follows bears the imprint of the arbitrariness at its source.

This would certainly be the case if our responsibility for criteria of action had the form of *choice*. Then we would face the problem of infinite regress at this point. But it is not a 'choice' in the plain sense of the word, i.e. where the one who chooses either has no reason at all for choosing this way rather than that, or does not know why this reason rather than another should have proved decisive.

Let us take an example. Imagine someone with a lucrative position within his grasp, who has only to spread a libellous report to put an obnoxious rival out of the running. He has a reason to do this, and he also has a reason not to do it. His reason to do it is his interest in 180 providing himself with a secure and affluent livelihood. Interests need no further reason to become motives for action. They are, as such, sufficient reasons prima facie. But in this case the prima facie reason may be deprived of force by a reason to the contrary, namely, that libel is forbidden. What kind of reason is this? What purchase does it have? In explanation for his failure to spread the report about his rival, he will say, perhaps, that it is 'not nice', even 'wrong'; that he would not like to be the object of such a libel himself; he would not like to be the kind of person who would do such a thing; he would get no satisfaction from the post if he acquired it by these means, and so on. Perhaps he may add, with a note of regret, that he lacks the temperament or upbringing to set these scruples aside. Other people are better at it. Or he may say that he does not want to risk his soul, or *karma*. All such explanations come back in the end to the first: it is not right. That is the only reason not to *want* to be the kind of person who does such things, the only reason it might risk one's soul or leave one feeling bad. That something is 'morally deplorable', i.e. wrong, is like a vital interest: it constitutes a sufficient reason in and of itself not to do something. The question 'Why not do something wrong?' can only be answered, 'Because it is wrong.'

Yet there is a difference between the moral reason and the vital interest. The moral reason is not a prima facie reason, such as could be trumped by another, given the right conditions. To be aware of a moral reason for acting this way and not that is to be aware that by its very nature it must be conclusive. Someone who allows his interest in professional advancement to be overridden when only an act of treachery can secure it, does not deny that interest in any way; no sacrifice of judgement or integrity is involved. Prima facie reasons must from time to time give place to other reasons, yet they continue to be prima facie reasons just the same. But it is quite a different thing to renounce the criterion of moral good. *This* reason-for-acting cannot submit to being overridden. Either it has the last word, or the agent denies something in himself, acts in opposition to his better 181 judgement. There is no need of a third reason to decide between these two motives-for-acting. The moral reason is not in competition with others, so as to require an arbiter. The moral reason either has the last word, or it disappears. The name we give a moral reason in conflict with our interests is 'conscience'.

III

Conscience confers a unique personal dignity, in that nothing else can make someone the judge of final instance in his own cause. But the person must be in a position to recognize the moral claim, must, that is, be able to exercise practical rationality. Conscience is not an irrational oracle that may substitute for practical rationality, although it may often happen that the deliveries of reason are anticipated by intuitive certainties.

Taken simply as rational entities, human beings are interchangeable. It makes no difference to the reason behind a judgement *whose* reason it is that reaches it. Were it not that individuals are prone to be clouded in their judgement by particular momentary interests, anyone could be the judge in any cause at any time, his or her own cause included. Because judgement may be clouded, however, and because there are many different angles to most causes, we are ready to distrust our judgement in our own cause, and in case of doubt to put it to the test of discussion with others. It is a mark of probity when we do so. The fact that reason is no respecter of persons does not entitle us to think our judgement better and more reliable than other people's. It is more plausible to think that for every reasonable individual there is one more reasonable still. The basic idea behind Plato's philosopher-ruler is that men should be ruled by reason, not by other men. 'Ruling oneself' can only mean, for Plato, being ruled by reason. That is why it is better for the unwise to be ruled by the wise than by themselves, i.e. by their irrational impulses.

The discovery of the conscience is the discovery that persons are not merely better or worse instances of a reason irrespective of 182 particular individuals, but that reason itself is concrete. That is to say, it terminates in judgements on particulars. To see the particular as falling under the universal is, as Kant demonstrated, not a performance that follows automatically from insight into the structure of the universal. This performance—'subsumption'—is assigned by Kant to the 'power of judgement'. Its deliveries are not irrespective of persons, though they make truth-claims just as universal propositions do. It follows that, where questions of practical reasoning are involved, they may be mistaken.

The problem posed by partiality and clouded judgement, whether it is short-term interests that prevail over long-term, or personal interests that prevail over those of other people, does not have to do with the knowledge of moral norms. It is a problem with sub-sumption. Other people's conflicts of interest are easier to judge fairly than those in which we are involved, unless, that is, they have a perilous resemblance to those in which we are involved. Partiality mostly takes the form of making a rule so precise that it applies to our own case only, or so general that our own case easily slips through as an exception. That was why John Rawls devised his 'veil of ignorance', which the prophet Nathan had made use of long before.[3] Only when the prophet had told King David the story of the rich man with his flocks and his theft, and led him to pronounce the penalty of death, did he apply the parable and deliver his *coup de grâce* with the subsumption, 'You are the man!'[4] But the point of the story is that David's conscience was stirred by this judgement. He accepted the subsumption. And that was something only David could do, especially since, as king, he could have said 'My position is different.'

The verdict of conscience, then, can be construed as the subsuming of an action under a rule of moral reason, which in turn is founded on a judgement of value. This subsumption has the character of a demand; it is a 'voice'. And it is important to notice that the 'voice' not only has to do with how the judgement is executed in action, but with the judgement itself. Universal value-judgements and universal moral norms provide the material of moral reason and insight. In the formation of these there can be many factors in play, but conscience is not yet involved. But when we exercise the power of judgement as Kant described it and 'subsume', judging 'this act of mine falls under this rule and not some other', there we have before us the material of conscience. Taking its rise from reason, conscience puts a stop to rationalization. It tells us, 'You are the man!' We speak with some point, then, of a 'judgement' of conscience. The phrase 'conscientious decision', on the other hand, is rather misleading. Decisions may comply with conscience, or they may fail to comply with it.

---

[3] *A Theory of Justice* (Oxford: Oxford University Press, 1972).
[4] 2 Samuel 12: 7.

When they comply, it does not mean the *conscience* has decided—simply that the agent has decided in accord with the judgement of conscience.

To speak of 'subsuming' an act under a rule is a reconstruction of the judgement after the event. The usual thing, after all, is to know what is right to do before we know what rule it conforms to. And we know it, often enough, with greater certainty than we know the universal rule. It is clearer to me that *I must not play this trick*, than that *no one should ever play a trick like that*. Yet, in the last analysis, conscience is concerned with its 'this', whatever that may be, under some specification; it is concerned with it *as a case of* such and such. Conscience warns us not to mistake our particular uniqueness for a difference of kind, not to refuse to subject our actions to the test of universalizability. The person realizes his or her uniqueness precisely in being a 'rational nature' in his or her own personal, irreplaceable way, and *therefore* included in a kind; yet not included as a mere unconscious *instance* but as a conscious *participant* in the universal. If we withdraw from the kind, if we refuse to govern our actions with reference to it, we relapse into the merely natural existence of an 'instance of...' something or other. Individualism cannot do justice to the uniqueness of the person. Persons prove their 'incommunicability' precisely by *not* demanding to be made exceptions of. Anyone, after all, can want to be treated as an exception!

There is only one legitimate form of exception, which is the one Kierkegaard explored.[5] This is a limiting case, an exception susceptible only of a religious interpretation. The voice that requires 184 Abraham to sacrifice his son is neither the voice of conscience nor of his individual nature, but the voice of one who transcends both, the creator of his nature and the source of his conscience. *This* voice, we are told, cannot be interpreted as a faculty of judgement subsuming cases under rules! There are no criteria to determine whether it is or is not the voice of God. The one who obeys it is, to the outside world, no different from a maniac. The 'exception' (in this sense) takes us beyond morality to its source, and so leads to utter isolation. But it is also part of Abraham's story that the voice that required him

[5] *Fear and Trembling*, tr. Howard and Edna Hong (Princeton: Princeton University Press, 1983).

to be ready to slay his son forbade him to do so in the end, so that morality is restored. It is the hypothetical exception that proves the rule. And the proving is what makes the rule, which is as such indifferent to the individual, decisive for the person. 'Persons', unlike 'individuals', are not elements in an encompassing whole; each person is an all-encompassing whole.

The absolute claim of conscience, then, is not to be understood as an objective entitlement demanding recognition, as though any judgement of the conscience were always bound to be right. It is simply that no one can impose on someone else the subsumption of his own case under a given universal rule. For the judgement that a case falls *under* a rule cannot be derived *from* a rule, which would lead to infinite regress: a procedural rule for treating cases under a rule would need a judgement that *this* was the right occasion to applying that procedure, and so on. The exercise of the faculty of judgement, we conclude, can never simply be a matter of following rules.

IV

The absolute claim of conscience is a formal one, which means we are not entitled to draw substantive moral conclusions from the autonomy of conscience. We are not to conclude, for example, that obedience or submission to socially binding decisions is wrong. We can be convinced that a given authority is properly constituted and legitimate, and that we are morally obliged to obey it. Far from 185 forbidding obedience, conscience requires it—except where the subject is sincerely persuaded that the bearer of authority is overstepping the bounds of his authority or demanding something inconsistent with the social norms from which his authority derives its legitimacy. In the first of these cases disobedience is permitted; in the second it is required.

A special question arises where one's judgement about what is morally required clashes not with a command but with another person's judgement. The voice of conscience is absolute because the person is absolute, representing the whole to itself. But this is only in so far as it can grasp its own relativity as an individual. There is no a priori reason to prefer one's own prima facie judgement in moral questions to the judgement of another person. There are often reasons to distrust it: either I am a party to the case, and therefore have reason to doubt myself, or the other person is, in my experience, wiser than I am. If I follow his judgement rather than my own, that does not mean that I am acting against my conscience and following his, but simply that I judge his judgement to be more reliable than mine. It is precisely *my* conscience that encourages me to follow *his* judgement. If I come to the conclusion that he is wrong, of course, I may decide not to follow him after all.

Conscience is absolute in the sense that without it, or in contradiction to it, it is impossible to live in a way that does justice to personality. It is not absolute in the sense that every life lived in conformity to conscience is a good life. Nothing that contradicts conscience is good, but not everything is good that conscience requires or permits. The voice of conscience—at once the voice from nowhere, the voice of God and the voice of reason—draws an individual into unity with him- or herself. That unity is, at the same time, a totality. There is nothing beyond it, nothing to which conscience could contribute as a part or as a function, no point of view from which the perspective of conscience could be relativized. To do *this*, and to do it *here and now*: that is what conscience approves in a final and unqualified way. But can conscience guarantee that what it approves is really good? If one said, 'whatever my conscience approves is good', one would have missed the true voice of conscience 186 altogether, since as the voice of practical reason conscience strives for a total perspective rather than simply standing its ground. It intends truth, and therefore can be mistaken. If the voice of conscience merely stood its ground, it would be indistinguishable from any other casual wish an individual might form. Such wishes come straight up against other wishes and against other people's wishes, with which they are naturally in competition, creating a parallelogram of forces within which they are all assumed. As rational beings we can comprehend this parallelogram and relativize our own wishes. We may try, perhaps, to be just. In grasping our relativity as individuals, we are more than particular individuals; we are rational beings, and as such we embark upon an open-ended discourse, yet without surrendering ourselves unconditionally to whatever may be the outcome of this discourse. Whether we allow the outcome the final word over our actions or anticipate it on our own responsibility, it is always our *own* decision to do the one or the other, and in this 'metadecision' it is at the behest of conscience, once again, that we follow our own best insight. Insight is not the result of introspection, but of an intuition that we reach at the conclusion of a process of rational deliberation, or by which we anticipate the conclusion. Since conscience claims validity for its judgement, its judgement may be wrong.

It is easy to form the impression that since a mistaken conscience has the same binding force as an unmistaken one, to follow it is always good. But if that were so, the judgement of conscience would not be *about* what is 'good' and 'bad' to do independently. It would be an opaque idiosyncrasy, and as such would have nothing to do with personality and possess no kind of dignity. At best, it would be a fallible judgement about what was the 'right' or 'wrong' thing to do in some non-moral sense, so that any action conforming to what was judged 'right' might be called 'good' without reference to the rightness or wrongness of the judgement itself. The words 'right' and 'wrong' are equivocal. There are numerous standards for judging right and wrong; even a murder can be performed in a right or wrong way! It is *moral* right and wrong that we call 'good' and 'bad'. If every judgement about moral right and wrong is true by definition, there is no *judgement* involved at all. And if it is good to follow one's own judgement in every case, the judgement (which may possibly be 187 wrong) cannot be *about the good*.

Yet, as we have seen already, it is always bad to act against the judgement of our conscience. So someone with a mistaken conscience cannot act rightly. That situation is called, in scholastic terminology, 'perplex', and it implies that a mistaken conscience is a moral failure, not merely an intellectual one.[6] And that in fact is the case. If someone experiences a sudden 'awakening' of conscience, and realizes that for years he has treated another person unjustly, he does not excuse his former conduct on the ground that he never realized it

---

[6] Cf. R. Schenk, 'Perplexus supposito quodam. Notizen zu einem vergessenen Schlüsselbegriff...', in *Recherches de Théologie ancienne et médiévale* 57 (Leuwen: 1990).

was wrong. He blames himself all the more *because* he never realized it was wrong. If this were not so, there would be no reason to test one's conscience, no reason to offer help, or seek it, in the clarification of one's conscience. It would be better to spare oneself and others the conflicts arising from such knowledge. So long as one had a good conscience about the wrong one did, one would be a good person. This amounts to a kind of moral hedonism: what matters is to feel good, which cashes out in this case as having a good conscience. It is obvious that this is not consistent with our understanding of conscience. By implication it is inconsistent, too, with the sort of interaction that we owe to persons. To hand oneself over regardless, and everyone else as well, to whatever one's conscience may happen to dictate, is to refuse to respect the human striving for reality, i.e. transcendence. It is to treat people as idiosyncratic individuals essentially incapable of giving an account of themselves, to impute to them no interest in moral truth, but only in keeping themselves warm.

It remains to ask how one can extricate oneself from a mistaken conscience. So long as one is trapped in it, one fails to see the mistake for what it is, and therefore sees no reason to attempt an escape. The very idea of self-extrication supposes that the mistaken conscience is seen as a moral fault, and that the one entrapped in it, experiencing self-contradiction, is ready in principle to break out of the limited and imprisoning perspectives of self-interest.

A mistake of conscience is no different from a theoretical mistake. 188 The Socratic path of theoretical enlightenment starts from the assumption that no mistake is really consistent and coherent. Someone who makes a mistake runs into a contradiction sooner or later, either with experience or with himself, and is actually not ready to endorse all the consequences that flow from his mistake. Socrates allows his partners in dialogue to discover their contradictions. So it is with the mistake of conscience. Its most usual cause is found in a failure to enquire of the conscience 'when the passions are silent'.[7] It can often be traced, moreover, to an initial struggle with the conscience that has gradually silenced or bent it. The mistaken conscience has a

---

[7] D. Diderot, 'Droit naturel', in *Encyclopédie* iii (*Œuvres Complètes* (Paris: Garnier, 1876), vii).

tendency to lead us further and further away from the requirements of practical reason. But as long as one is alive as a person at all, one can discover the precipitous direction in which one is headed, and can 'be converted'. The safest way to extricate oneself from the mistakes of conscience is to follow the conscience, that is to say, to follow what we *believe* we have grasped of the good, as 'conscientiously' as possible. Then the conscience displays a dynamic tendency towards self-enlightenment. We learn to recognize a mistaken conscience as a moral fault, a hindrance on the path to becoming a person. Conscientiousness includes the readiness to test our convictions in discussion, and especially with those who do not flatter us— not with accomplices, that is, but with tried friends.

V

Conscience is a paradox, and its paradoxical character expresses, as nothing else can, the constitution of the 'person'. What we intend in conscience is something objective and unqualified, something good in itself, not merely in appearance, a good to be done, or an evil to be left undone, right here and now. The judgement of conscience lays claim to unqualified obedience. As an act of the faculty of moral judgement it may defend its claim in argument, but not establish it 189 beyond all possibility of challenge. When our actions or omissions hurt others, whether individuals or communities, it does nothing to enhance their legitimacy if what we do is a 'conscientious protest'. For in the first place there is no transparent criterion that establishes the sincerity of conscientious conviction as a public fact. In the second place, legal requirements are, of their essence, subject neither to whim nor conscientious scruple. If a state allows *non-performance* of certain civic obligations on the ground of conscience, that is an act of toleration that may be conceded if no very great mischief may be expected to follow. But illegal *actions* on the ground of conscience cannot be tolerated by any state. Conversely, it is a measure of the sincerity of conscientious protest that the protester has taken the probability of punishment into consideration. Conscience must understand itself as the voice of practical reason, not as an idiosyncracy; a dissident acting on conscientious grounds must believe the laws prohibiting his act unjust and the legislator mistaken—and mistaken not because the right of *dissent* is not respected, but because certain laws are viewed as just which in the dissident's view are unjust. The conscientious protester wants nothing to do with toleration, but for justice, as he or she understands it, to be the basis of the universal law.

Respect for the sanctity of the person, i.e. for the conscience, does not prevent us from inducing someone to act unconscientiously. If we judge certain actions or omissions wrong objectively, we shall try to induce the agent to do what is right instead, without enquiring into what his conscience says. We shall try to deflect terrorists from an act of terror by bribery if necessary, and we shall use threats to induce them to betray associates. We may always hope that their conscience, which is interested in the good by definition, will rid itself of its confusion, or what we take to be such. It is *actions* that merit public interest, while others' consciences remain forever hidden from us. There is, however, one proceeding that is simply ruled out: the use of physical torture to destroy another person's capacity 190 to be the subject of his or her own acts, to induce performances that could not be described as acting freely. To threaten death does not destroy anyone's freedom. Life may be the price one has to pay for refusal to perform certain acts. It has always been regarded as a proof of sincere conviction, indeed, to be willing to accept death on its account. But torture does not aim to prove freedom but to eradicate it, and it is incompatible with the a priori relation that obtains between persons.

That apart, respect for another's conscience in a state of conflict assumes a predominantly symbolic character. A situation of conflict is a situation of combat, and combat may be about life and death. A good conscience is the conviction that one has right on one's side; but giving effect to this right is not simply a matter of letting the spiritual might of right prevail of itself. That can happen only when the opponent is persuaded, or when one comes round to revising one's own view. Political conflict, which may always spill over into measuring physical force against physical force, takes over where the uncoercive spiritual might of truth is insufficient to prove itself; but the medium of physical force is indifferent to right and wrong, the stuff of conscience. In physical combat the right of the stronger prevails, and it is a matter of chance whether the stronger is also the better. Anyone who takes the sword may perish by the sword. If physical combat is to remain an encounter between persons, we must not confuse physical weapons with moral ones. Given the possibility that our opponent may be eliminated physically, we are not entitled to demand his moral elimination at the same time. We may eliminate morally only those whom we do not eliminate physically. The moral elimination of Cain, the first fratricide, goes hand in hand with the command: 'If anyone slays Cain, vengeance shall be taken on him sevenfold.'[8] Physical combat is compatible with human dignity only when accompanied by the mutual respect of the combatants, who, in exposing themselves to the risks of combat, permit *each other* to follow their consciences. If it were not so, the combatant would simply be a hangman.

[8] Gen. 4: 15.

15

Recognition

I

The way persons are available to one another's knowledge determines how they interact. But *how* they are available to one another's knowledge is something we shall not understand if we rely on the analogy with how natural objects are known. It is the other way round: the way natural objects are available to knowledge derives from our knowledge of persons. A person is not exhaustively accounted for in terms of how he or she can be known. With persons, *esse* is not the same as *percipi*; there is 'something more' to them. How we explain that 'something more' marks a decisive parting of the ways among the philosophical schools.

Our observation of living creatures offers an immediately attractive explanation. A higher animal, at least, is a being-in-itself, an inwardness essentially eluding our objectification. There is continuity, to be sure, in the enjoyment of life: 'Delight was given to the worm and the cherub face to face with God,' as Schiller wrote.[1] Yet it is paradoxical to speak in this connection of continuity, since the peculiar mark of the living creature is its monadic separation from everything else. Drive, together with the pleasure and pain that accompany it, constructs an inner room without a window. No *other* creature can register the pain or pleasure felt by *this* creature. Registering it would be nothing less than experiencing it. That is how the Cartesians came to deny that non-human animals experience pain; for though animal behaviour presses the analogy of experience on us,

---

[1] F. Schiller, *Ode to Joy*.

we cannot be made to accept it. Inwardness, which living creatures have in common with human beings, and human beings in common with living creatures, makes it possible for humans to extract themselves from this community and treat non-human animals as mere objects. To recognize being-in-itself is never anything less than an act of freedom. All of which applies to the recognition of persons, too, though in a qualitatively higher way.

So it is tempting, at first glance, to understand personal being as a heightened form of inwardness, a reflection in which human beings 192 relate to their own vitality. But it really will not do. This type of self-understanding cannot be characterized as just another variety of inwardness—'solitude' (*Für-sich-sein*), in Hegel's term. If persons *know* themselves to be solitary, that can only mean they have recognised their solitariness as 'a fact' (*an sich*); they have taken the step from *cogito* to *sum*. Yet it is, at the same time, an immediate datum of their consciousness (*für sie*) that they exist for others, that they have an outer surface. The perception of the inner–outer difference, which lies at the root of human speech, cannot simply be assigned to the realm of the subjective any more than the structure of speech itself can. The recognition that a person is 'someone' is not reached by analogy. It is not like the belief that animals are impelled by drive and are capable of pain—a subjective conviction of what is objectively no more than probable. What we are dealing with in that case is a decision to attribute properties to animals which (though the matter cannot be settled one way or the other) they either have or do not have. If, next, we wonder whether other humans are in pain, this is something we can ask them and they can give us the information we ask for, since everyone enjoys a privileged access to his or her own inwardness. But with being a person it is quite a different matter from both these examples.

Being a person is not an objective occurrence like the capacity for pain. We enjoy no privileged access to our own personal being. Whether someone is in pain is something she, and only she, can tell us conclusively. But there is something she cannot judge on her own; and that is whether she understands the meaning of the word 'pain' correctly. To reach that judgement she needs the collaboration of a conversation-partner; the two of them must work together to see whether they have achieved a mutual understanding about pains with the aid of words. And so it is, too, with the question whether another being, let us say, a visitor from Mars, is capable of reflection—capable, that is, of the inner distance on its own states that is the hallmark of the person—and so is the subject of intentional acts. Such acts, as we have seen, are not psychological occurrences that may be established objectively. They can only be taken note of through cooperative performances. The being from Mars cannot answer our question about its capacity for reflection with a straight yes or no. It can answer it only by *understanding* the question—and by observing what a pointless question it was to ask!

That Lise is a person, then, is not something that we first suspect 193 and then, as our suspicions grow stronger, reach a judgement on, so that finally we recognize her personal status. Only as we recognize Lise as a person can we even conceive of her being one. Recognition is not a conclusion founded on analogy, as when we conceive from our own pain what the pain of another creature must be like. On the contrary, we can only conceive of ourself as a person if there is someone else whom we conceive as one. We do not find out first whether we understand a language, and then whether anyone else understands it, too. To be a person is to occupy a place within a field where other persons have their places. The occupation of our own place does not depend on being assigned it by those who were ahead of us. Each human being assumes his or her place *suo iure*, as of birthright. But neither does the occupation of the place comes first, as a prior empirical *datum*; for the place itself cannot be identified apart from recognition. That is why, as I have observed already, you cannot first assert that John is a person and then protest that persons matter no more to you than monarchs do. To acknowledge personal status is already to express respect, which is the specific way in which persons are accessible to one another. This, of course, is paradoxical. Respect, recognition, and so on are species of activity, which would seem to presuppose a moment of receptivity in which persons were identified as persons. Apparently, and not least because it is a question of perceiving another centre of being, the perceiver needs to be in a completely receptive posture. But that is not the case, and for a very clear reason: a centre of being is, by definition, not something available to knowledge as a phenomenon.

Objective qualities are available as phenomena. Acts, on the other hand, which make these qualities their object, are not available as phenomena. They are available to the extent that we engage in them, whether actively or by reflective imagination. Even to know another life requires a certain sympathetic engagement, for life is noticed only by the living. It is simply that this engagement involves a resonance of which we are not aware and which we can only call 'free' in the sense that we can stand back from it intellectually. But it is different with persons. It takes a deliberate personal act to treat *them* as objects, an act with a specific character, 'wickedness'. As a person I can define 194 myself only in relation to all others. Persons are beings that other persons *speak to*. It is no simple matter, then, to treat them as things merely *spoken of*. The other's gaze meets mine; I cannot refuse it without assuming a cold, humiliating manner, which is in itself a manner of *personal* dealing.

The alternative way of dealing is to recognize the other as a centre-of-being. This presumes, of course, a measure of passive availability to knowledge first: the other must be an object of sense-perception, construed as 'human being' in the way that other living creatures are construed as what they are. But the personal existence of the other is not construed like that, but 'noticed' by an act of free recognition. There is an ambiguity in the word 'notice', which comes into play here.[2] We say that we 'take note of' another person's interests when we make them our own and defend them before third parties. This is the sense in which persons can be said to be 'noticed'. All obligation begins with noticing persons. It is not an imperative or norm that requires us to deal with persons in a certain way. Imperatives are exposed to the question, why obey? All axioms of moral argument, indeed, when stated as obligations, are open to that question. Even arguments deriving obligation from the principle of consistency run aground when they treat consistency as an obligatory requirement. The voice of God which seeks Cain out after the murder of his brother does not ask whether he has infringed a moral norm or prohibition. It asks, 'Where is your brother Abel?' It demands that

[2] [The author comments on the semantic range of the verb *wahrrnehmen*, which in this place I have translated 'notice', or 'take note of'—not entirely doing justice to the argument, which requires a sense such as 'act on behalf of'.]

Cain should know where his brother is. The answer, 'Am I my brother's keeper?' refuses even this imposition.[3] To fail to know the other's place, according to this story, amounts to a confession of murder.

II

Duties to persons are derived from the duty to notice them as persons. Yet this cannot, strictly speaking, be formulated as a duty. Duties need justifications, but noticing persons is the ultimate justification of every duty. Besides duties, of course, there are values of a non-personal kind. We can act better or worse, morally or immorally, by conformity or disconformity to such non-personal values. But in speaking of duties we have persons in view.

We sometimes say that persons have rights against other persons, but that is only another way of saying that persons have duties to other persons. These two expressions are strictly reciprocal. There is no sense in speaking of a human right if no one can be identified as having a corresponding duty, even if only a duty to desist. Were that the case, we would have to agree with Grillparzer: 'Hunger and hardship, my friend, these are the rights of man!'[4] Duties of one to another are generated by the moment of recognition in which one person notices another. Prior to this moment there is no obligation. On the contrary, obligation follows from noticing the person, which is one and the same as recognizing another as 'like myself'. Yet to recognize a person is not to *posit* one, as if we owed our personal existence to someone else's recognition. I recognize because recognition is due, yet I do not *first* know it is due, *then* recognize. To know that it is due is no more and no less than to recognize.

There are two misunderstandings to which the recognition of another human being as 'like myself' is exposed. It may be taken to mean no more than that the other is of the same species, *homo*

---

[3] Gen. 4: 9.

[4] F. Grillparzer, *Ein Bruderzwist in Habsburg, Werke* ii (Munich: Carl Hanser, 1971), 327.

sapiens. If this were all that was meant, there would be some basis for the objection to 'speciesism': it would be simple *parti pris* for one's own kind. But recognition of a human being as a *person* means something more—even if we make it a point of principle to recognize each human being as a person without further ado, even, in fact, if 'person' is taken to have exactly the same field of reference as 'human being'. Belonging to one species affords grounds for a certain vague solidarity against the rest of the world; but it does not explain how the recognition due to each and every person forbids the sacrifice of this or that member to the interest of the species as a whole. This prohibition cannot be reached from the claim that humans are more valuable than other animal species. It can only be derived from a claim of incommensurable value—incommensurable even with the dignity of other human beings. That is why we prefer to speak of human 'dignity' (*Würde*) rather than human 'value' (*Wert*). The *value* of ten people may be more than that of one, but ten are no more than one in point of dignity. You can't tot up persons. They form a system of relations in which each is uniquely situated in relation to every other. 196

Failure to comprehend this relation gives rise to a second misunderstanding. 'Like myself' contains a paradox. It is not *similarity* of others to myself that is in view, but the *same incomparable uniqueness.* Human beings, *qua* human beings, may be more or less similar; but as persons they are not similar, but equal—equal in their distinctive uniqueness and incommensurable dignity. The second misunderstanding, therefore, is to take the phrase as though it gave priority to self-recognition, so that we noticed other persons on the basis of an analogy with ourselves. 'Person' means the occupant of a unique position in the relational field of persons; so it is one and the same moment of perception by which we notice that we ourselves occupy such positions, and that other people do, too. To take note of a human being as a person is precisely this: to take note of the a priori relational field that personality constitutes. Only in the context of this field do we discover ourselves as persons.

What it means to enter the sphere of the personal is expressed by Kant in the second formulation of the categorical imperative: 'So act that you use humanity, whether in your own person or in the person of any other, always at the same time as an end, never merely as a means.'[5] There is a self-restraint required, on the basis of a shift in perspective. The animal—and the human animal like any other—constructs its own specific universe of which it is the centre. The significance of each encounter is programmed by instinctual 197 organization and determined by its function in the system. As living creatures, human beings construct their own universe in which significance and function coincide, defined by the interests of the individual human. Not, of course, only selfish interests. The survival of the species—or should we say, the optimal reproductive prospects for our genes?—is anchored in the structure of our drives. But so is a certain solidarity with those connected to us closely by family or culture or spontaneous sympathy—even, in a weak sense, with all our conspecifics. Up to a point our well-being is inseparable from theirs. But entry into the sphere of the personal is a qualitative leap beyond this, a step into a wholly new form of relation. This need not mean that the step has the character of a breach. Even natural egocentrism is not egotistic, but includes a tendency to self-transcendence. *Amor benevolentiae* can develop from *amor concupiscentiae,* and so create the impression of continuity.

What is new about personal relations, however, can best be illustrated in the case where continuity of interest is not evident, i.e. where there is no 'pathological' motive (in Kant's sense), no motive of sympathy to assist the overcoming of self-centredness, so that personal relations assume the elementary form of justice.[6] To recognize a person means pre-eminently to restrain my own potentially unlimited urge for self-expansion. It means to resist the inclination to see the other only as a factor in my own life-project. That is 'respect': respect for one who can never be made an object, never a means subservient to my own universe of significance.

III

What does 'respect' mean? The practical application of the term is not easy to determine. Attempts to define it usually accomplish too

[5] *Groundwork of the Metaphysics of Morals, AA* iv. 429. (*Practical Philosophy,* ed. and tr. Gregor, 80.)
[6] *Critique of Practical Reason, AA* v. 75. (*Practical Philosophy,* ed. and tr. Gregor, 200–1.)

much or too little, so that respecting every person as an end, i.e. as a subject of ends, appears either vacuous, imposing no restriction at all 198 on our field of action, or so restrictive as to be inconsistent with our self-preservation. And what does 'as an end' mean? Does it mean permitting and facilitating their pursuit of their own ends? We may do no less in rearing animals—until, of course, we send them to the abattoir! If we gave them no forage they would cease to be of use; if we gave them no mating opportunities, they would die out.

Or does it mean that we should not make use of others' actions for our own ends—should not, that is to say, 'instrumentalize' another person? That would make human life impossible. Human existence is bound up with human nature, which, like every other nature, lives at others' expense, including that of conspecifics. It has been a consistently cherished ideal that humans, being related to each other, should organize their endeavours cooperatively, understand their interests as common interests, never instrumentalize each other or compete, but cooperate as effectively as they can through a discursive communication about the common good. Equally consistently, every attempt to implement this ideal has led to disillusion. If we understand what a person *is*, we shall understand why the attempt must fail. Nothing could demonstrate this more clearly than the way the communitarian ideal itself sets us at odds with one another as nothing else can. Precisely in the name of this ideal personal recognition is refused to those who oppose it: 'Whoe'er these truths will not maintain, doth not deserve to be a man.'[7] No ordinary conflict of interest ever sacrificed such a hecatomb of victims as the ideal of overcoming conflicts of interest. It wants to take the wings of a dove, and fly away from human nature.

The wings it will employ are those that constitute the specific difference of human nature: that is to say, reason. Reason, since Plato, is *to koinon*, the common, indifferent to individual interest. As a creature of pure reason, mankind had to be capable of under- 199 standing its interests as common. 'When good comes to the light of day,' we read in the *Gorgias*, 'it is common to all.'[8] But persons are, to

---

[7] E. Schickaneder and W. A. Mozart, *The Magic Flute* 15.
[8] 505E, κοινὸν γὰρ ἀγαθὸν ἅπασι φανερὸν γενέιθαι αὐτό.

the highest degree, individuals, which is evident precisely in their capacity to form *individual* views of the *common* good. The way in which we each understand the common opposes us more sharply than our individual interests do. Individual interests, moreover, contribute imperceptibly to our conception of the common—which is the subject-matter of the critique of ideology. The great political conflicts of history were grounded in irreconcilable aspirations to the universal.

What, then, can 'recognition of the person' mean when set in a context of profound disagreement? Obviously not a readiness to facilitate the attainment of another's goals as one does one's own. That is impossible, for the simple reason that in such circumstances attaining the one goal is incompatible with attaining the other. The modern constitutional state has recognized the legitimacy of political conflict, and has domesticated it. It has laid down the rules of play, and has imposed observance of them as a condition of participation in legitimate conflict. Observance of the rules of play is the institutional form that personal recognition takes within the context of political disagreement. For what recognition means is that personality goes deeper than reason. Reason, as understood by Plato and the eighteenth century, was the means to universal agreement and resolution of antagonisms; but in the age of the two world wars reason itself became a cause of disagreement. One universalism confronted another in the name of reason. To deal with this the modern constitutional state formulated Fundamental Laws that were at the same time rules for regulating conflict, each of these two aspects needing to be seen in connection with the other. The rules of procedure are not to be understood as purely pragmatic devices. It is not a matter of replacing justice with value-neutral rules of procedure, but of recognizing the persons involved in every conflict of justice, persons who have the right to uphold their view of the right against other 200 views and to promote their implementation to the extent that the rules allow.

Naturally, this imposes certain disabilities on universal visions, treated by analogy with private interests, which is certainly not how they see themselves. That cannot be helped. The idea that rational human nature, in leaving conflicts of interest behind, had to become, as Marx imagined it, a 'species-animal' (*Gattungswesen*), rests on a false understanding of what it is to be a person. To an incomparably higher degree than living creatures of kinds, persons are 'individuals', and that because of, not in spite of the fact that each represents a vision of the universal and the common, not merely her own or his own private interests. The confrontation of private interests is now reproduced at a higher level in terms of the definition of the common good. A definition of the common good is not a common definition. When, as in the plural constitutional state, there is in fact a definition held in common, it is a second-order definition that does not pretend to supersede the various competing universal visions, but to recognise their competition and domesticate it. Persons are recognized within such a state as creatures that are not exhaustively accounted for by their natural particularities and perspectives. They can relate to their particularities, then, as to something that they have. They may have convictions incompatible with other people's, and may respect convictions they see as erroneous without putting their own in question, in that they respect the person who has them. No person is simply identical with everything he or she may happen to have.

How strongly one identifies with any aspect of one's endowment is a matter for personal freedom. To identify oneself wholly with every opinion one has makes one invisible as a person—as though for fear of abusing one's freedom one refused to use it to identify oneself. Where such ultimate existential decisions are concerned, naturally enough, there is an end to respect for rules of procedure. And that is true not only for those whose existential decisions are incompatible with the rules, but for those who defend the rules. The rules exist to domesticate conflict and subject it to respect for persons, but that 201 does not rule out life-and-death struggle. In the face of a resolute attack on the constitutional state its supporters may be left with no alternative but to operate outside this scheme for personal recognition, to meet opposing force with force, and to kill its opponents if they are finally driven to it.

And does that put an end to personal recognition, too? Do natural antagonisms force it to surrender in the end? Was it always conditional on a certain measure of good behaviour on the part of those one respected, or at least on a principle of mutuality? It is of the utmost importance to see that that is not the case. If the formulation, 'use humanity, whether in your own person or in the person of any other ... never merely as a means', does not imply a kind of recognition that amounts substantially to taking note of persons, it is a contradiction. If I attach conditions, it means I do not treat the other as an end in himself; I accommodate him by virtue of a certain compatibility between the demands of his life and will and of mine; which is to say, I subordinate him to my own ends. But is that not unavoidable, if strife itself is sometimes unavoidable? No: if personal recognition is unconditional, it must be sustainable in the face of life-and-death struggle. That is why we cannot let any theory of the person pass which ignores the possibility of strife or mentions it only to condemn it.

IV

The name we give to the special relation between persons is 'peace'. The Semitic greeting, 'Peace be with you!' has a twofold sense: it 'concludes peace' with the other, and it wishes him to be 'at peace'. 'Peace' is a correlative term; no condition or relation could be described by it without reference to some contrasting condition. Peace means the absence of war, strife, and conflict—and not their bare absence from such causes as indifference or exhaustion, but the express and active *ending* of war, what we call the 'conclusion' of peace. To conclude peace implies reciprocal recognition of what persons have—'have', in the sense that they invest their being in it and are not prepared to be separated from it. Since the existence of a person is a having, personality can only be recognized in what it has: life, physical existence, vocation, possessions, and the space needed for self-realization. In its original form this claim is unconditional, and may collide at any time with demands made by others. But a 'concluded' peace is what we call a state of right. It converts claims into rights by limiting them. Possessions become property. The a priori space in which every person assumes a place uniquely his own and defined as such, demands of its very nature to be instituted as a state of right, where personal incommensurability takes the form of an equal right to otherness. Recognition means precisely that I see the other as one who does not owe his existence to me, just as I do not owe my existence to him. To give effect to recognition means to secure this independence, so that being recognized does not depend on someone's whim. That is why an order of right is compulsory; by imposing it, right-bearers indicate that they are *giving effect* to mutual recognition, and do not merely propose to bestow it gratuitously. Anyone who is prepared to withdraw recognition has not conferred it in the first place.

Thinkers of the eighteenth century set up a contrast between the state of nature and the state of right—too sharp a contrast, which left a hint of the mythological surrounding the transition from the one state to the other. This hint can be dispelled by the concept of the person, which makes it easy to understand how the state of nature persists in a weaker form *within* the state of right.[9] The pair of terms, 'state' and 'society', points to this continuing polarity. Liberal and totalitarian theories are often agreed in making the state an agency in the service of social forces, from which the totalitarian conclusion may be drawn that the state has an all-encompassing competence over the whole of society. But personal existence implies an inner structure—the human individual in possession of self, nature, and life—and it is easily seen how this structure must unfold in a bipolar, not a unipolar form. Recognition is essentially an order of formal 203 equality, yet this order never becomes real and alive without the unfolding of human life within it. This must always have the character of competition and conflict—including conflict over the juridical framework for handling conflict, for the way that framework is constructed has consequences for the way social processes work out. Peace cannot escape being a focus of conflict, for the form peace takes is always controversial.

That is why no juridical order can approximate to the Kingdom of God in which all disagreements are left behind, which acquires, therefore, the character of imperishability. No juridical order can secure itself definitively in perpetuity. The community that takes form in it is a factor in the consciousness of each participating individual; so each and every participant may raise questions about its form and provoke conflict about the rules for conflict resolution.

[9] Cf. Robert Spaemann, *Rousseau, Bürger ohne Vaterland: von der Polis zur Natur* (Munich: Piper, 1980).

No remedy can be found for this that would not have the effect of abolishing personality and changing men into thinking beasts. Persons are, as they always will be, a risk.

Does that imply—to approach the question from a new angle—that the recognition of a person, the taking note of of his or her personal status, cannot be sustained outside a juridically protected order of peaceful society? Is such an order the one and only form of personal recognition, so that conflict necessarily proceeds on an impersonal basis? Not at all. True, every actual conflict between two human subjects arises from a breach of actual communication, i.e. the relation in which our mutual demands meet with mutual consent. But it does not mean, where persons are concerned, that in the event of conflict we no longer put the question of what is reasonable and just. It means simply that we have to answer that question unilaterally and on our own. In a conflict of private interests what personal recognition means is that we restrict measures to defend our 204 interests within the legal rules. But where conflicts are more fundamental, and the whole point of the struggle is to bring the opponent's efforts to nought, what is needed is a conviction of the rightness of our cause: that is, that the consequences of success would be those an impartial observer would judge fair to all parties. Fairness does not imply that the opponent must actually consent to them. Anyone could captiously refuse consent in order to block a just settlement, on the one hand; on the other, people might consent to unreasonable exactions because their position was too weak, or because they were unclear what was involved. The duty of justice, like all duties, is primarily a duty of each person to him- or herself. Generally speaking, breaking off communication can be assumed to be justified if there are honest-minded people ready to offer a public defence of the struggle, which means that they will defend it to the opponent, too. But that implies a readiness to hear and weigh any new arguments that may be raised. The conclusion is paradoxical: in order to break off communication and 'resort to other means', one needs a particularly firm conviction of one's right. It is part of the logic of struggle that to cultivate doubts about the rightness of one's cause is detrimental to success. Yet doubt is never more pressing than in the circumstance where, given the breach of communication, the established tests for impartiality are unavailable. The temptation is to suppress the doubt with a thunderous *stet pro ratione voluntas*, or 'my country, right or wrong!'

It was, therefore, a significant advance when 'just cause', while continuing to be a recognized moral requirement in war, was qualified in modern international law by the idea of 'right on both sides', requiring the enemy to be credited with good faith as to the justice of his cause. For this reason, war was no longer to be conceived as punitive, but as a contest between moral equals. (Hence the interest of all those who disturb the peace in being recognized as belligerents.)

A final criterion for personal respect is the way the dead are treated, not least dead enemies. In death everything 'qualitative', everything that distinguishes men from one another, falls away. Honour is due 205 to the dead—to each one—in his or her unique identity as a person. It is the capacity to make this distinction that enables one whom death has spared to be recognized as a person himself.

V

Our reflections up to this point may seem to breathe a certain air of unreality in relation to our historical situation. The peaceable order of political society has been treated as a structure of interpersonal relations; international conflicts and political uses of force have been viewed as though they were ancient battles in which persons measured themselves against other persons. We have spoken of Cain and Abel, of Creon and Antigone, while in the modern world institutions have long since placed themselves on an independent footing, so that it is difficult to see today how their relations to the individual, and their mediation of relations between individuals, can be talked about in personal categories at all. Political entities once obeyed a prior logic that could be interpreted, at the level of protagonists at least, in personal terms. Today that is no longer so. Personalities at the head of governments may or may not 'hit it off together', and this factor may expedite the smooth running of their bureaucratic systems, but the essential realities that direct political processes are unaffected. Globalized markets have given a further impulse to depersonalization.

The political is, as such, a personal category, since it enables personal identification and restrains a purely economic logic. With the collapse of Marxist systems these controls have disappeared. Large-scale events seem to be no one's responsibility any more, and begin to assume the appearance of natural phenomena. In a book on persons it may seem anachronistic to persist in discussing large-scale institutions at all—like discussing physics, on the plta that as human beings persons must obey the laws of physics like any other material object.

Yet there really is a place for speaking about physical laws in 206 connection with persons, for they touch on questions of central importance, such as how self-determination is compatible with the principle of conservation or with the postulate of a closed universe of processes. What would follow, then, if institutions were merely impersonal constructions running in accordance with their own laws? That would present a real challenge to any theory of the person. Such entities would relate to persons as to constituent elements, and the juristic or contingent relations of those elements would be no more than raw material for events that proceed irrespective of the tendencies of their parts. But would this amount to a refutation of personal self-understanding? That could not be the case, because the person is never so merged into an event or a given state of things that it will disappear when it is no longer in control of things. To be in control of things is the tendency of all living creatures—but persons can adapt themselves to not being in control. This self-distancing can assume various, sometimes incompatible forms. It can consist in resignation, in romantic transmutation of external events, in anarchic resistance, or in patient efforts to defend the personal side of politics against material compulsion, retaining the awareness that compulsion cannot be total for those with their own fundamental options to fall back on. It is true that the undeclared options of the majority and the systematic dissimulations they involve may take on the character of a fate against which the individual has no recourse. The mere fact of surviving on the terms the system has dictated, having to make use of the resources for life which the system has provided, can be claimed as an indication of the individual's consent. But no one can compel any person to accept this representation. Modern systems of civilization that ignore the state of nature and subject essential resources to social control are no longer in a position to distinguish parasitic behaviour. They can hardly expect, at any rate, that this distinction should be a point of principle with those involved!

What demands our personal loyalty to large-scale institutions is not their role in social provision, but their political and juridical character. Institutions remain 'political' for just as long as the demands they make are expressions of personal will, whether the collective will of a historical community or the will of a legitimate authority. The expression of will, however, must be upfront, and its rejection of alternatives must be explicit. For example, any country is free to open its borders at will; it may decide in favour of a multi-cultural society. But if such a fundamental decision is not made formally, but merely inferred by presuming upon some unspoken consensus, its claim upon the loyalty of its citizens is eroded. Niklas Luhmann has argued that it is a primary trait of the modern state not to make its claim to legitimacy openly through representative persons but by implication from correct adherence to agreed procedural rules.[10] As far as the *stability* of systems goes, this is certainly correct. Conformity is a more reliable mode of discipline than obedience, for obedience is a personal act that can always be refused. But we must be clear that stability achieved in this way is not the same as legitimacy. It undermines legitimacy, in fact, for legitimacy is a personal category that lays claim on the loyalty of persons. Depersonalization dispenses with such claims, in the reasonable expectation that things will run smoothly enough—perhaps more smoothly—without them.

In this connection one especially offensive phenomenon, calculated to rob the personal dimension of its means of expression, is the all-pervasive use of personalized vocabulary that engulfs us on every side. Kindly expressions of good will assail us on advertising hoardings and computer screens. Directions blared out by public address systems never fail to thank us in advance for our understanding and cooperation. Any child can see that friendliness, good nature, consideration, interest in others' welfare, gratitude, and suchlike dispositions are being used as oil to keep the engine of business running and have virtually nothing to do with interpersonal relations. One mark

---

[10] *Legitimität durch Verfahren* (Frankfurt: Suhrkamp, 1963).

of respect that persons could reasonably look for from the systems programmers would be a return to materially precise and impersonal vocabulary. Then we might recover a sense of the real value of a smile from the girl at the cash-desk to the customer before her—even if the firm does profit from it. The smile is, after all, *her* smile; it is not 208 the firm the customer feels grateful to, but her.

Institutions exerting material or spiritual power must in the first place, then, make their *political* character apparent, especially when they lay claim to loyalty or moral support. The second condition is that they must have a fundamentally *juridical* character. By this we mean not primarily that they should observe given rules of practice, but that they should afford real protection to the personal status of each human being within the sphere of their institutional power—which is what it means to be a 'state'. The relational sphere of personal interaction is universal; from which it follows that the exclusion of even one person from the scheme of recognition brings the personal character of the whole system tumbling down. This occurs, as we shall show in a later chapter, the moment any qualitative criteria are imposed, over and above bare membership of the human race, for recognizing a someone as a someone and for co-opting him or her into the community of persons. A political system that imposes such restrictions loses its juridical character and its claim to loyalty. From that point on we can deal with it only through canny calculation. Of course, rights of citizenship are for any country to confer on whom it will; that is a matter on which there can be no obligation to treat everyone equally, no objection on the ground of arbitrariness. But rights of citizenship are worth nothing at all unless the country also affords human rights (and supremely the right to life) the fullest and most unrestricted protection that the state's power is capable of assuring.

16

Freedom

I

The idea of the person is inseparably bound up with the idea of freedom. To speak more precisely, the idea of the person adds a new dimension to that of freedom, the dimension of 'free will'. But free will has been a perennial storm-centre of controversy. To say that someone has free will is to say that the reason she acts in one way and not another lies in herself. Not in the minimal sense that her action is the necessary consequence of antecedent conditions beyond her power that determine what she is like. It means that what she is like is something she is responsible for, since it is the product of her actions. Decisions about particular actions are, at the same time, decisions about the kind of individual one wills to be. How are we to understand this radical development of the idea of freedom? And how should we evaluate it?

First we must ask what is meant by speaking of freedom in the first place. Freedom is a reflexive term. It does not refer to anything that can be identified ostensively; it reflects on the absence of something, usually something harmful. You are free of fever, or free of an addiction; a territory is free of malaria, a people of foreign domination or tyranny. To recognize clearly what is absent, we must first conceive the harm as a real possibility. It must either have occurred in fact, or have presented an evident threat. Alternatively, we must be able to observe it in others, comparing their condition with those who are not affected. We can sensibly say that a room is 'bug-free' when there are bugging-devices about. We speak of 'freemen' only in societies where serfdom or slavery is established. Freedom is 'freedom from' something, or else it has no content at all.

But harm, and reflection on the absence of harm, are a consider- 210
ation only for beings that 'go out for' things. Freedom, therefore, is also 'freedom for' the development of some implicit tendency. Animals are 'born free' in the wild. 'Free fall' is an Aristotelian expression supposing a 'tendency' in bodies to fall downwards until they meet resistance. The idea of freedom, therefore, is modulated by specific possibilities of development. A swallow is not free in water, and neither is a trout on the river-bank.

Yet that does not mean that any development whatever will count as freedom. Addiction is an example of an immanent tendency that makes us unfree. Why is that? Because it is unnatural. And on what basis can we call it unnatural? Because freedom and unfreedom are predicated only of beings with a 'nature', that is, in Aristotle's defini-tion, a 'source of rest and motion in themselves'.[1] Such beings 'go out for' things—their own continued existence, first of all. But human nature is incomparably flexible, and possesses considerable scope for manoeuvre among the movements open to it. This scope for man-oeuvre is structured by education, speech, morality, and habit, all of which we sometimes refer to as a whole by the name, 'second nature'. Second nature, the custom of living appropriately, was what *eleutheria*, freedom, amounted to for the Greeks of the sixth century BC. Someone who stood in the way of it was reckoned a tyrant. Antigone was not deprived of freedom by the ancient requirement that she should bury her brother, but by Creon's innovative demand that she should not do so.

With the sophists there emerged a new thought, which was explored in depth by Plato: morality, too, can make someone unfree, and can do so just when the second nature finds itself in conflict with the first. This is the case even if one has so internalized the tendencies of the second nature as to be unaware of the tendencies of the first. Slavery, too, is internalized; but that does not make a slave free. To be free one must be able to do what one wills; but to be able to do what one wills, one must know what one wills. Unfreedom, then, does not consist merely in having something imposed. It can have to do with

---

[1] *Physics* 192^b 13–15.

one's own 'inauthentic' will, as in the case of addiction. Behind the inauthentic will, according to Plato, lies a distorted perception of 211 reality and of what should be desired.

'Nature', as the Greeks used the term, is the standard for evaluating different practices, i.e. for recognizing them as really appropriate to the occasion. The 'natural' (in this sense) is what is worthy of humanity. It encourages an emancipatory understanding of freedom. The first nature is emancipated from the second, or at least, as in Aristotle, the second nature is criticized by a standard of consonance with the first.

But does such a test have any meaning? Must not 'human nature', if it means anything at all, simply be whatever asserts itself over secondary habits and motives? Like software supported by hardware, secondary systems can establish and sustain themselves, it would seem, only if they are compatible with the flexible nature of the human being. This sceptical objection, however, fails to carry its point. Higher animals are not faced with a simple choice between overcoming dangers and succumbing to them. Higher animals, as Aristotle puts it, are characterized by the difference between living and living well.[2] They can suffer losses without suffering outright extinction. The addict lives, but lives badly. His health suffers, his circle of interests shrinks, his dependence grows. As distinct from the habits we call virtues, vices are bad habits that hinder us from doing what our insight would otherwise incline us to do. Second nature may relate to the first harmoniously or unharmoniously—that is clear. We call those 'free' in whom the relation is harmonious, where the first nature is not suppressed by the second, but trained to develop in keeping with its own insight and achieve a particular historical form.

The same goes for social *nomos*. For a 'naturalistic' theory of society, a social order will count as 'natural' if it arises from a natural 212 parallelogram of forces, expressing the natural power-struggle of the strong to subject and suppress the weak. For the antelope eaten by the lion death may be 'violent' rather than 'natural'. But it is natural to the lion to eat the antelope, and an ecological system where lions eat antelopes is called a 'natural system'. All domination seems as

---

[2] *De anima* 434^b 21.

natural as its opposite. Nature is simply 'how one thing relates to another'.[3] But the nature of human beings is to *relate* to how one thing relates to another. We consider such natural processes as eating and being eaten now from the point of view of the eater, now from the point of view of the eaten; and where human beings are involved as agents, we draw conclusions about what it is right to do. This follows from the specific difference of the person, which is to relate to its own nature, condition and state. We have described it as 'having' its nature.

But our own nature, condition, and state cannot be defined without reference to everything else. To relate to one's nature means to relate to the world as a whole. Identification with the cosmos was, the Stoics thought, the solution of the problem of freedom. Assent to what will happen anyway delivers one from the role of victim. Human beings merely play, so to speak, the part of the victim, while their real interest, if they are wise, lies in the success of the show as a whole. Nothing can occur to frustrate my will if I bring it into harmony with fate, extending my natural interest in survival to encompass the whole, which is in no danger anyway. But the liberation the Stoic has achieved from his own individual nature is not as such an act of *freedom*. It does not result from a free conversion at the level of motive, but from the discovery of necessity. That is the meaning of Stoic 'wisdom'. The wise man, and only the wise man, achieves freedom. So freedom is not the product of free decision. Reason, not personal freedom, affords the condition for being free.

With Christianity, at length, there arises the thought of a conversion within the world that, rather than following on from new discovery, paves the way for it. Paul directs this thought specifically against Stoic wisdom. 'If I understand...all knowledge, and...if I give away all I have to the poor, and if I deliver up my body to be burned, and have not love, I gain nothing.'[4] The Stoic is prepared for everything the Christian is prepared for, and needs no fundamental conversion of the will to be prepared for it. The natural will for self-assertion, guided by insight, prompts an expansion of the self

---

[3] Cf. Robert Spaemann, *Das Natürliche und das Vernünftige* (Munich: Piper, 1987).
[4] 1 Cor. 13: 2–3.

to a cosmic scale, overcoming the particularity of this individual nature. Quite differently from this, love—in the sense of the New Testament's *agapē*—does not mean a cosmic expansion of *oikeiōsis*, 'identification', the owning of the world through the self. It means a radical change of viewpoint, described by Paul with the aid of the metaphor, 'dying'.[5] What this change amounts to is that the other— *as* other, not merely as a feature in my world—is as real and important to me as I am to myself; which leaves open the possibility that our interests may conflict. When Christians pray, they do not have the answer to their prayer already; and that is what distinguishes their attitude from that of the Stoic wise man. He does not pray for a hostile fate to be removed. Indeed, he does not *pray* at all, for he has overcome anxiety. Of death he is unafraid, and from the torments of death he can escape by means of suicide. He does not renounce his own for another's will, but forestalls the other will, when it is armed with greater strength than his, by assenting to it, making it his own in view of the pointlessness of resisting. This requires no decision and no love, only insight.

The reason for the difference is easy to see. Stoics do not reckon with God's will as a factor in reality. Their idea of divinity is not personal, their idea of the world not that of a product of will, a contingent entity. The All can be no other than it is, and I myself am an element in it. Intelligent beings can know that much about themselves. They know the play in which they have a part, and can play their part in the full knowledge that it *is* a part. In doing so they are more than mere elements; they are one with the Logos of the All.

But when this All is conceived as contingent, the product of a free act of creation, even, everything is different. Face to face with that, there is no such thing as insight into necessity. New attitudinal possibilities appear on the horizon: questioning, petition, thankfulness, alienation, reproach, and the choice between defiance and trusting love. It is not a matter of universal *oikeiōsis*, the identification of the I with the Whole, but of a relation to an Unnegotiably Other. And for this relation there are two possibilities, mutually exclusive, self-assertion and self-transcendence. In the one case man asserts his centrality, seeing all structures of meaning as subservient

[5] Colossians 3: 3, for example.

to it. In the other case he recognizes another centre of meaning, which he can affirm as he affirms himself, or many others, distinct from himself and from each other, not sunk in a higher unity that swallows their identities.

II

If we suppose an absolute centre of meaning, which is to say, a divine centre, it will claim our unconditional assent. Self-assertion must capitulate before it. Augustine speaks of *amor Dei usque ad contemptum sui,* 'love of God to the extent of contempt of self '.[6] When other finite persons are brought into the reckoning, however, the conclusion is not *contempt* of self, but the *relativizing* of self. For they are to be loved 'as yourself'. The first thing that implies is that relations shall proceed on the basis of justice, so that one's own interests do not outweigh others' a priori. The practice of justice assumes, of course, agenda and interests, which are to be brought into an equitable settlement. But it also requires that an individual's conduct should not simply reflect the lie of his private interests, but take cognizance of the interests of all affected, so that they, too, can be offered a 'justification' of what is done.

To a degree, it is built into our natural constitution to attend to the interests of others. These interests may be reckoned, then, among our natural interests. Ties of belonging and of sympathy are natural ties. Persons, however, can step outside natural sympathy in one of two directions. They can break free of natural ties and constraints, and decide for radical, uncompromising egoism—not necessarily abandoning relations based on sympathy, but adopting a strictly 215 calculative approach to them in terms of the material, psychological, or emotional benefits they yield. A storm of passion will not modify this approach, for then the other person figures as an element in the satisfaction of letting passion run its course. It is not, in truth, the other person who is the object of *fruitio,* the source of joy. Our real

---

[6] *De civitate Dei* 14. 28.

telos is and remains the enjoyment of our passion. That is why sympathetic relations of this kind may, as experience shows, transmute without warning into brutality.

That is one way in which persons, set free by reflection from the immediate promptings of nature, can be seen to 'have' their nature, rather than merely 'being' it. Creatures that simply inhabit their nature live in the perpetual innocence of *intentio recta*, extroverted, focused on others without conceiving them *as* others. They identify with others in elementary *oikeiōsis*, reach out to them and invest them with a meaning in their own life-context. Only one type of creature is capable of a reflection on its own experience that consciously subordinates others to their contributory role in its own experience, and that is the creature which, knowing the otherness of the other and its difference from the self, turns back reflectively on itself as its own final object. The *cor curvatum in se* is a theme of the Augustinian tradition. Only persons can be radical egotists. But there is an alternative: building on the reflective recognition of the other as independent of one's own life-context, deliberately to will, respect, and love the other as such, and to situate one's own perspective as one among many perspectives. Persons are capable of unselfish benevolence. And the lowest and most basic level of benevolence is justice.

A decision between these alternative motivations is 'arbitrary' in the sense that there is no more basic motivation to account for it, no general measure by which one or other of the two contending forces can be shown to be stronger. It is true that anyone who wills the good knows why he wills it: he wills it because it is good. But there is no reason why that reason should be decisive for him. Any further reason would, in effect, undermine that reason. To be sure, human 216 nature is disposed a priori to find the moral demand self-evident. There is such a thing as spontaneous sympathy, and among rational beings capable of speech there is sensitivity, no less spontaneous, to the elementary demands of reciprocity. Radical egoism is not our first and most spontaneous motion. Since Plato philosophy has striven to prove the fundamental identity of the objective and the subjective good, and the promises of religion point in the same direction. It is true that the concept of reward may appear at first glance to subordinate God to self-love. Yet this suspicion is overcome

when talk of reward is parsed by the divine word, 'I am your reward'.[7]
Anyone who finds it strange that justice and love should be sufficient
motives on their own will not be drawn by this reward, which
depends entirely on the love of God. To renounce egoism is not to
renounce oneself as a person, but actually to realize oneself. The
point of the promise is to allay anxiety before the leap into the
unknown—for a leap is what we are talking about here. As rational
beings we have actually made that leap already. We already stand in
'the light that lights every man that comes into the world'.[8] But as we
stand in that light, so we flinch from it, fearful of losing something
if we give ourselves up to it.

The decision which of the two motives to follow is a fundamental
one. It is not a 'choice', since a choice needs a reason. To be able to
make rational choices is the freedom that marks men and women out
not as persons but as 'rational animals'. This freedom, as Aristotle has
described it, is constituted by the fact that human beings are not
programmed to act instinctively in ways that serve biological functions they are unconscious of.[9] Human beings understand the biological function of hunger and the sexual appetite. They know why
they build a house. And because they know it, they can make a choice
among different courses of action. It is not simply a matter of
selecting means to ends on the basis of a transparent utility-calculus,
for, given the limitations upon strength and time, the whole range of
other ends is affected by the decision to pursue any one activity. Only
rarely, then, do calculation, consideration, and deliberation assume 217
the shape of a deduction from which a particular imperative will
emerge compellingly as a conclusion. Each end can be placed in a
wider context as a means to further ends, but what we hope to
achieve *overall* cannot be stated as an end to which all particular
actions are means. These particular actions, taken together, are
the sum total of our life, and what we hope to achieve overall is
something that embraces all these activities, something we can only
refer to by an imprecise phrase such as 'making a success of life'.
The Greeks used to speak of *eudaimonia*. Far from encouraging a
simple-minded utility-calculus, this term identifies a problem,
namely what the 'success of life' actually consists in.

---

[7] Gen. 15: 1.   [8] John 1: 9.   [9] *Nic. Eth.* 1109^{b}30–1115^{a}3.

A tradition that began in antiquity and persisted into the Middle Ages located the realm of free choice, *liberum arbitrium,* in the space opened up by the willing of means to ends. *Eudaimonia* was the 'last end', but not in the sense that one could simply choose it. It was an end that was 'natural' to pursue. But it opens up a space for choice, a space that in principle cannot be hemmed in by calculations of utility for the very good reason that the choice of means and the interpretation of the end come at this point to one and the same thing. In making this choice we decide at one and the same time who we are. Or ought we rather to say, *we reveal* who we are?

Ancient philosophy never posed this question clearly, for it would have meant going back behind the ontological primacy of *physis.* Plato saw very well that anybody's character could be observed from the way he understood happiness. *Qualis unusquisque est, talis finis videtur ei,* says Thomas Aquinas still: 'According to the character of a man, so does the end appear to him.'[10] But why does someone have the character he does? *Agere sequitur esse,* runs another medieval saying, 'action follows being'.[11] But in the case of persons does the contrary not also hold true? Do their actions not affect what they are? Antiquity was familiar with this point, too; it was known that virtues, as habitual dispositions to act, were acquired by acting. But why does one person acquire them and another not? The answer, well-grounded empirically, ran as follows: one was conditioned to do so, 218 another was not; one had a better disposition than another. Education and inheritance were the two conditioning factors that determined what the individual agent was. Yet we hold the agent, not only his progenitor and educator, responsible for his good and evil deeds. This was as commonplace to Aristotle as to us, but antiquity can offer no theoretical account of the fact, and its lack of one does not prompt it to a new line of thought.

Not until Augustine do we find it clearly stated that there is no third love lying behind the two loves, no single encompassing motive to decide between the alternative directions of the will. True, Augustine holds to antiquity's conception of *eudaimonia,* and it is

[10] *De malo* 2. 3, tr. Jean Oesterle (Notre Dame, Ind.: University of Notre Dame Press, 1995), 57.
[11] e.g. *Summa contra Gentiles* 3. 69.

clear to him, too, that only *amor Dei,* and not *amor sui,* leads to
happiness. 'This is what you have ordained... that every soul that
sins brings its own punishment on itself,' we find him saying in the
Confessions.[12] Enlightened self-interest can never justify contempt of
God, and since *curvatio in se ipsum* makes no one happy, since the
lost son ends up among the troughs of pigswill, there is a strong
natural motive for conversion. Yet 'if I dole out all I possess to the
poor' out of self-love, that does not mean I have love. The conversion
of the heart is not an organic development; it is a prior moment of
decision that fixes the direction in which any possible development
shall go. It belongs at the level of 'secondary volitions', i.e. how we
orient ourselves to the concrete objects of our will.

III

These 'secondary volitions' should rather, I would think, be called
'primary will'; but however that may be, there are two questions that
they pose. First, is this will free? Or better, perhaps, how can we
conceive of it as free? Second, has this will a real influence on our
concrete acts of will, or does it amount to no more than an inconsequential reflection, free, to be sure, but impotently wishful?
Aristotle thinks that this first human will is *not* free, not in the
sense that it could be willed otherwise. And anyway the 'meta-will' 219
to be happy implies no clear prescription for specific concrete actions
and will-acts. Not only do different people conceive happiness differently; the operations of reason, as we saw above, create space in
principle for deliberation. To determine oneself to act in ways
consistent with a basic will for happiness is not a matter of deductive
inference, but of practical judgement associated with the power of
decision. Certainly, there is no reason not to call *these* actions free. It
is usually but not always the case that a decision to act in this way or
that follows the conclusions reached in deliberation as a matter of
course, but we can, in fact, act against them. We can do this either
from weakness, i.e. an urge that leaves us incapable of following the

[12] *Confessions* 1. 12. 19.

insight we have attained, or from an instinctive assertion of the basic will itself, which may supplant the conclusions we have reached through deliberation with the wholly intuitive conviction that there is something wrong with them: some other decision will turn out in the end to be the right one, even if the reasons do not become apparent to us until later. There is no reason to think of any act as unfree if it is consistent with our conviction, however we may have come by it—not even if we share Aristotle's view that our basic will, the meta-will, is not free but naturally (*physei*) conditioned.

With discussions like that of the freedom or unfreedom of the will, which go to and fro for century on century and always end up in stalemate, it is reasonable to suspect that the question has been framed wrongly, and that the object whose existence or non-existence is at stake has not been described properly. We often do something because we want to do it—nobody doubts that. And nobody doubts that we are often responsible for wanting to do that rather than something else. When we are asked why we did this or that, we give reasons that we found persuasive, not circumstances that *caused* us to find those reasons persuasive. Does that mean we don't allow for causation at 220 this point? And what does it mean to say that 'we' are responsible?

There are two possible interpretations of this 'we'. With John Eccles and Karl Popper we may posit a distinct 'self', an entity responsible for decision in some interactive relation to the brain.[13] Or we may treat the *whole* person as an entity which, like every being equipped with drive, rises above the conditions of its appearance rather than simply being continuous with them. In resolving the problem of freedom there is, in fact, no advantage conferred by the dualist route of isolating this superior entity and locating it *within* the human being, instead of identifying it *with* the human being as a body–soul totality. For we would have to ask the same question about this 'self', this 'I', this 'mind', as we ask of the human subject as a whole: what does it mean to define oneself 'above' one's conditions of appearance? How are we to conceive of that?

Even if freedom is incompatible with determinism, indeterminacy and randomness are not a sufficient condition for freedom. Random decisions are the very opposite of free. But a decision cannot be free if

---

[13] Eccles and Popper, *The Self and its Brain.*

it is a necessary consequence of something in the agent that is either a necessary consequence of its existence or a chance accident that befell the agent. Nothing is gained for 'freedom', then, by assuming a dualist interaction of spirit and body, for the question is simply shifted along to reappear in a new guise: what can it mean for such a 'self' to determine itself? Eccles's most effective argument survives if we transfer it from a dualist context to a holistic one: the proof that the direction of neuronal processes can be determined non-physically, or 'mentally', without damage to the law of the conservation of energy, will be just as valid if the determination is due not to causation by a distinct 'self' but simply to the fact that neuronal processes are vital functions in human beings, and are therefore not mere physical events. The causation would be 'formal', in Aristotle's terminology, rather than 'efficient'. Eccles's quantum-mechanical 221 considerations might even carry more weight in this case, since they enable us to conceive causality formally, in terms of a whole in relation to its parts without presuming another entity, and so to reconcile it with the conditions for existence established by physics.[14]

But, as I said before, the fact that quantum mechanics is open to such possibilities is not decisive. It does not authorize a conclusion about the reality of self-determination, whether we understand this as determination by 'a' self, or by 'him-' or 'her-' self. In fact, the concept of self-determination, together with that of freedom of the will, have two different applications, depending on whether it is concrete decisions resulting from deliberation that we have in mind, like Aristotle, or decisions about good and evil, which are more clearly a matter of conviction when the agent has not had to engage in deliberation about them.

IV

We shall consider the first of these two applications first. In these concrete decisions the general motivation is assumed, and is not up for decision. From it we derive criteria for our decision, which allow

[14] J. Eccles, *How the Self Controls its Brain* (Berlin: Springer, 1994).

us to rank alternatives in order of preference. Sometimes this ranking leads to a clear decision immediately. On other occasions deliberation yields no clear result. For the most part this is either because the decision is largely inconsequential and can be settled by 'where the fancy of the moment leads', or because the consequences, though they may weigh gravely on the whole of life thereafter, are too remote to be clearly made out. These cases require intuitive decision and risk-taking. The latter type may sometimes be prompted by a definite instinctive sense of what is right to do—a sense that is not infallible!—but sometimes, too, by a feeling of inadequacy in the absence of good and sufficient reasons. What decisions of this sort really amount to is a resolve to rely upon a kind of mental random-selection, which could easily be replaced with an outward form, such as tossing a coin. The material decision in such cases does not merit the epithet 'free', but the 222 decision—reasonable in itself—to make a decision without reasons does merit it. This decision, too, of course, can be the result of chance, as when something happens to force a decision on us one way or the other, which we have no means of putting off.

The determinist thesis is that not only intuitive decisions, but conclusions of reflection and calculation too, are unambiguously determined by neurophysiological processes. Even if we allow an element of chance, decisions are simply chance outcomes. It is a matter of chance that this or that course of action strikes us as supported by compelling reasons. Naturally, more recent versions of determinism take account of the fact that information can be determinative. But here they exploit an ambiguity in the concept of information. On the one hand it can be understood in a purely physical sense as 'negentropy'; the content of information is then identical with its digital transport. On the other hand, information may be *what* is communicated, something in the order of 'significance', that is, which can only be interpreted semantically. On the determinist account, determination by reasons, i.e. by meaning, is 'really' physical causality. Freedom, then, is a self-interpretation which, as the product of physical causes, can only sustain itself if it does not see through itself.

Three arguments work in rebuttal of the determinist account, as applied even to the ordinary conduct of life which does not require a radical notion of self-determination.

The first argument runs thus: If it were true that acting on conviction was merely a necessary consequence of processes in which the condition of the agent was the chief factor determining the conviction, the account itself could make no claim to be true; it would only be evidence for the condition of whoever was advocating it. A truth-claim could not be taken to mean what it said, but merely noted as a datum of information about the person who made it. But this datum of information in turn could not be taken to mean what it said, since it would only be a digital process. And so on. Every understanding is a misunderstanding. A clash of arguments between rival theories would in reality be a physical conflict between two electronic systems—though even talk of systems, of course, makes sense only in relation to living beings that can identify physical processes as systems and so treat them analogously with organisms. Materialist determinism leads to *reductio ad absurdum* so quickly that it could hardly have survived without the dogmatic determination to account for the universe in exclusively physical terms, arguments notwithstanding. One of its protagonists, Daniel C. Dennett, has recently admitted as much in so many words.[15] The persistent weakness of antideterminism is due to its inability to compete with the materialist boast to offer the most economical explanation of everything. That this boast is purely utopian and can never be made good, seems, surprisingly, not to carry much weight.

But not all determinism is of the materialist variety. Psychological motivation can be thought of in a strongly determinist way. Deliberation is conceived as a process in which motives based on fundamental preference-structures play into a parallelogram of forces that yields a decision. Alternatively, where the weighting of motives does not produce a clear result, we end up leaving it to 'chance', and it is immaterial in that case whether chance motivations correspond to fully determined neuronal processes or whether there are chance reactions at the level of neuronal infrastructure, too. It is redundant, in any case, to assert—or even imagine—a personal subject deciding

---

[15] Dennett explains: 'I adopt the apparently dogmatic rule that dualism is to be avoided *at all costs*. It is not that I think I can give a knock-down proof that dualism, in all its forms, is false or incoherent...' (*Consciousness Explained* (London: Penguin, 1993), 37).

what weight to give to different motives. Psychological determinism, unlike materialism, is not immediately vulnerable to *reductio ad absurdum*, but is no less utopian and no less liberal with boasts that are in principle unredeemable.

This leads us, then, to the second argument. It is wrong to conceive of thoughts and wishes as 'motives' exerted in a psychological parallelogram of forces. Motives are not motives until they motivate. The 'weighing up' of motives for action is not at all like a 'conflict of motives'. There are, to be sure, competing wishes, and we may 224 experience their competition as a conflict of a kind. But until a given wish actually prevails, there is no sense in which it can be called the 'stronger' motive. A psychologically less pressing wish may at any time win support from a rational argument and gain a decisive advantage. The empty boast of determinism could only be made good if we could observe motives before they motivate, calculate them as independent variables, and so predict the outcome of their interaction. This is exactly what we cannot do, and not only because our knowledge is too limited in fact. We cannot do it in principle. That is because our consciousness is distinctively temporal. Every causal law assumes that the factors can be classified as instances of temporally invariant 'kinds'. Without this assumption it is impossible to formulate general laws. Within the stream of human consciousness there are, of course, temporally invariant structures we may identify, but these are only abstractions from a process that is unique as a whole. Its phases cannot be viewed as repeatable wholes. A repetition of a feeling we had before, of a thought we had before, or of an action we performed before, is a quite different psychological event from what it repeats; and that is because of the temporality of conscious life, which is to say that what happened before is recollected, or, if forgotten or suppressed, still colours the way we encounter the present. The present coloured by the past is never the same as the past. It can never be viewed independently, which is what would be needed in order to speak of it as the 'effect' of some 'cause'. The exact repetition of a given reaction by a given person has never happened. Any attempt to predict such a repetition on determinist grounds is therefore impossible, there being no earlier examples to go on. In general terms, precedents for action can give rise equally well either to custom or to tedium.

In its essentials this argument was developed with painstaking care by Bergson.[16] But Bergson made the mistake of thinking that it 225 amounted to a proof of freedom. What this antideterminist argument demonstrates is not that there is freedom in the sense of self-determination, but that the outcomes of freedom obey no laws and cannot be ordered into isolated events that will allow of causal connections between one kind and another. States of consciousness are not classifiable in 'kinds', but are unique. A fortiori this applies to the states of consciousness of persons; for persons, simply by reflecting on the repetitive character of their states, ensure that they cannot be compared precisely with earlier or later states. Deliberation implies this kind of reflection, and so delivers us from determination of every kind, even our own free self-determination if we are to think of it as initiating a predetermined process. To deliberate is not to initiate a process. It is to find ourselves already moving within the horizon of 'going out for' things. There is always something at stake for which we act, something we have not voluntarily chosen for ourselves. What we do voluntarily is to act within the frame of this horizon. This or that is what seems to us should be done, *given* that we are who we are. The question whether the process that led to that decision was a necessary one is wrongly posed.

This brings us to the third argument. Determinism presumes on the concept of necessity, and necessity presumes on the concept of possibility, since necessity is neither more nor less than the absence of alternative possibilities. But when discussing freedom of action it makes no sense to deny categorically that there could be other possibilities. By possibility we mean something that could be the case, but is not. The Megarians attacked the whole idea of possibility by arguing that the only possibility is one for which the conditions of realization are met—but if they are met, it must be realized, and is therefore a necessity. But we have one experience of possibility which is of a different order, and that is being the subject of the verb 'can'. We are aware of actions that we can perform if we wish to perform them. 'Can' is not a real property of anyone, for it has no definition apart from the act that we may or may not perform. The experience 226

---

[16] 'The Organization of Conscious States of Free Will', *Time and Free Will*, 140–221.

of 'can' is what possibility *is*. The pianist's assertion, 'I can play the piano,' is not disproved by the fact that he cannot play when there is no piano available. He will agree that he can play only when there is a piano, but that changes nothing; for 'can' is a possibility that opens up an alternative possibility, namely its own non-realization.

For any condition of an event it is true that alternative outcomes remain open for as long as not all the conditions are met. But actions are not like conditions for their outcomes. The outcome is part and parcel of the action. Again, the will to act is not one among other conditions for the realization of the act. The will is the immediate beginning of the act. 'Can' as distinct from 'must' means: if all the conditions are met, it rests with us either to act or not to act. Persons are aware that they could have done things that they did not actually do. This counterfactual possibility lies at the root of all our pronouncements about causal necessity. What distinguishes the statement, 'B followed A' from the statement, 'A is the partial or total cause of B, B the necessary consequence of A + X'? The distinction is this: in the second statement we say that B *would not* have happened if A had not happened. But what can be the point of this conditional statement, if everything that happens is *eo ipso* necessary? The question 'what if?' loses its intelligibility. Yet the question is unavoidable, because as *agents* we cannot avoid putting it. We ask what happens if we do this or that, and what happens if we do not do it. In order to be able to act at all, we have to think of ourselves as causes, but the only way we can think of ourselves as causes, is to think of ourselves as initiating chains of necessary events, rather than as links in such chains. Determinism itself, in any case, has presupposed this pragmatic view by reflecting upon the conditions for the efficacy of our active intervention into the course of things. Its attention to our act, however, is such as to subvert its presuppositions. It objectivizes it by treating it as a field for the active intervention of others. Thus it 227 merely displaces the problem—for what can it say about the acts of these others?

Our conclusion up to this point is that human activity cannot be understood in naturalistic categories. It cannot be understood as an effect of antecedent conditions determined by regular laws. Our knowledge of a cause cannot be the effect of that same cause; for us to know the causes of our acts of will, therefore, would immediately deprive these causes of their causative force. In knowing them we would relate to them; and our relation to a cause cannot be caused by the very cause we relate to.

V

We return, then, to the radical concept of freedom-of-the-will, or self-determination, that we owe to early Christianity. We have already seen that this radical freedom is superfluous in accounting for day-to-day activity, which demands no more than a freedom to act-for-reasons rather than acting-from-causes. Motives, or reasons-for-acting, are sufficient explanations on their own, because we are constituted so as to 'go out for' things. This constitution is not itself the result of free decision, but sets the horizon of our deliberations. The course we follow is whichever seems best among those presented to our view; but the reason it seems best is simply that we are who we are.

A more radical self-determination does not come into question until, over and above the conclusions reached by deliberation, to do this or not do that, we add another level of decision: *who* we are, and what we want *fundamentally*. This is the level of 'secondary', which I prefer to call 'primary', volition. In this decision the human being is fully visible as a person, which is why antiquity knew nothing of it. Such decisions differ from every day choices with their assumed criteria, in three ways:

1. They are not *moments* in the continuum of life and consciousness, but decide the meaning of life as a whole. What the decision is about 228 is whether the individual realizes his or her personality by grasping life in an act of self-transcendence that sees the world as more than an ecological *niche*; or whether, alternatively, he or she falls back into a natural, biological, and non-personal self-centredness.

2. Acts that decide upon the horizon of life create caesuras in life's continuity that assume the character of new beginnings. When someone is 'converted' and changes direction, a new beginning is apparent. A subsequent relapse into self-centredness, by contrast, is

not a new beginning, only a resubmersion in the stream of nature. Conversion implies abiding by the moral decision one has made, perpetuating the new beginning, which continues to be 'new' in relation to the stream of nature. Staying in love is never explicable by the law of inertia; on the contrary, it is opposed to it.

3. The decision about the direction of the will is not itself an act of will. That Aristotle saw correctly. An act of will needs a motive, but what motive could there be for deciding what will *count* as a motive? That would produce an infinite regress. Directing the will is not one more thing that we do by act of will; it springs from a disposition best described, with Max Scheler, as 'love and hate'. Long ago Augustine spoke of two poles of love by which the meaning of every personal life, human or angelic, is decided. 'Where your treasure is, there will your heart be also', the New Testament tells us.[17] It is not that will decides what we love, but that love decides what we will. Because love is not subject to the will, it appeared to Kant as an unfree, morally irrelevant feeling. But he also saw that there can be no will to will things; it needs a prior disposition—which he thought of as another 'feeling'—to provide a motive for acts of will. With love dismissed as irrational, Kant replaced it with 'a feeling that is produced by an intellectual ground', 'respect for the law'. This feeling, whose rational origin is apparent from the fact that it 'strikes down self-conceit', must be distinguished from all other feelings, which, in Kant's mind, are lumped together as mere subjective states.[18]

229

Love of God, in Augustine, similarly reaches 'to contempt of self'.[19] But love is different from respect for law. It is not an expression of 'man's rational nature', but of personality. It is the opening of the person in spontaneous affirmation of all other members of this a priori universal community. This lies behind all the particular will-acts that the person performs. It is definitely not itself an act of will, but an immediate qualification of the person's being, the source from which acts of will proceed. How, then, do we first confront the alternative between love's two possible directions?

[17] Matt. 6: 21.
[18] *Critique of Practical Reason, AA* v. 73, in Kant, *Practical Philosophy,* ed. and tr. Gregor, 199–200.
[19] Augustine, *City of God* 14. 28.

Only in connection with concrete situations, especially those where conflicting interests arise. Schiller argues that we need at least one conflict between duty and inclination if we are to discover our freedom and become aware of the 'dignity of our calling'.[20]

But if the love behind every act of will is not itself an act of will, how can we call it free? And how can we call the person free in respect of the direction of his or her heart? It might seem that we were left with the modest Aristotelian sense of freedom after all. There seems no point of responsibility for the basic structure of motivation that gives the will its fundamental direction. What pushes us into this dilemma is the idea of personal autonomy. On the one hand, we do not love because we will to love, but we find ourselves already loving or not-loving. Love, when true, is felt as a spontaneous answer to the being and nature of others: I experience the other as the ground of my love, not myself. On the other hand, we do not experience ourselves as the ground of others' love when we are its object. If they perceived that that was what we thought, they would find it impossible to love us. We are thankful for the love of others as a gift although, or because, we do not think they love us just because they will to. We are thankful that our being arouses love in others. The freedom we look for in love is not 'freedom of will', in the sense of autonomy.

Freedom, as we saw at the outset, is first and foremost freedom *from* something; but what is the *person* free from? Only from his or her own nature. A person 'has' a nature, but that nature is not what the person *is*, because the person has the power to relate freely to it. But this power is not innate; it comes through encounter with other persons. Only the affirmation of other centres of being, through recognition, justice, and love, allows us the distance on ourselves and the appropriation of ourselves that is constitutive for persons—in sum, 'freedom from self'. This we experience as a gift. It is simply the emotional and practical side of that opening up, that light in which persons see themselves placed and in which they see whatever encounters them as what it is in itself, not merely as an element in their world serving their organism and their interests. The human

---

[20] 'Über die notwendigen Grenzen beim Gebrauch schöner Formen', *Werke* (Nationalausgabe) 21. 27.

capacity for truth is the opposite of autonomy. It is a step into the open, a step towards freedom, where the existent reveals itself as itself.

If 'autonomy' is often used as a synonym for freedom in this context, it is because this freedom, too, obviously enough, may be refused. The gift of open space is not forced upon us. We may, if we will, refuse to recognize the life and feeling of a living animal and treat it as a kind of machine, though machines in fact simulate living creatures. Because the reason we possess shatters our original symbiotic unity with the rest of reality, we may deny recognition to other centres of being that disclose themselves, we may withdraw into the *curvatio in se ipsum*. And because we may do this, we seem to stand, as it were, above the parting of the ways between good and evil, to have them at our command to choose, or to decide, between them. This decision necessarily appears motiveless. But that is an illusion.

Most of the antinomies surrounding freedom of the will spring from this illusion. It is not we who reveal ourselves in our decision, but reality that reveals itself to us; we are on the receiving end of revelation. That is the origin of love, and it may be refused. We find 231 ourselves in the open space, but we incline to refuse and pull back into ourselves. We could say that it is our nature that pulls us back, for our nature, like every other living nature, is self-centred, 'egocentric'. But natural egocentrism is innocent and morally neutral in itself. Our egocentrism is no different from that of everyone else, and as persons we can deal with our own in the same way that we deal with theirs, as a simple fact of life that does not prejudice what we really will and do. Our nature, however, resists the neutralizing of its tendency; it creates a motive in contradiction to love. Not a 'rational' motive, since there is no rational ground to think of oneself more highly than of anyone else, though there may be good grounds to give prior attention to self and near neighbours in many cases, since that is what is implied in the realization of our nature, which we grant to others as to ourselves on the basis of the *ordo amoris*. But if we go beyond this and think of ourselves at the level of secondary volition as really more important, it is not nature that bears the responsibility, but will—a will to claim for nature the central place which is renounced in the open space of the community of persons. The will to be *merely* natural is not a natural will; it is arbitrary, and therefore evil.

All explanations of evil, therefore, are circular, explaining how evil is possible, but not why it occurs. One may identify a cause for someone's evil deed—and there are always causes to identify, since evil consists precisely in giving up acting for reasons and withdrawing into the realm of simple causation. But for this withdrawal itself there is no explanation. If there is a simple *cause* determining it, we do not speak of 'evil' at all, but simply think of the agent as unable to plead, incapable of bringing his personality to expression. Evil is that for which there is no reason, which cannot be comprehended. What can be comprehended about it is precisely what is not evil about it. And in this sense there exists no such thing as *pure* evil. Something desirable is in view when one gives up something yet more desirable. Freedom as autonomy is the freedom to refuse (for no reason) to 232 enter the space of freedom. Because this is possible, even the step into freedom can be thought of as autonomy. But to take this step is to experience it in the opposite way, as an 'awaking to the light', as Plato put it. And no man can waken himself.

VI

We can now situate the specific problem of the freedom of the will more precisely. It does not lie with our repeated acts of considered choice derived from established motives. Nor is it to do with decisions about our basic motivation itself. The problem is whether the primary will (Harry Frankfurt's 'secondary volitions') has the power to determine our concrete will effectively, or whether it amounts to no more than impotent reflection and wishful thinking. Can we actually will what we will? Does a person's distance on all her attributes imply that she really 'has' herself? Or is it merely that, whatever she wills and does, she can always assume a distance afterwards?

In our experience we are most wholly free when we can identify with ourselves, when self-distance is no more than an abstract, remote possibility. At the opposite extreme is the condition of non-identity that we experience as enslavement. The Apostle Paul gave this its classical expression, when he wrote: 'I do not do what I will, but I do the very thing that I hate,' adding: 'So now it is no longer I who do it, but sin that dwells within me.'[21] The impotence of the primary will to provide an effective motive is what we call 'weakness of the will', though this phrase creates more puzzles than it solves, for it is a real question whether love that cannot motivate the concrete will effectively is love at all. Precisely for that reason we view this 'weakness' as culpable, in just the same way that we blame ourselves and others if we, or they, have forgotten to do something important. It is not that the omission was intentional; but it shows that we set too little store by the matter.

The problem of the freedom of will, in the sense we are exploring it here, is apparently that of focusing our attention. It is not as though persons have at their disposal a reserve of energy to be thrown into the scales against the deadweight of nature; but what they can do is direct their attention on an object, fill their thoughts and imagination with it, regardless of life's necessities, and concentrate more protractedly upon it than they would have done without a definite resolve. 'It is an idea to which our will applies itself, an idea which if we let it go would slip away, but which we will not let go. Consent to the idea's undivided presence, this is effort's sole achievement.'[22] This thesis of William James is the most illuminating thing said about the freedom of the will before or since. It can never, James concedes, be proved or disproved by empirical investigation or psychological reflection that at some point we could have paid more attention than we did. But philosophy, as we have seen, can show us what is lost if we give this belief up. We lose, among other things, a reason to exert ourselves to prove the belief wrong.

In our reflections the connection between freedom and attention forms a natural corollary to the concept of the person. The alternative that confronts the primary will is not, as Frankfurt assumes, either to fashion our concrete acts of will directly or to observe and criticize them ineffectually.[23] Neither can the primary will replace the concrete will, taking over its function and countermanding its decisions. The best illustration of its role is as a court of appeal in

---

[21] Rom. 7: 15, 17.

[22] William James, *The Principles of Psychology* (London: Macmillan, 1890), ii. 564.

[23] Frankfurt, *Journal of Philosophy* 68 (1971), 5–20.

relation to a court of first instance. The appeal court may overturn the lower court's judgment, but it cannot substitute its own; it can only refer the case back, drawing attention to what, in its view, has been overlooked. This much our 'secondary volitions' can do; and it is what we normally understand by 'freedom of the will'.

Whether that really establishes radical freedom as we have con- 234 ceived it in this chapter, turns on what kind of ideas we attend to. If someone forces himself to keep an eye on the stock-market reports when he is in love, that is because he is interested in the growth or the protection of his investment. This interest is as natural as the interest that draws his thoughts to the beloved—less immediately compelling, but (for this individual, obviously) no weaker for that. It counts among his long-term interests, which prevail against immediate interests only with the aid of reason. Reason is here placed at the disposal of nature, but nature is not converted by reason but continues wholly wrapped up in its vital egocentricity.

It is quite different with ideas that do not represent a natural subjective interest, but are themselves the reason for the attention they attract. Attention in this case is not directed by vital interests; for the interests of a particular human being are not in question, only the idea itself. What kind of interest do we have in preserving the last tigers in Russia from extinction? We shall never see them anyway! What kind of interest moves an artist to labour at perfecting his masterpiece without thought for his strength or life expectancy, though hardly anybody, perhaps, will ever appreciate it? What kind of interest drives someone to keep a promise when there are attractive prospects in view, with nothing to stand in their way except the promise and the trust another has placed in it? What kind of interest makes a man, even on his deathbed when the deception is inconsequential, want to know the truth rather than accept the consolation of a well-intentioned lie?

In all these cases the interest that draws our attention to an idea, is an interest in the truth of the idea. To open oneself to its claim is to let oneself go, to renounce the natural demand for autonomy. And that is the condition for personal freedom.

17

Promise and Forgiveness

I

Persons are capable of promising. That means that on their own initiative they can make engagements. Engagements create expectations; expectations demand satisfaction. Animals, too, have expectations, and we have expectations of animals. We have expectations even of objects, natural or artificial; we expect, for instance, that the sun will rise tomorrow. These expectations are based on experience and on the assumption that the regularities of the world will not suddenly change. Expectations are built on universal natural laws and specific characteristics of given objects. When they are disappointed, as from time to time they are, the cause lies in ourselves: our calculations were subject to error, or else we hazarded a bet and lost. We had no *claim*, at any rate, to have our expectation fulfilled. It is a measure of maturity when someone learns that the world is not obliged to satisfy his expectations of it. Neither are animals so obliged; the so-called 'punishment' of animals has no point other than to condition those that are capable of learning new behaviour.

Experience is a factor, too, in our expectations of promises. We will not bank on a promise which experience teaches is impossible to fulfil, and we will place no confidence in someone who, in our experience, never keeps promises. But that does not change the fact that what we base our expectation on is precisely the promise. Promises create and justify expectations prima facie, because they give rise to claims. If a promise is easy to keep, we will even trust a stranger's word—give him a letter to post, for instance, in the nearest box, though he has no reason to do it apart from his promise. Yet if the letter were specially important, we might hesitate, however transparent the impression the stranger made on us. A promise licenses a claim that is peculiarly unconditional; but if our expectation of its fulfilment is not quite so unconditional, that is because we do not know how well any given individual will measure up to its unconditionality. Moral necessity is not physical necessity Whether it is as compelling as physical necessity depends on who it is that undertakes the obligation.

'Depends on who it is...'—what does that mean? It means, it depends on *what kind* of individual makes the undertaking. Does it follow that someone who says, 'That's just the way I am!' has produced an acceptable excuse? Obviously not. 'That's just the way you *shouldn't* be!' we think. We assume that human beings are responsible for their competence to promise, or at the very least, if they cannot rely on themselves, responsible for not making promises they are not competent to make. Promises found a variety of claims; but the claim not to be misled by a promise is a claim that every person can make against every other, constitutive for interpersonal relations. And since, as we have seen, every person relates to every other as participant in a community, this community is marked *inter alia* by the fact that every person can make a promise to every other without generating an infinite regress: 'I promise to keep my promise to keep my promise...' Such a chain of meta-promises could not be drawn out *ad infinitum;* somewhere we would have to reach a promise that the promiser had made but not promised to keep, so that he might say he had no reason to keep his promise. If we replied that every promise includes an undertaking, he might wriggle out with the same gambit: 'I undertook it as a matter of expediency, and feel no obligation to observe my undertaking.' Why does this not satisfy us? What is wrong with an infinite regress of guarantees? How can a promise bind 237 without further promises to hold it in place? Yet how, on the other hand, could we possibly insist on an infinite series of guarantees, and allow that in default of it promises have no binding force?

The distinctive feature of moral obligation seems to be that it rules out a reflective train of thought that is in itself perfectly possible, by which we may wriggle out of any obligation at all. To renounce this train of thought seems to be the very essence of the moral act. In renouncing it, the human subject realizes him- or herself as a person, and that is the irreducible presupposition of the train of thought itself. One takes upon oneself the promise which, as a person, one already *is*. By speaking and demanding to be understood, one has engaged in the same personal relation that is presumed in each separate act of promising. The question of how to secure the promise no longer arises. The final security is the refusal to pose that question, a refusal already made when human beings recognize each other, and claim recognition from each other, as persons. The person is a promise. To be a person means to assume a place in the community of all persons. Intelligent creatures have no choice whether or not to assume this place together with its associated obligations and claims. They can neither refuse the claims nor denounce the obligations. The person is autonomous; but there is no autonomous act giving rise to personal autonomy, no autonomous discretion to which that act is subject. Our legal order invalidates a contract in which one party purports to renounce civil and human rights. Even less is it possible to unburden oneself of one's duties. Entry to the community of the free is not itself a free act. Consent is presumed, as is the agreement of others to the equal membership of each new arrival in the human species. There is no act of co-optation, but everyone takes a place in this community by birthright. We have already commented on the very important fact that this non-natural community of persons comes into being and perpetuates itself wholly by natural means. 238 The original promise undergirding all subsequent promises stands beyond the reach of question or challenge, simply because it was never a free action performed in time. It is an intelligible postulate, the meaning of which is nothing more or less than our actual situation in the community of persons.

II

So the practice of promising throws a shaft of light on what it is to be a person. Since the original promise cannot be situated in time, person-hood, though ascribed on the basis of certain properties, is not iden-tical with any properties but prior to them all. It is something of which we take cognizance only by recognizing it. When we make an actual promise in history, on the other hand, we rise above our normal immersion in the stream of time. We do not leave it to the course of events to decide what we shall do at a given point in the future, nor do we leave it to whatever attitude or state of mind, wishes or priorities we may happen to have at that time. We take advance purchase on that moment, and decide *now* what we shall do, or not do, *later*, making any subsequent revision of our present resolution morally impossible. We place the matter beyond our own control by grounding another person's claim to have our decision implemented. Of this general paradigm a contract is a special case. This is clear enough when a contract imposes a reciprocal burden that the other person must discharge to require performance of us, but that hardly gets to the core of the matter, since unconditional promises, too, may be given a contractual form, as in the case of deeds of gift and legacies. In normal speech contracts are distinguished solely by the fact that the claim they confer is a legal, not simply a moral one. In making the promise, we arm the claim with sanctions to enforce its implementation. The expectation is thus 239 anchored psychologically and physically within the causal structure of reality, in the promiser's own 'nature' and in the reality of the world.

Apart from the case of a contract reinforced with sanctions, the new reality brought into being by a promise is not at all easy to describe. The fact that someone close to me has definite expectations of me may motivate me to do what I would not otherwise do. But such expectations can be created without promising—for example, I may often have gratified this person in some way in the past, and regular patterns of behaviour, like all regularities, create precise expectations. However, a promise creates something more than this: it creates a *claim* to have the expectation fulfilled. The category of claim, like that of obligation, is of a different order, not psychological but moral. Obligation and claim are independent of whether those involved are presently aware of them. Forgetting one's promise does not derogate from the obligation to keep it. One *ought not* to forget it. Nor is a claim extinguished by the beneficiary's failure to keep his entitlement in mind.

Yet obligation exercises its control only through certain psychological impulses. Kant speaks in this context of 'respect' as a 'feeling produced solely by reason'.[1] Our responsibility is not directed

---

[1] *Critique of Practical Reason, AA* v. 76. (*Practical Philosophy,* ed. and tr. Gregor, 201).

primarily, as utilitarianism suggests, towards an indefinite number of human beings, self included, who benefit from the convention of promise-keeping. It is a personal responsibility to a particular individual, created by a promise that may now perhaps interfere with my wishes, needs, and preferences. But that is precisely what is implied in a personal relation to one's natural condition, in 'having' a nature. This is no merely formal or transcendental relation to one's state that leaves it unaffected, rather as some philosophers and theologians imagine a relation between God and world in which God never acts 240 in the world 'categorially'. The will to keep one's promise is *unconditional*, but at the same time *conditioned*, by education, disposition, and even by short-lived emotional states, and that notwithstanding the fact that rising above short-lived emotional states is the essential point in keeping promises. The knowledge that one has bound oneself by a promise is a modifying factor in one's psychological state, and so is the knowledge that personal existence is already a promise. That knowledge is called 'conscience'.

To make conscience a reliable factor—and in cases of conflict, a conclusive factor—in one's psychological make-up, is a task only beings with 'secondary volitions' can confront, those who can take a view of their impulses as a whole, i.e. persons. The purpose of this effort is what we call 'virtue': conditioning one's nature to reliable self-determination, integrating the various impulses with the goal of actually achieving what one wishes to achieve. What is at stake is the ability to rely on oneself. The abstracted consciousness has, as we have seen, only an instantaneous identity with no dimension in time. Inwardness recollected is 'out there', yet it is still *inwardness* that is 'out there'. There is a meantime, and we can determine how we have become different in the course of it. If identity were merely a matter of isolated consciousness, we could understand 'becoming different' as 'becoming *someone* different'. But that would make ourselves disappear as persons relating to other persons; for in other persons' eyes we can only be identified, as other things and animals are, in space and time. Other things are continually 'becoming different' in the sense of 'altering'. And persons alter, too.

A promise fences a decision off from alteration by giving another person the right to rely on its performance, so as to be able to presume upon it safely in his or her own plans for action. How is it possible to fence oneself off from alteration in the course of time, especially if there is no legal contract to bar the possibility of promise-breaking? 241 We make it 'morally impossible'—but what does that mean? It means that I tie the content of the promise to the promise that I, as a person, *am*. To break the one promise, I must break the other. I must make myself disappear as a person. The truth of this is expressed in the proverb, 'False spoken once, forsworn for aye!' Here, of course, nothing is said of the possibility of regret and repentance. But could we believe someone who, while showing no regret for past breach of promise, merely assured us he would keep his promise this time? The most we could do would be to gamble on the chance that his interests might lie in the other direction this time.

I do not propose to go into the casuistry of promising here. Of course, there are promises from which we excuse ourselves on the ground of urgent necessity that imposes duties inconsistent with them—a type of case in which we need to be clear that the other party does not insist on the keeping of the promise. The point, however, is that it can never be a reason for non-performance that the promiser simply asserts that he has changed his mind. That was precisely what the promise was meant to exclude. The way in which the person is distinctively present in a promise is especially clear in the case of promises to the dying. Once they are dead they can enforce no claim; yet precisely for that reason we feel we owe it to ourselves to perform. Our promise otherwise would have been no more that a palliative expedient, disrespectful of the other's personal transcendence, treating him or her solely as a 'phenomenon of nature' to be pacified and handled with kid gloves. We can only recognize another's personhood by actualizing our own. Conversely, we can only realize our own personal standing by recognizing persons.

III

A distinctive yet paradigmatic case of promising is the *marriage vow*. 242 Marriage is no ordinary promise to perform something, which one can still go through with when one has no mind to, or no longer feels the special interest that inclined one to the promise in the first place. With the marriage vow two people tie their fortunes together irrevocably—or that, at any rate, is what the vow intends. This promise could hardly be kept if one were in fact to change one's mind fundamentally. It is only possible to make it, then, if it includes an undertaking not to change one's mind. But how is that possible? Simply by virtue of the peculiar capacity of persons to assume a secondary relation to their own make-up, their 'nature'.

By virtue of this capacity we encounter growth not merely as something that happens, but as something that happens to the extent that we are open to it. The nature of every living being is subject to change, and persons, who 'have' a nature, are not exempt from this law that governs every nature. But they can relate to it in such a way that their growth is not merely a function of spontaneous natural energy, but subject to the higher law of personal identity. The promise of marriage is a promise not to view the growth of one's own personality as an independent variable that may or may not turn out to be compatible in some degree with the growth of the other's personality. For if that were all there were to it, the successful sharing of two destinies would be a matter of luck and chance, and no promises could be made. But in fact it is possible to set parameters for one's growth compatible with the growth of another person. At every stage of one's growth one is aware of the meaning it has for the other and for the other's growth. This is a very considerable restriction of our room to manoeuvre, but it is not a restriction of our *freedom*. For we could not in any case exhaust the whole range of possibilities. With every 243 possibility we choose, we cancel others. If we do not wish to pay that price, we can never grasp the possibilities we have, and so never actually realize freedom. The marriage vow cancels a vast number of possibilities, but what it accomplishes can only be accomplished in this way. It is like a duet, which requires two singers or players, or even an improvization in which two players listen to each other and fit in with each other, so that neither part is the same as it would be if played independently. This is only a metaphor, of course; the cooperation of two musicians in a given performance can be brought to an end. The essence of marriage is that two lives, two whole biographies, are tied together so as to become one history.

Marriage is predicated on the capacity of persons to create a structure for their life that is independent of unforeseen occurrences, delivering themselves from the control of chance by deciding once and for all in advance how such occurrences will be dealt with. This is true in general of religious vows, too. But in marriage the actualizing of this personal capacity brings the other's otherness into play, so that the meaning of one's own life for the life of another becomes a central shaping element in it. When this happens consciously with the assent of the emotions and the will, we speak of love. Love is not constitutive of marriage, but the point of marriage cannot be realized without it.

In principle all this applies to every kind of friendship. Yet not every friendship is a marriage. It is not essential for friendship that there should be lifelong sharing of destinies. The specific unity of the marriage partnership is expressed in the New Testament by the saying that 'the two shall become one flesh'. The lifelong horizon of this partnership and the fact that the couple form a legal person, is all of a piece with the sexual difference and natural complementarity of the two persons that goes with it. Their relationship includes sexual intercourse with its a priori ordering towards the objectification of 244 the union in children that belong to them both. Being father and mother to one and the same child means objectively a lifelong relation between a man and a woman, and it lies a priori in the child's interest that the relationship should have a form matching the personal identity of their common child. The distinctive character of the marriage vow is only conceivable on the basis of the specific complementarity of persons of opposite sex, on which the handing on of human life and the continuance of the human race rely. If personhood consists in having a human nature, it consists of necessity in having either a male or a female nature, which is to say, a nature with its own ordering towards a person of the other sex. The person as such is not endowed with a sex. Its relations are simply to other persons. But this specific and exclusive bond, formed by exchange of promise as a new and permanent union without room for substitution, builds on the sexual relation of two partners of opposite sex. Persons of the same sex can feel erotically attracted to each other. But their sexual relation remains their 'private affair'. It lasts for as long as each wants it to last. It does not create an objective and new unity. The two do not become 'one flesh'.

Sexual relations are in one sense the most impersonal relations imaginable. They have an element of disindividuation, of immersion into the sub-personal stream of life. That is why there is a definite suspicion of the sexual in a philosophical tradition oriented to the ideal of autonomy. The force of mutual attraction between the sexes obviously weakens individual autonomy, and the state of being in love is famously one of utter helplessness, 'losing one's head'. But precisely this helplessness can be understood as a prerequisite for the new, strong unity that emerges from personal and physical union. The personal communion of life freely founded by promises supplies the framework within which the two can let go without losing themselves, since they can count on one another. At this point chaos may be fruitful, the source of living order.

The promise of marital fidelity is essentially a promise of sexual 245 exclusiveness. The point of this exclusivity is to guarantee children a safe family setting in the first place, in which mother is uniquely related to father and father to mother and the relation of siblings to one another is perfectly clear. But there is a further point, which is to exclude a particular threat to marriage itself. A loving relationship leading to sexual union, if it is worthy of personhood, contains in itself a tendency to exclusivity, permanence, and the uniting of the two destinies. Lovers' vows point in this direction spontaneously. The partner is generally likely to experience it in this way, and that is why an extramarital affair is generally concealed. In German we speak of adultery as a 'breach' of marriage (*Ehebruch*), even though not every marriage is actually broken by it. When adultery is not concealed, but the partners have agreed on mutual permissiveness, the case is rather different, though no better. Either we are not talking about a marriage in the sense of a lasting communion of lives and destinies, or the agreement imposes an asymmetric shape on the other affairs: they are not seen as personal relations at all, or else they are meant to take more than is given, to hoodwink other sexual partners. That is why the promise of sexual exclusiveness, though difficult to keep and frequently broken, is an essential constituent of the marriage vow, the promise which expresses the human type, the 'natural person', more than any other.

IV

The self-possession that constitutes the person also—and not acci-
dentally—has the character of self-expression. Promising gives something of ourselves away. We clear the way for someone else to make a
claim on us. That is the only way we can be delivered from being at
the mercy of our natural condition, for, as Wittgenstein demonstrated, it is impossible to follow a purely private rule, but rules are
what we need if we are to rise above the heteronomous laws of
natural process. Freedom comes only from engaging with social 246
groups established by mutual claims, claims that we either recognize
or have ourselves given rise to.

Regularity in obedience to moral rules is modelled on the
regularity of laws of nature. One formulation of Kant's categorical
imperative runs: 'Act as if the maxim of your action were to become
by your will a universal law of nature.'[2] Unlike the better-known first
formulation, which states that we should act so as to be able to *will*
the maxim of our action as the maxim of a universal law, this one
speaks of acting 'as if'. We cannot will this universal law to be a new
law of nature in fact, because we know that is impossible. We cannot
even *wish* it, since our freedom to obey the rule would disappear if
the rule were transformed into a law of nature. The maxim is not to
become a law of nature, but to be as much like one as possible *in
respect of its regularity*. The one serves as a model for the other.

Regularity has two roots. Its specific and peculiar root is personal
trust, the faith reposed in the word and free commitment of the
promiser. The object of this trust is the other's freedom, and trust is
clearer and stronger when backed by the conviction that the other
was really free from impulsive inclinations, independent of natural
determinants, 'master of himself'. The more the will is independent
of nature, the more it corresponds to the model of a law of nature.

The other root is exactly the opposite. It arises from a realistic,
even sceptical evaluation of free human self-determination. It
amounts to a confidence precisely about the *nature* of the promiser.

---

[2] *Groundwork of the Metaphysics of Morals*, AA iv. 421 (*Practical Philosophy*,
ed. and tr. Gregor, 73).

It assumes that promising is not so opposed to natural inclination that keeping it involves great effort and gives rise to lasting inner conflicts. We are more ready to rely on someone's word when the 247 person who gives it will suffer no great loss in keeping it. This kind of reliance does not really deserve to be called 'trust'. It is not specifically personal, but rather compensates for the mistrust which we have all acquired from experience, and which finds its simplest expression in that expression from the Psalms that Paul quotes in Romans: 'All men are liars.'[3]

Sidera inclinant, non necessitant. From this ancient piece of astrological lore Thomas Aquinas concluded that astrology was capable of statistical pronouncements, since most people follow their inclinations, but not of definite predictions for individual cases, since no one is compelled to follow his inclinations.[4] In making a promise one must be aware of this, and mistrust oneself. In making a promise one must be willing to cultivate in oneself the right inclinations to support promise-keeping. One must assent, furthermore, to the legal sanctions that make breach of promise disadvantageous. They will not disadvantage oneself unless one intends to break one's promise. But the knowledge that they *could* affect oneself helps one to do what one anyway intends to do simply for the promise's sake. Here, too, we see that 'having a nature' does not make a person *independent* of human nature. Freedom is a particular way of relating to one's nature, not of growing out of one's nature and leaving it behind.

Regularity in promising leaves open the possibility of a breach. What the promise creates is not nature, not even when there is the greatest imaginable resemblance between the ideal and nature. In a breach of promise there is a shattering of personal identity, a victory of entropy over freedom. How is that possible? If weakness were not, as it were, 'to blame for itself', were not the product of freedom, no such action as promising could be conceived. But there is another action we could not conceive of in that case, one that, again, is possible only in dealing with persons: I mean forgiveness.

---

[3] Ps. 116: 11 LXX, alluded to at Rom. 3: 4.
[4] *STI.* 1. 115, repeated at *Contra Gentiles* 3, 82–7, *De iudiciis astrorum, De sortibus* 4.

V

Forgiveness presupposes guilt—which implies the exercise of per- 248 sonal freedom. It is the personal 'self', not some state in which the self finds itself, that underlies the behaviour in question. But there is another side to it: forgiveness presupposes that the wrong decision has not placed the person in a state that is definitively settled. Of course, *I* am the person who did *this,* and will always be so. My personal identity is not something apart from my innate or acquired attributes; it is the whole of which my attributes are qualifications. Yet the meaning of these qualifications for the whole—for the Being of the person—is not settled once and for all. The person is always more than the sum of the attributes. The person cannot make what has happened not to have happened, and must reckon with what he or she has become. But it makes a difference how this reckoning is done. Disowning a deed in repentance is a way of reintegrating what has happened by re-evaluating it.

Self-transcendence in regard for other persons is, as we have seen, how persons realize themselves. Rising above the egocentricity of our vital instincts is possible for us because as human beings we have the experience of recognition by others. Persons exist only in the plural. That applies also to when it is a question of finding their way back to resume their life-journey when it has been interrupted by the guilty *curvatio in se ipsum.* If the interruption is to be be put behind them, it requires the help of others. And what that help consists in is their readiness, and especially the readiness of the injured party, not to identify the offender with what he has become in fact, but to permit him to redefine himself in relation to his deeds. This permission we call 'forgiving', and it has to be asked for. Here there is a peculiar asymmetry: a duty to forgive corresponds to no right to be forgiven. The guilty party has no claim on forgiveness, and can only plead for it; yet the 'creditor' very definitely has a duty to respond to the plea. If he should fail in this, he too would fall into *curvatio,* his own personality would vanish from sight. For to identify someone defini- tively with any of his predicates means to refuse him recognition as a 249 person, which is to say, a subject free in respect of all its predicates. The guilty person needs the permission of others to exercise this freedom—and that is his punishment. But one who refuses it, excludes himself, too; for the community of persons is in principle all-inclusive.

Forgiveness may be qualified by conditions, e.g. that the harm intended should be made good. Where the political community is involved, making good may even consist in accepting punishment, since punishment serves as a deterrent, preventing other similar offences. Yet punishment, as Hegel said, is 'the honouring of the offender', i.e. as a person.[5] Having served his penalty he is restored to equal membership of the civil community as of right. The guilt is 'erased'. Even life imprisonment can be understood in principle as the efface-ment of guilt, an address to the person as a person, not merely a measure for dealing with him or with the situation. His place as a subject is not eliminated. On antique executioners' swords are engraved the words: 'Whene'er the blade I lift on high, I pray the sinner heavenward fly.' Naturally, an institution cannot offer forgiveness in the full sense of the word. It can only shape its procedures to make the possibility of forgiveness evident—which means that the procedures must permit and encourage the individual to achieve a distance on his own deed.

The question remains, which comes first, the permission or the inner distance? Both are plausible. Someone who finds himself per-manently cast in other people's view as the one who did this thing or that, has no alternative but to make it a point of honour to define himself that way, 'to stand by what he did' as the phrase goes. He cannot go on for ever begging to be recognized as what he would like to be, while having no claim to be recognized. He really is the one who did what he did; he cannot require anyone to look at him in a new light, as he would look at himself if he were permitted to. On the other hand, how can anyone look at him in a new light if he does not 250 do so himself? How can I forgive an injury if it is persisted in? How can I forgive someone who does not ask for forgiveness?

Can we escape the stalemate of each side waiting for the other to go first? We saw in our discussion of evil that though it does not arise from innocent ignorance (for nothing from that source could be evil in the true sense), evil is, nevertheless, shrouded in a kind of

---

[5] *Philosophy of Right* 100, tr. T. M. Knox (Oxford: Clarendon Press, 1952), 71.

ignorance, depriving the agent of clarity. This is what makes conversion possible, because conversion is a return to clarity and there is a natural undertow pulling towards clarity. This, too, is what makes possible the first softening of the heart towards forgiveness, even the first step towards forgiveness itself. 'Forgive them, for they know not what they do!'[6] The Socratic intellectualist has nothing to forgive, since he takes evil to be no more than a mistake. But neither can someone who demonizes evil forgive, since evil willed as evil is unforgiveable, and conversion from it is impossible. But that guilty blindness which is evil's mode of appearing in the world of time and history always involved a moment of entanglement. To be set free from entanglement is a possibility, provided it is 'permitted', provided the victim is prepared to view the offender as someone other than the perpetrator of the offence, which is to say, to forgive him. One who forgives abandons the right to take the offender as he found him, and gives the offender the opportunity to take himself differently, too. Until this opportunity is seized, forgiveness is no more than an exploratory probe. For if we say, 'I know you are not like that!', we may be beaten back by the response, 'I am like that, and I will go on being so!' Forgiveness is then brought to a stand.

That forgiveness may anticipate a change of attitude and smooth the way for it, turns on what I have elsewhere called 'ontological forgiveness'.[7] We are finite and natural creatures, and we fail to live up to the promise our personhood presents. Which means we cannot treat everyone as they deserve to the same degree. That was why we had to make a promise in the first place, so that someone could rely 251 on us in this or that instance: our sheer existence did not give reason enough for reliance. The 'ontological promise' of our existence is no more than a ground for relying on promises that we actually make. 'Ontological forgiveness' is the acknowledgement that the other person, being finite, cannot really put himself in the right with us. Simply as the finite and natural beings they are, persons stand in need of forbearance. Moral forgiveness offered 'on account' takes a step further, out of the transcendental sphere and into the categorial, out

---

6 Luke 23: 34.

7 Robert Spaemann, *Happiness and Benevolence*, tr. Jeremiah Alberg (Notre Dame: Notre Dame University Press, 2000), 189.

of the ontological into the moral. Forgiveness reaches its goal in reconciliation, and in arriving at that point, makes itself redundant by bringing to an end the moral asymmetry on which it stands and re-establishing equality of mutual recognition.

Equality, however, can only be re-established because it was never completely destroyed. Nobody, however bad his conduct, can finally annihilate himself as a person while still alive. Nobody can become an 'un-person', the difference between personal identity and attributes reduced to zero. While someone lives, there is someone there to forgive. No one, on the other hand, is absolute freedom or pure subjectivity, rising above natural and finite perspectives. No one really knows what he does when he does wrong. That is why one cannot wait to forgive until the divergent perspectives have been merged, and the difference in how we see things is overcome. Since everyone is caught in his own perspective, irreconcilability is a sin in itself in that it refuses transcendence. It means locking oneself up in the prison of one's own finitude, putting oneself out of reach of others' forgiveness. It is profoundly significant, therefore, that the petition for forgiveness in the Lord's Prayer is immediately expanded with a profession of readiness to forgive.

So forgiveness is the mark of personality, complementary to promising. Both confirm the difference between personal identity and the attributes and qualities that we display in real time. Promise underwrites the independence of personal identity from absorption in actuality. Forgiveness evokes this independence in the teeth of actuality. It is, in an eminent degree, an act of creation.

18

Are All Human Beings Persons?

I

Human beings have certain definite properties that license us to call them 'persons'; but it is not the properties we call persons, but the human beings who possess the properties.

There are, it is clear, human beings who do *not* possess these properties; so it may seem that these human beings are not persons, and can make no claim to be recognized as such. This thesis, which goes back to Locke, is currently argued by Peter Singer and by Norbert Hörster.[1] If persons are individuals who possess a 'rational nature', it would seem that human beings are not persons when they do not command the powers of rationality and intentionality—'not' meaning 'not yet', 'no longer', or 'never'. That is to say, small children are not persons; the seriously handicapped are not persons; and neither are we persons while we are asleep.

And then, if a person is not an instantiation of a concept or a member of a class but a participant in a community of mutual recognition, how do we enter that community? The answer that immediately suggests itself is that personal status arises with *acceptance*. In practice a child develops the characteristic indices of a person only as it is accepted and experiences the appropriate attention from its mother. The attention seems to come first, and personal existence seems to depend on it. From which it follows that we have no need to justify refusing it. Only persons can demand

---

[1] Peter Singer, *Practical Ethics* (Cambridge: Cambridge University Press, 1993²); Norbert Hörster, *Neugeborene und das Recht auf Leben* (Frankfurt: Suhrkamp, 1995).

that we justify the way we treat them; but recognition is what constitutes personality in the first place.

This, however, is a misconception of what 'recognition' means. Recognition is a free and spontaneous act, certainly, and may be refused. Yet when we recognize something, we do not see our attitude as one we equally well might or might not have adopted. It is the appropriate response. That is how it is, for example, when we recognize the force of an argument. Nothing can compel this recognition, and if we are determined enough, we can refuse to recognize even the most 'compelling' arguments. And at the other extreme there is such 253 a thing as capitulation, when we abandon our objections from exhaustion, fear, or complaisance. But true recognition is a response to the claim the argument has made. We are free when we acknowledge someone is right; but we acknowledge it because he *is* right. It is the same with recognizing persons. When we recognize someone's claim to a place in the community of persons, it is not an act of co-optation. The criteria for it are not set by those who are already recognized as members.

Who can make this claim, and on whose behalf can it be made? What properties must someone possess to have the right to recognition as a person? But that is the wrong way to pose the question, because it uses the word 'someone'. Anything that is 'someone' is a person. We would do better to ask, When is some-*thing* some-*one*? But that is still wrong. Some-thing is never some-one. To be 'some-one' is not a property of a thing, whether animate or inanimate; it is not a predicate of some previously identified subject. Whatever we identify, is identified either as someone or as something from the word go. 'Is anyone there?', we ask when we hear a noise, or 'Who is that?' And when we discover it was the wind shaking the shutter or the dog scratching at the door, we realize that the answer to the first question was 'No', and that the second was based on a misapprehension, since we asked 'who?' instead of 'what?' (A dog, however, may cause us some hesitation. It is neither 'someone' nor 'something', but a kind of adjunct to humanity. But that would require a separate discussion to sort out.)

If being a person is a *modus existendi*, there is no *genus proximum*, no more general category that the concept of 'person' could specify. But may we not say, 'Some living things are persons'? No, that proposition is misleading. Personality appears in it as species within a genus, distinguished by its own specific difference. But that does not fit personal existence. The name of the species to which we ascribe personal existence is (without wishing to exclude the possibility that there could be others) 'human being'. So now the question sounds like this: Are *all* human beings persons? Are the rights of persons the same as human rights, or must we exclude a portion of the human race from the sphere of persons, and so abandon the term 254 'human rights' altogether, as has recently been suggested? In support of this it is argued that since the properties of rationality and self-consciousness are the ground for designating living things as persons, it is not very clever to call human beings persons and accord them personal recognition if in fact they do not possess these properties.

This challenge assumes a nominalistic view of natural kinds. It recognizes universal predicates such as 'self-consciousness' and 'rationality', and so ascribes a generic meaning to the concept of person. But it denies such a thing as a universal human nature with any more content than a genealogical connection among individuals, the majority of whom have certain features as adults that entitle us to call them persons. This genealogical connection is assumed to be self-evidently irrelevant to what they are as individuals; nor does it provide a basis for the community of persons that we customarily call 'humanity'. One does not enter that community by being begotten or born, only by becoming self-aware and being co-opted by other members.

In what follows I should like to give six reasons why this conception is untenable, six reasons that argue for the truth of our intuitive conviction that all human beings are persons.

II

1. The concept of a natural kind is not univocal. It works differently in relation to physical objects and artefacts on the one hand and to animate beings on the other. Inanimate objects are classified as instances of a kind on the basis of likenesses. The relation of likeness is paratactic. Inanimate objects that share likenesses are grouped together indirectly, not directly. This happens either through a

sequence of ideas, in which one instance suggests the thought of the next, and so comes to be thought together with it as a unity; or, as in the Platonic theory, when a particular thing is seen as an instance of a 255 Universal, and is classified together with other instances of the same Universal. These elements need no direct relation to each other. It makes no difference to one member of a class whether there exist any others, and if so, how many.

With living species it is quite different. The instances of such species are connected by a genealogical relation that is constitutive. One member of the species could not exist without others, nor without definite ties of affinity. Among the higher forms of life this relation has a sexual component. The community of the species is a reproductive community first and foremost. Phenotypical similarity is a secondary factor. This goes for human beings, too. All human beings are related to one another, and to a greater extent than palaeontological discoveries had led us to suspect. According to the findings of geneticists, all human beings alive today are the descendents of a single woman who lived about 200,000 years ago.

But does that have any significance for the way we are connected? Is it not merely a biological fact, irrelevant to the question of the personal status of each human being? What this separation of the biological from the personal fails to grasp, is that personhood is situated in the *life* of human beings. Fundamental biological functions and relations are not apersonal; they are specifically personal performances and interactions. Eating and drinking are personal acts (*actus humani,* as the scholastics said, not merely *actus hominis*).[2] They are embedded in rituals, they provide the focus of many forms of community life, they stand at the centre of many cults. Something similar applies to sexual intercourse. Here, too, the biological function is integrated in a personal context, often as the highest form of expression of a relation between persons. The kinship-connections of mothers and fathers to sons and daughters, of grandparents to grandchildren, of siblings and cousins to one another, are not merely a biological given, but personal relations of a typical kind, relations 256 which as a rule last for life. Human personality is not something over

---

[2] e.g. Thomas Aquinas, *ST* I–II. 1. 3; 17 4.

and above human animality. Human animality, rather, never was mere animality, but the medium of personal realization. The nearer and more distant kinship relations in which human beings stand to one another are of personal, and so of ethical, importance.

Failure to recognize this gives rise to such extreme utilitarian proposals as Peter Singer's, that biological relations must be excluded from the criteria for distribution of scarce resources in times of need.[3] The same logic underlies his criticism of what he calls 'speciesism', the privileging of human beings as such. But members of the species *homo sapiens sapiens* are not merely exemplars of a kind; they are kindred, who stand from the outset in a personal relation to one another. 'Humanity', unlike 'animality', is more than an abstract concept that identifies a category; it is the name of a concrete community of persons to which one belongs not on the basis of certain precise properties objectively verified, but by a genealogical connection with the 'human family'. ('Humanity', in Kant, combined these two points of reference: on the one hand, the family of human beings, on the other, the quality that makes a human being a person. So he writes of 'humanity, whether *in* your own person or *in* the person of any other...')[4] Belonging to the human family cannot depend on empirically demonstated properties. Either the human family is a community of persons from the word go, or else the very concept of a person as 'someone' in his or her own right is unknown or forgotten. Fathers in pagan Rome actually had the right to decide whether they wished to confer on a newborn baby the legal status of a legitimate child, and with it that of a human being; but that merely proves that the Romans had not discovered the community of persons, in which no one is obliged to anyone for his rights, but every one is *sui iuris*. Which can only mean, a member from birth.

2. Recognizing a person is not merely a response to the presence of specific personal properties, because these properties emerge only where a child experiences the attention that is paid to persons. To 257 enable elementary personal reciprocity, the mother undergoes an instinctive regression—automatic, but not unfree—by which she

---

[3] Singer, *Practical Ethics*.

[4] *Groundwork of the Metaphysics of Morals*, AA iv. 429. (*Practical Philosophy*, ed. and tr. Gregor, 80).

puts herself on the child's level. The mother, or her substitute, treats the child from the start as a subject of personal encounter rather than an object to manipulate or a living organism to condition. She teaches the child to speak, not by speaking in its presence but by speaking *to* it. Attempts to teach the children of deaf and dumb parents to speak with the help of videos have been unsuccessful. To understand words, which means understanding that they *are* words, cannot be taught. Nobody can explain what it means that something 'means something', because every explanation supposes a capacity to grasp explanations. When we speak with an infant we make this supposition counterfactually, in order for it to become true. But the mother is conscious of no pretence, no acting *as though* what she wanted were already the case. We never consciously 'make' persons. Personal existence is in the highest sense existing 'out of one's origin', something unsusceptible to external inducement. It means that the mother can, and must, be authentic in relating to the child, so that the child grows up psychologically healthy. If the theory were true that personal existence is conferred by recognition, we should have to take great care that those who did the recognizing were kept in the dark about the theory; for it would seriously inhibit the authenticy and spontaneity of recognition.

One could reply that this argument was purely pragmatic. Philosophy, after all, implies a breach with the natural instincts. Yet a breach with natural instincts can be on a secure footing only if it opens up a hitherto unrealized theoretical perspective, from which we can gain a new and higher viewpoint on the natural instincts. What we see from that viewpoint will not in any way affect what occurs, and must occur, at the level at which the instincts operate. The theory of the person which we oppose here does not function at this philosophical-phenomenological level. It is a practical theory, with immediate implications for practice. It is not a *reflection* on the spontaneously creative power of recognition which may or may not be implicit in natural instinct, but simply a *misdescription* of the act 258 of recognition itself, a misdescription that will encourage us not only to think differently about it but to change our habitual practices. This theory, in other words, operates on the territory of natural instinct and proposes to eliminate the phenomenon of recognition on its own ground.

We could put our critique like this: there is no graduated transition from a 'something' to 'someone'. It is only because we treat human beings from the start as someone, not as something, that the majority of human beings actually develop the properties that then justify the way we have treated them.

3. We can attain unqualified certainty about the presence of intentionality; we do so constantly, whenever we engage in immediate personal communication. But we cannot reach the same certainty about its absence. Recognizing rationality and interpreting human acts *as* human acts can be shown to involve an element of evaluation.[5] To credit someone with rational action (i.e. with action, simply) implies sympathy with some of his or her supposed intentions. Intentional action is recognized, therefore, only through its rationality (or at least, its partial rationality). It may happen in fact that someone acts intentionally without this being recognizable to observers. Consider, for example, Malvolio, who sets out to woo Olivia with entirely false assumptions about what will make her admire him. The innocent observer cannot know what he hopes to achieve with his yellow cross-garters, or even whether he hopes to achieve anything at all. But that does not mean Malvolio cannot be acting intentionally. Responsibility and the capacity to calculate results must thus, as Scheler observed, be kept quite separate.[6] It may happen that we are unable to identify the meaning of an action for someone who is psychologically ill, and so cannot hold him responsible for its effect. His practical intentions and theoretical intentions, his purposes and his view of how the world is constructed, are such that we cannot trace the connection from one to the other. Yet he can have his own practical rationality and be capable of distinguishing clearly between good and evil. He can be responsible—if not to human judgement, at least to God—just as a 'rational' 259 person is.

4. But what about human beings so severely disabled that they cannot even co-ordinate their movements, or infants who have not

---

[5] D. Davidson, *Essays on Actions and Events* (Oxford: Oxford University Press, 1980), 83 ff.

[6] Max Scheler, *Formalism in Ethics and Non-formal Ethics of Value*, tr. M. S. Frings and R. L. Funk (Evanston, Ill.: Northwestern University Press, 1973[5]), 472–3.

yet learned to? Have we any rational ground for viewing them as 'someone' and for treating them as such—a more expensive and more sacrificial course of action than disposing of them on a purely utilitarian basis? The fact that we are prima facie inclined to make such sacrifices is attributed by Peter Singer to 'speciesism', i.e. a rationally groundless partisanship with everything that belongs in purely biological terms to our own species.

Let us take the severely disabled first. Are we dealing with a thing? Or with an animal of a different kind? Of course not. We are dealing with a *patient*. If the severely disabled patient were not 'someone', but something *else*, he or she would have to possess a special kind of normality, a non-personal existence that assured an ecological *niche* in the world. But a disabled individual with whom we can never have personal communication is inevitably treated not as a normal being but as a sick one. A broken chair does not strike us as other than a chair; it is simply a chair broken. And so it is with a human being incapable of personal expression, i.e. of the expression of intentionality: we see him or her as a sick human being in need of help. We look for ways of helping if we can, for ways of restoring 'nature', providing an opportunity to take that place reserved for him or her in the community of persons until death. The severely disabled are not, as animals are, at one with their nature, their mode of existence. They 'have' a nature; but because their nature is defective, so is their way of having it. We do not know what it is like to be such a person— we do not understand the *modus essendi*—any more than we know what it is like to be a bat. But we perceive immediately that the severe defective has not regressed into the animal kingdom. In ancient times such people would have been treated as numinous, there being no other categories to regulate dealings with them. How we treat them shows in a quite distinctive way whether we have come to terms appropriately with what being a person means. Their existence is the 260 acid test of our humanity. They are human beings, and human beings are a kind of creature whose nature it is to 'have', not simply to 'be', its nature. The human being, the being that 'has' its mode of existence, is *ipso facto* a mystery, never merely the sum of its predicates. In cases of aphasia we have no access to its thoughts. Where this is aggravated by lack of controlled movement, we have no other proof of an intentional inner life. And yet we presume that this inner life continues. With severely disabled persons we do not know what to presume. But since it is a property of human nature to be 'had' in a personal way, we have no reason to view this nature, when it is severely deformed, in any other light.

We can easily conduct a thought-experiment to the contrary. Let us imagine a creature born to human parents but very unlike other human beings. Let us suppose its conduct gives no suggestion of any kind of mutually reinforcing practical and theoretical intentionality. Let us conceive, furthermore, that this creature seems quite healthy, moving through the world normally and functioning as an animal equipped with all those instincts for survival that mankind characteristically lacks. It stands in need of no external assistance to survive. It is uninterested in, and of course incapable of, communicating with other human human beings. Since it shows no signs of sickness, such a creature will inevitably present the appearance of a new and hitherto unknown variety of animal. It will not be a person, will not belong to the human race. The severely disabled are different. They do belong to the human race, and they participate in the community of persons simply as recipients of physical and moral support, though they themselves may be incapable of recognition and all that follows from it.

In fact, however, they give more than they get. They receive help at the level of sustaining life. But for the hale and hearty portion of mankind giving this help is of fundamental importance. It brings to light the deepest meaning of a community of persons. Love or recognition directed to a human being is not, as we have seen, directed merely to personal properties, though it is the personal properties that allow us to grasp that a person is there. Friendship and erotic love develop mainly in response to the beloved's individ- 261 ual personal properties. A disabled person may lack such properties, and it is by lacking them that they constitute the paradigm for a human community of recognizing *selves*, rather than simply valuing useful or attractive *properties*. They evoke the best in human beings; they evoke the true ground of human self-respect. So what they give to humanity in this way by the demands they make upon it is more than what they receive.

5. As for small children, the nominalistic argument declares they are only *potential* persons. To become persons-proper, they need to be co-opted into the community of mutual recognition. One side of this argument we have dealt with already: to recognize someone presupposes there is someone to be recognized. But something further needs to be said about the concept of a 'potential person'.

There are, in fact, no potential persons. Persons possess capacities, i.e. potentialities, and so persons may develop. But nothing develops *into* a person. You don't become some-one from being some-thing. If personality were a condition of affairs, it could arise bit by bit. But a person is a someone situated *in* this or that condition; the condition is always a predicate of the person, the person always presupposed by the condition. The person is not the result of modification; it simply 'presents itself', like substance in Aristotle. The person is substance, because the person is the mode in which a human being exists.

The person does not begin its existence after the human being, nor does it end its existence before the human being. It takes quite a time before a human being starts to say 'I'. But what does he or she mean by 'I'? Not '*an* I', but simply the selfsame human being who *says* 'I'. So we say, 'I was born on such and such a date', or even, 'I was conceived on such and such a date', though the being that was conceived or born on that date did not say 'I' at the time. That is no reason for saying, 'On such and such a date there was born some thing from which I later developed.' *I was* this creature that was born. Personality is not the result of development, but its framework. Since persons are not totally accounted for by their present condition, they can understand their own development as that of a unified 'self' over time. This unified self is the 'person'.

To speak of potential persons is meaningless, furthermore, because the concept of potentiality itself can arise only on the supposition of an underlying personality. Persons are the transcendental meaning of possibility. Ever since the pre-Socratics there have been objections to saying that something that is not the case is 'possible': if the (merely) possible is defined by the absence of at least one condition of actuality, then it is simply *im*-possible; if, on the other hand, possibility arises only as all the conditions are met, it is not possible but actual. One paradigm case, and one only, blocks this line of argument: the consciousness of freedom. I can be free to do something only if it would be possible not to do it. And what it means for it to be 'possible' not to do it can only be defined in a circular fashion, referring back to the consciousness of freedom. But the consciousness of freedom—the concept that at bottom defines possibility—cannot itself be thought of as mere potentiality. Persons *are*, or they *are not*. If they are, they are actual, *semper in actu*. They are like Aristotelian 'substance', the *protē energeia* or first reality, which contains in itself the possibility of a multitude of further actualizations. So although it makes good sense to speak of intentionality as 'possible' or 'actual', since intentional acts emerge from the stream of consciousness and gradually assume a propositional structure to become distinct and separate items, when we speak of 'potential intentionality' we presume the existence of real persons as its subjects.

6. To acknowledge personal existence is to acknowledge an unconditional demand. This unconditional demand could only be an illusion if in practice it could materialize only on certain empirical conditions, which might or might not be fulfilled.

This situation does in fact arise in some theoretical contexts. There are propositions which, if they are true at all, are logically and necessarily true—all propositions of arithmetic are of this kind—yet it is open to dispute whether any given proposition belongs to this class of necessary truths. But it is not the case with practical propositions. They cannot be conclusive while their conclusiveness lies open to doubt. It must always be possible to know a concrete moral obligation when we see one. If we could not know such a thing 263 with certainty, we could not be obligated *in concreto*, here and now. In situations of objective uncertainty there must be rules for negotiating the uncertainty that are not themselves subject to the same uncertainty. (Descartes's 'provisional morality' is a collection of such rules.) If, as I say, it were a matter of fine judgement to recognize a human being as a person, either because the criteria for personal existence were controversial or because doubt could arise as to whether they were met in a given case, the obligation to recognize persons 'unconditionally' would be an illusion, the term 'unconditional' a mere rhetorical flourish.

But it is not the case that we have first a general rule requiring unqualified respect for persons, and then apply that rule to particular cases—with possible difficulty at one or another point in applying it. We encounter the demand for unconditional respect primarily and fundamentally in some particular person or in some particular group of people. We cannot grasp the unconditional nature of the demand without being convinced that *this* is unconditionally an instance of it. The unconditional 'Thou shalt not kill!' presents itself in a particular human countenance every time. It is clearer to me that I may not kill *him*, I may not kill *her*, I may not kill *them*, than it is that I may not kill anyone. 'Person' is not a generic term; it is the way in which individuals of the human genus exist. Each of these individuals occupies an irreplaceable position in the community of persons that we call 'mankind'. As the occupant of this position they can be taken seriously as persons by another occupant. If we make the ascription of this position depend on certain prior qualitative conditions, we have done away with the unconditional demand. No one occupies the position by co-optation, only by being born to membership of the human race. The rights of persons are neither accorded nor ascribed, but demanded, and demanded with precisely the same right by each and every person. 'By each and every person' means: 'by each and every human being, at least'. In sum, the rights of persons can be unconditional only if they do not depend on satisfy- 264 ing the existing members of the community of rights that certain qualitative conditions are met. The human community cannot be a community of rights if it operates a 'closed shop'. For in that case even such a basic rule as *pacta sunt servanda* ('promises must be kept') would protect only those already recognized as fit subjects of rights by the majority.

There can, and must, be one criterion for personality, and one only; that is biological membership of the human race. The beginning and end of personal existence cannot be taken apart from the beginning and end of human life. If someone exists, that someone has existed since the individual human organism existed, and will continue to exist for as long as the organism continues to live. What it is to be a person is to live a human life. There is no sense in saying such things as, 'Brain-death means the death of the *person*, even if the *human being* is still alive.' The person cannot die before the human being, for the person is the human being, not a property of the human being. The question of the person's beginning and end is decided on the same terms as that of the biological beginning and end of human life.

The rights of persons are human rights. Yet if there exist within the universe other natural species of living beings possessing an inner life of sentience, whose adult members usually command rationality and self-awareness, we would have to acknowledge *not only those instances but all instances* of that species to be persons.

All porpoises, for example.

Index